Constantine the Great

John Firth

Published 2017 by Jovian Press

All rights reserved.

10 9 8 7 6 5 4 3 2 1 0 00 000 0

CONTENTS

THE EMPIRE UNDER DIOCLETIAN

THE catastrophe of the fall of Rome, with all that its fall signified to the fifth century, came very near to accomplishment in the third. There was a long period when it seemed as though nothing could save the Empire. Her prestige sank to the vanishing point. Her armies had forgotten what it was to win a victory over a foreign enemy. Her Emperors were worthless and incapable. On every side the frontiers were being pierced and the barriers were giving way.

The Franks swept over Gaul and laid it waste. They penetrated into Spain; besieged Toledo; and, seizing the galleys which they found in the Spanish ports, boldly crossed into Mauretanian Africa. Other confederations of free barbarians from southern Germany had burst through the wall of Hadrian which protected the Tithe Lands, and had followed the ancient route of invasion over the Alps. Pannonia had been ravaged by the Sarmatae and the Quadi. In successive invasions the Goths had overrun Dacia; had poured round the Black Sea or crossed it on shipboard; had sacked Trebizond and Chalcedon, and, after traversing Bithynia, had reached the coast at Ephesus. Others had advanced into

Greece and Macedonia and challenged the Roman navies for the possession of Crete.

Not only was Armenia lost, but the Parthians had passed the Euphrates, vanquished and taken prisoner the Emperor Valerian, and surprised the city of Antioch while the inhabitants were idly gathered in the theatre. Valerian, chained and robed in purple, was kept alive to act as Sapor's footstool; when he died his skin was tanned and stuffed with straw and set to grace a Parthian temple. Egypt was in the hands of a rebel who had cut off the grain supply. And as if such misfortunes were not enough, there was a succession of terrifying and destructive earthquakes, which wrought their worst havoc in Asia, though they were felt in Rome and Egypt. These too were followed by a pestilence which raged for fifteen years and, according to Eutropius, claimed, when at its height, as many as five thousand victims in a single day.

It looked, indeed, as though the Roman Empire were past praying for and its destruction certain. The armies were in widespread revolt. Rebel usurpers succeeded one another so fast that the period came to be known as that of the Thirty Tyrants, many of whom were elected, worshipped, and murdered by their soldiers within the space of a few weeks or months. "You little know, my friends", said Saturninus, one of the more candid of these phantom monarchs, when his troops a few years later insisted that he should pit himself against Aurelian, "you little know what a poor thing it is to be an Emperor. Swords hang over our necks; on every side is the menace of spear and dart. We go in fear of our guards, in terror of our household troops. We cannot eat what we like, fight when we would, or take up arms for our pleasure. Moreover, whatever an Emperor's age, it is never what it should be. Is he a grey beard? Then he is past his prime. Is he young? He has the mad recklessness of youth. You insist on making me Emperor; you are dragging me to inevitable death. But I have at least this consolation in dying, that I shall not be able to die alone". In that celebrated speech, vibrating with bitter irony, we have the middle of the third century in epitome.

But then the usual miracle of good fortune intervened to save Rome from herself. The Empire fell into the strong hands of Claudius, who in two years smote the Goths by land and sea, and of Aurelian, who recovered

Britain and Gaul, restored the northern frontiers, and threw to the ground the kingdom over which Zenobia ruled from Palmyra. The Empire was thus restored once more by the genius of two Pannonian peasants, who had found in the army a career open to talent. The murder of Aurelian, in 275, was followed by an interregnum of seven months, during which the army seemed to repent of having slain its general and paid to the Senate a deference which effectually turned the head—never strong—of that assembly. Vopiscus quotes a letter written by one senator to another at this period, begging him to return to Rome and tear himself away from the amusements of Baiae and Puteoli. "The Senate", he says, "has returned to its ancient status. It is we who make Emperors; it is our order which has the distribution of offices. Come back to the city and the Senate House. Rome is flourishing; the whole State is flourishing. We give Emperors; we make Princes; and we who have begun to create, can also restrain". The pleasant delusion was soon dispelled. The legions speedily reassumed the role of king-makers. Tacitus, the senatorial nominee, ruled only for a year, and another series of soldier Emperors succeeded. Probus, in six years of incessant fighting, repeated the triumphs of Aurelian, and carried his successful arms east, west, and north. Carus, despite his sixty years, crossed the Tigris and made good— at any rate in part—his threat to render Persia as naked of trees as his own bald head was bare of hairs. But Carus's reign was brief, and at his death the Empire was divided between his two sons, Carinus and Numerian. The former was a voluptuary; the latter, a youth of retiring and scholarly disposition, quite unfitted for a soldier's life, was soon slain by his Praetorian prefect, Arrius Aper. But the choice of the army fell upon Diocletian, and he, after stabbing to the heart the man who had cleared his way to the throne, gathered up into his strong hands the reins of power in the autumn of 284. He met in battle the army of Carinus at Margus, in Moesia, during the spring of 285. Carinus was slain by his officers and Diocletian reigned alone.

But he soon found that he needed a colleague to halve with him the dangers and the responsibilities of empire. IIe, therefore, raised his lieutenant, Maximian, to the purple, with the title of Cesar, and a twelvemonth later gave him the full name and honours of Augustus. There were thus two armies, two sets of court officials, and two palaces, but the edicts ran in the joint name of both Augusti. Then, when still further division seemed advisable, the principle of imperial partnership was extended, and it was decided that each Augustus should have a Cesar attached to him. Galerius was promoted to be the Cesar of Diocletian; Constantius to be the Caesar of Maximian. Each married the daughter of his patron, and looked forward to becoming Augustus as soon as his superior should die. The plan was by no means perfect, but there was much to be said in its favor. An Emperor like Diocletian, the nominee of the eastern army alone and the son of a Dalmatian slave, had few, if any, claims upon the natural loyalty of his subjects. Himself a successful adventurer, he knew that other adventurers would rise to challenge his position, if they could find an army to back them. By entrusting Maximian with the sovereignty of the West, he forestalled Maximian's almost certain rivalry, and the four great frontiers each required the presence of a powerful army and an able commander-in-chief. By having three colleagues, each of whom might hope in time to become the senior Augustus, Diocletian secured himself, so far as security was possible, against military rebellion.

Unquestionably, too, this decentralization tended towards general efficiency. It was more than one man's task, whatever his capacity, to hold together the Empire as Diocletian found it. Gaul was ablaze from end to end with a peasants' war. Carausius ruled for eight years in Britain, which he temporarily detached from the Empire, and, secure in his naval strength, forced Diocletian and Maximian, much to their disgust, to recognize him as a brother Augustus. This archpirate, as they called him, was crushed at last, but whenever Constantius crossed into Britain it was necessary for Maximian to move up to the vacant frontier of the Rhine and mount guard in his place. We hear, too, of Maximian fighting the Moors in Mauretania. War was thus incessant in the West. In the East, Diocletian recovered Armenia for Roman influence in 287 by placing his nominee, Tiridates, on the throne. This was done without a breach with Parthia, but in 296 Tiridates was expelled and war ensued. Diocletian summoned Galerius from the Danube and entrusted him with the command. But Galerius committed the same blunder which Crassus had made three centuries and a half before. He led his troops into the wastes of the Mesopotamian desert and suffered the inevitable disaster.

When he returned with the survivors of his army to Antioch, Diocletian, it is said, rode forth to meet him; received him with cold displeasure; and, instead of taking him up into his chariot, compelled him to march alongside on foot, in spite of his purple robe. However, in the following year, 297, Galerius faced the Parthian with a new army, took the longer but less hazardous route through Armenia, and utterly overwhelmed the enemy in a night attack. The victory was so complete that Narses sued for peace, paying for the boon no less a price than the whole of Mesopotamia and five provinces in the valley of the Tigris, and renouncing all claim to the sovereignty of Armenia.

This was the greatest victory which Rome had won in the East since the campaigns of Trajan and Vespasian. It was followed by fifty years of profound peace; and the ancient feud between Rome and Parthia was not renewed until the closing days of the reign of Constantine. Lactantius, of whose credibility as a historian we shall speak later on, sneers at the victory of Galerius, which he says was "easily won" over an enemy encumbered by baggage, and he represents him as being so elated with his success that when Diocletian addressed him in a letter of congratulation by the name of Cesar, he exclaimed, with glowing eyes and a voice of thunder, "How long shall I be merely Caesar?". But there is no word of corroboration from any other source. On the contrary, we can see that Diocletian, whose forte was diplomacy rather than generalship, was on the best of terms with his son-in-law, Galerius, who regarded him not with contempt, but with the most profound respect. Diocletian and Galerius, for their lifetime at any rate, had settled the Eastern question on a footing entirely satisfactory and honorable to Rome. A long line of fortresses was established on the new frontier, within which there was perfect security for trade and commerce, and the result was a rapid recovery from the havoc caused by the Gothic and Parthian irruptions.

Though Diocletian had divided the supreme power, he was still the moving and controlling spirit, by whose nod all things were governed. He had chosen for his own special domain Asia, Syria, and Egypt, fixing his capital at Nicomedia, which he had filled with stately palaces, temples, and public buildings, for he indulged the dream of making his city the rival of Rome. Galerius ruled the Danubian provinces with Greece and Illyricum from his capital at Sirmium. Maximian, the Augustus of the West, ruled over Italy, Africa, and Spain from Milan; Constantius watched over Gaul and Britain, with headquarters at Treves and at York. But everywhere the writ of Diocletian ran. He took the majestic name of Jovius, while Maximian styled himself Herculius; and it stands as a marvellous tribute to his commanding influence that we hear of no friction between the four masters of the world.

Diocletian profoundly modified the character of the Roman Principate. He orientalised it, adopting frankly and openly the symbols and paraphernalia of royalty which had been so repugnant to the Roman temper. Hitherto the Roman Emperors had been, first and foremost, Imperators, heads of the army, soldiers in the purple. Diocletian became a King, clad in sumptuous robes, stiff with embroidery and jewels. Instead of approaching with the old military salute, those who came into his presence bent the knee and prostrated themselves in adoration. The monarch surrounded himself, not with military prefects, but with chamberlains and court officials, the hierarchy of the palace, not of the camp. We cannot wholly impute this change to vanity or to that littleness of mind which is pleased with pomp and elaborate ceremonial. Diocletian was too great a man to be swayed by paltry motives. It was rather that his subjects had abdicated their old claim to be called a free and sovereign people, and were ready to be slaves. The whole senatorial order had been debarred by Gallienus from entering the army, and had acquiesced without apparent protest in an edict which closed to its members the profession of arms. Diocletian thought that his throne would be safer by removing it from the ken of the outside world, by screening it from vulgar approach, by deepening the mystery and impressiveness attaching to palaces, by elaborating the court ceremonial, and exalting even the simplest of domestic services into the dignity of a liturgy. It may be that these changes intensified the servility of the subject, and sapped still further the manhood and self-respect of the race. Let it not be forgotten, however, that the ceremonial of the modern courts of Europe may be traced directly back to the changes introduced by Diocletian, and also that the ceremonial, which the older school of Romans would have thought degrading and effeminate, was, perhaps, calculated to impress by its stateliness, beauty, and dignity the barbarous nations which were supplying the Roman armies with troops.

We will reserve to a later chapter some account of the remodeled administration, which Constantine for the most part accepted without demur. Here we may briefly mention the decentralization which Diocletian carried out in the provinces. Lactantius says that "he carved the provinces up into little fragments that he might fill the earth with terror," and suggests that be multiplied officials in order to wring more money out of his subjects. That is an enemy's perversion of a wise statesman's plan for securing efficiency by lessening the administrative areas, and bringing them within working limits. Diocletian split up the Empire into twelve great dioceses. Each diocese again was subdivided into provinces. There were fifty-seven of these when he came to the throne; when he quitted it there were ninety-six. The system had grave faults, for the principles on which the finances of the Empire rested were thoroughly mischievous and unsound. But the reign of Diocletian was one of rapid recuperation and great prosperity, such as the Roman world had not enjoyed since the days of the Antonines.

THE PERSECUTION OF THE CHURCH

UNFORTUNATELY for the fame of Diocletian there is one indelible blot upon the record of his reign. He attached his name to the edicts whereby was let loose upon the Christian Church the last and—in certain provinces—the fiercest of the persecutions. Inasmuch as the affairs of the Christian Church will demand so large a share of our attention in dealing with the religious policy of Constantine, it will be well here to describe, as briefly as possible, its condition in the reign of Diocletian.

It has been computed that towards the end of the third century the population of the Roman Empire numbered about a hundred millions. What proportion were Christians? No one can say with certainty, but they were far more numerous in the East than in the West, among the Greek-speaking peoples of Asia than among the Latin-speaking peoples of Europe. Perhaps if we reckon them at a twelfth of the whole we shall rather underestimate than overestimate their number, while in certain portions of Asia and Syria they were probably at least one in five. Christianity had spread with amazing rapidity since the days of Domitian. There had been spasmodic outbreaks of fierce persecution under Decius,—"that execrable beast", as Lactantius calls him,—under Valerian, and under Aurelian. But Aurelian's reign was short and he had been too busy fighting to spare much time for religious persecution. The tempest quickly blew over. For fully half a century, with brief interludes of terror, the Church had been gathering strength and boldness.

The policy of the State towards it was one of indifference. Gallienus, indeed, the worthless son of Valerian, had issued edicts of toleration, which might be considered cancelled by the later edicts of Aurelian or might not. If the State wished to be savage, it could invoke the one set; if to be mild, it could invoke the other. There was, therefore, no absolute security for the Church, but the general feeling was one of confidence. The army contained a large number of Christians, of all ranks and conditions, officers, centurions, and private soldiers. Many of the officials of the civil service were Christians. The court and the palace were full of them. Diocletian's wife, Prisca, was a Christian; so was Valeria, his daughter. So, too, were many of his chamberlains, secretaries, and eunuchs. If Christianity had been a proscribed religion, if the Christians had anticipated another storm, is it conceivable that they would have dared to erect at Nicomedia, within full view of the palace windows, a large church situated upon an eminence in the centre of the city, and evidently one of its most conspicuous structures? No, Christianity in the East felt tolerably safe and was advancing from strength to strength, conscious of its increasing powers and of the benevolent neutrality of Diocletian. Christians who took office were relieved from the necessity of offering incense or presiding at the games. The State looked the other way; the Church was inclined to let them off with the infliction of some nominal penance. Nor was there much difficulty about service in the army. Probably few enlisted in the legions after they had become Christians; against this the Church set her face. But she permitted the converted soldier to remain true to his military oath, for she did not wish to become embroiled with the State. In a word, there was deep religious peace, at any rate in Dio-cletian's special sphere of influence, Asia, Egypt, and Syria.

It is to be remembered, however, that there were four rulers, men of very different characters and each, therefore, certain to regard Christianity from a different standpoint. Thus there might be religious peace in Asia and persecution in the West, as, indeed, there was—partial and spasmodic, but still persecution. Maximian was cruel and ambitious, an able soldier of the hard Roman type, no respecter of persons, and careless of human life. Very few modern historians have accepted the story of the massacre of the Theban Legion at Agauna, near Lake Leman, for refusal to offer sacrifice and take the oath to the Emperor. According to the legend, the legion was twice decimated and then cut to pieces. But it is impossible to believe that there could have been a legion or even a company of troops from Thebes in Egypt, wholly composed of

Christians, and, even supposing the facts to have been as stated, their refusal to march in obedience to the Emperor's orders and rejoin the main army at a moment when an active campaign was in progress, simply invited the stroke of doom. Maximian was not the man to tolerate mutiny in the face of the enemy.

But still there were many Christian victims of Maximian wherever he took up his quarters—at Rome, Aquileia, Marseilles—mostly soldiers whose refusal to sacrifice brought down upon them the arm of the law. Maximian is described in the "Passion of St. Victor" as "a great dragon", but the story, even as told by the hagiologist, scarcely justifies the epithet. Just as the military prefects, before whom Victor was first taken, begged him to reconsider his position, so Maximian, after ordering a priest to bring an altar of Jupiter, turned to Victor and said "Just offer a few grains of incense; placate Jupiter and be our friend". Victor's answer was to dash the altar to the ground from the hands of the priest and place his foot triumphantly upon it. We may admire the fortitude of the martyr, but the martyrdom was self-inflicted, and the anger of the Emperor not wholly unwarranted. "Be our friend", he had said, and his overtures were spurned with contempt.

We may suspect, indeed, that this partial persecution was due rather to the insistence of the martyrs themselves than to deliberate policy on the part of Maximian. When enthusiastic Christians thrust their Christianity upon the official notice of the authorities, insulted the Emperor or the gods, and refused to take the oath or sacrifice on ceremonial occasions, then martyrdom was the result, and little notice was taken, for life was cheap. Diocletian, as we have seen, rather patronized than persecuted Christianity. Maximian's inclinations towards cruelty were kept in check by the known wishes of his senior colleague. Constantius, the Caesar of Gaul, was one of those refined characters, tolerant and sympathetic by nature, to whom the idea of persecution for the sake of religion was intensely repugnant; and Galerius, the Caesar of Pannonia, the most fanatical pagan of the group, was not likely, at any rate during the first few years after his elevation, to run counter to the wishes of his patron.

What was it, then, that wrought the fatal change in the mind of Diocletian and turned him from benevolent neutrality to fierce antagonism? Lactantius attributes it solely to the baleful influence of Galerius, whom he paints in the very blackest colours. "He was a wild beast, a savage barbarian of alien blood, tall in stature, a mountain of flesh, abnormally bloated, terrifying to look at, and with a voice that made men shiver". Behind this monster stood his mother, a barbarian woman from beyond the Danube, priestess of some wild deity of the mountains, imbued with a fanatical hatred of the Christians, which she was forever instilling into her son. When we have stripped away the obvious exaggeration of this onslaught we may still accept the main statement and admit that Galerius was the most active and unsparing enemy of the Christians in the Imperial circle. This rough soldier, trained in the school of two such martinets as Aurelian and Probus, who enforced military discipline by the most pitiless methods, would not stay to reason with a soldier's religious prejudices. Unhesitating obedience or death—that was the only choice he gave to those who served under him, and when, after his great victory over the Parthians, his position and prestige in the East were beyond challenge, we find Christian martyrdoms in the track of his armies, in the Anti-Taurus, in Coele-Syria, in Samosata.

Galerius began to purge his army of Christians. Unless they would sacrifice, officers were to lose their rank and private soldiers to be dismissed ignominiously without the privileges of long service. Several were put to death in Moesia, where a certain Maximus was Governor. Among them was a veteran named Julius, who had served in the legion for twenty-six years, and fought in seven campaigns, without a single black mark having been entered against his name for any military offence. Maximus did his best to get him off.

"Julius", he said, "I see that you are a man of sense and wisdom. Suffer yourself to be persuaded and sacrifice to the gods".

"I will not", was the reply, "do what you ask. I will not incur by an act of sin eternal punishment".

"But", said the Governor, "I take the sin upon myself. I will use compulsion so that you may not seem to act voluntarily. Then you will be able to return in peace to your house. You will receive the bounty of ten denarii and no one will molest you".

Evidently, Maximus was heartily sorry that such a fine old soldier should take up a position which seemed to him so grotesquely indefensible. But what was Julius's reply?

"Neither this Devil's money nor your specious words shall cause me to lose eternal God. I cannot deny Him. Condemn me as a Christian".

After the interrogation had gone on for some time, Maximus said: "I pity you, and I beg you to sacrifice, so that you may live with us."

"To live with you would be death for me", rejoined Julius, "but if I die, I shall live".

"Listen to me and sacrifice; if not, I shall have to keep my word and order you to death".

"I have often prayed that I might merit such an end".

"Then you have chosen to die?"

"I have chosen a temporary death, but an eternal life".

Maximus then passed sentence, and the law took its course.

On another occasion the Governor said to two Christians, named Nicander and Marcian, who had proved themselves equally resolute: "It is not I whom you resist; it is not I who persecute you. My hands are unstained by your blood. If you know that you will fare well on your journey, I congratulate you. Let your desire be accomplished".

"Peace be with you, merciful judge", cried both the martyrs as the sentence was pronounced.

The movement seems gradually to have spread from the provinces of Galerius to those of Maximian. At Tangiers, Marcellus, a centurion of the Legion of Trajan, threw down his centurion's staff and belt and refused to serve any longer. He did so in the face of the whole army assembled to sacrifice in honor of Maximian's birthday. A similar scene took place in Spain at Calahorra, near Tarraco, where two soldiers cast off their arms exclaiming: "We are called to serve in the shining company of angels. There Christ commands His cohorts, clothed in white, and from his lofty throne condemns your infamous gods, and you, who are the creatures of these gods, or, we should say, these ridiculous monsters". Death followed as a matter of course. Looking at the evidence with absolute impartiality, one begins to suspect that the process of clearing the Christians out of the army was due quite as much to the fanaticism of certain Christian soldiers eager for martyrdom, as to any lust for blood on the part even of Galerius and Maximian.

But what we have to account for is the rise of a fierce anti-Christian spirit which induced Diocletian — for even Lactantius admits that he was not easily persuaded—to take active measures against the Christians. It is certainly noteworthy that about this time the only school of philosophy which was alive, active, and at all original, was definitely anti-Christian. We refer, of course, to the Neo-Platonists of Alexandria. Their principal exponent was the philosopher Porphyry, who carried on a violent anti-Christian propaganda, though he seems to have borrowed from Christianity, and more especially from the rigorously ascetic form which Christianity had assumed in Egypt, many of his leading tenets.

The morality which Porphyry inculcated was elevated and pure; his religion was mystical to such a degree that none but an expert philosopher could follow him into the refinements of his abstractions; but he had for the Christian Church a "theological hatred" of extraordinary bitterness. The treatise—in fifteen books— in which he assailed the Divinity of Christ apparently set a fashion in anti-Christian literature. We hear, for example, of another unnamed philosopher who "vomited three books against the Christian religion", and the violence with which Lactantius denounces him as "an accomplished hypocrite" makes one suspect that his work had a considerable success. Still better known was Hierocles, Governor at one time of Palmyra, and then transferred to the royal province of Bithynia, who wrote a book to which he ave the name of The Friend of Truth, and addressed it, "To the Christians". Its interest lies chiefly in the fact that its author compares with the miracles wrought by Christ those attributed to Apollonius of Tyana, and denies divinity to both. Lactantius tells us that this Hierocles was "author and counsellor of the persecution", and we may judge, therefore, that there existed among the pagans a powerful party bitterly opposed to Christianity, carrying on a vigorous campaign against it, and urging upon the Emperors the advisability of a sharp repressive policy.

They would have no difficulty in making out a case against the Christians which on the face of it seemed plausible and overwhelming. They would point to the fanatical spirit manifested, as we have seen, by a large number of Christian soldiers in the army, which led them to throw down their arms, blaspheme the gods, and deny the Emperors. They would point to the anti-social movement, which was especially marked in Egypt, where the example of St. Antony was drawing crowds of men and women away into the desert to live out their lives, either in solitary cells as hermits, or as members of religious communities equally ascetic, and almost equally solitary. They would point to the aloofness even of the ordinary Christian in city or in town from its common life, and to his avoidance of office and public duties. They would point to the extraordinary closeness of the ties which bound Christians together, to their elaborate organization, to the implicit and ready obedience they paid to their bishops, and would ask whether so powerful a secret society, with ramifications everywhere throughout the Empire, was not inevitably a menace to the established authorities, The Christians were peaceable enough. To accuse them of plotting rebellion was hardly possible, though the most outrageous calumnies against them and their rites were sedulously fostered in order to inflame the minds of the rabble, just as they were against the Jews in the Middle Ages, and are, even at the present day, in certain parts of the Continent of Europe. But, at bottom, the real strength of the case against the Christians lay in the fact that the more enlightened pagans saw that Christianity was the solvent which was bound to loosen all that held pagan society together. They instinctively felt what was coming, and were sensible of approaching doom. Christianity was the enemy, the proclaimed enemy, of their religion, of their point of view of this life as well as of the next, of their customs, of their pleasures, of their arts. Paganism was fighting for existence. What wonder that it snatched at any weapon wherewith to strike?

The personal attitude of Diocletian towards religion in general is best seen in the edict which he issued against the Manicheans. The date is somewhat uncertain, but it undoubtedly preceded the anti-Christian edicts. Manichaeism took its rise in Persia, its principal characteristic being the practice of thaumaturgy, and it spread fast throughout the East. Diocletian ordered the chiefs of the sect to be burned to death; their followers were to have their goods confiscated and to suffer capital punishment unless they recanted; while persons of rank who had disgraced themselves by joining such a shameful and infamous set of men were to lose their patrimony and be sent to the mines. These were savage enactments, and it is important to see how the Emperor justified them. Fortunately his language is most explicit. "The gods", he says, "have determined what is just and true; the wisest of mankind, by counsel and by deed, have proved and firmly established their principles. It is not, therefore, lawful to oppose their divine and human wisdom, or to pretend that a new religion can correct the old one. To wish to change the institutions of our ancestors is the greatest of crimes". Nothing could be clearer. It is the old official defence of the State religion, that men are not wiser than their fathers, and that innovation in worship is likely to bring down the wrath of the gods. Moreover, as the edict points out, this Manichaeism came from Persia, the traditional enemy of Rome, and threatened to corrupt the "modest and tranquil Roman people" with the detestable manners and infamous laws of the Orient. "Modest and tranquil" are not the epithets which posterity has chosen to apply to the Roman people of the Empire, but Diocletian's point is obvious. Manichaeism was a device of the enemy; it must be poison, therefore, to the good Roman. Such an argument was born of prejudice rather than of reason; we shall see it applied yet again to the Christians, and applied even by the Christian Church to its own schismatic's and heretics.

It was during the winter of 302 that the question was carefully debated by Diocletian and Galerius-, the latter was staying with the senior Augustus at Nicomedia—whether it was advisable to take repressive measures against the Christians. According to Lactantius, Galerius clamored for blood, while Diocletian represented how mischievous it would be to throw the whole world into a ferment, and how the Christians were wont to welcome martyrdom. He argued, therefore, that it would be quite enough if they purged the court and the army. Then, as neither would give way, a Council was called, which sided with Galerius rather than with Diocletian, and it was decided to consult the oracle of Apollo at Miletus. Apollo returned the strange answer that there were just men on the earth who prevented him from speaking the truth, and gave that as the reason why the oracles which proceeded from his tripods were false. The "just men" were, of course, the Christians. Diocletian yielded, only stipulating that there should be no bloodshed, while Galerius was for burning all Christians alive. Such is Lactantius's story, and it does credit to Diocletian, inasmuch as it shows his profound reluctance to disturb the internal peace which his own wise policy had established. As a propitious day, the Festival of the Terminalia, February 23, 303, was chosen for the inauguration of the anti-Christian campaign. The church at Nicomedia was leveled to the ground by the Imperial troops and, on the following day, an edict was issued depriving Christians of their privileges as full Roman citizens. They were to be deprived of all their honours and distinctions, whatever their rank; they were to be liable to torture; they were to be penalized in the courts by not being allowed to prosecute for assault, adultery, and theft. Lactantius well says a that they were to lose their liberty and their right of speech. The penalties extended even to slaves. If a Christian slave refused to renounce his religion he was never to receive his freedom. The churches, moreover, were to be destroyed and Christians were forbidden to meet together. No bloodshed was threatened, as Diocletian had stipulated, but the Christian was reduced to the condition of a pariah. The edict was no sooner posted up than, with a bitter jibe at the Emperors, some bold, indignant Christian tore it down. He was immediately arrested, tortured, racked, and burnt at the stake. Diocletian had been right. The Christians made willing martyrs.

Soon afterwards there was an outbreak of fire at the palace. Lactantius accuses Galerius of having contrived it himself so that he might throw the odium upon the Christians, and he adds that Galerius so worked upon the fears of Diocletian that he gave leave to every official in the palace to use the rack in the hope of getting at the truth. Nothing was discovered, but fifteen days later there was another mysterious outbreak. Galerius, protesting that he would stay no longer to be burnt alive, quitted the palace at once, though it was bad weather for travelling. Then, says Lactantius, Diocletian allowed his blind terrors to get the better of him, and the persecution began in earnest. He forced his wife and daughter to recant; he purged the palace, and put to death some of his most powerful eunuchs, while the Bishop of Nicomedia was beheaded, and crowds of less distinguished victims were thrown into prison. Whether there was incendiarism or not, no one can say. Eusebius, indeed, tells us that Constantine, who was living in the palace at the time, declared years afterwards to the bishops at the Council of Nicaea that he hail seen with his own eyes the lightning descend and set fire to the abode of the godless Emperor. But neither Constantine nor Eusebius was to be believed implicitly when it was a question of some supernatural occurrence between earth and heaven. The double conflagration is certainly suspicious, but tyrants do not, as a rule, set fire to their own palaces when they themselves are in residence, however strong may be their animus against some obnoxious party in the State.

A few months passed and Diocletian published a second edict ordering the arrest of all bishops and clergy who refused to surrender their "holy books" to the civil officers. Then, in the following year, came a third, offering freedom to all in prison if they consented to sacrifice, and instructing magistrates to use every possible means to compel the obstinate to abandon their faith. These edicts provoked a frenzy of persecution, and Gaul and Britain alone enjoyed comparative immunity. Constantius could not, indeed, entirely disregard an order which bore the joint names of the two Augusti, but he took care that there was no over-zealousness, and, according to a well-known passage of Lactantius, he allowed the meeting-places of the Christians, the buildings of wood and stone which could easily be restored, to be torn down, but preserved in safety the true temple of God, viz., the bodies of His worshippers. Elsewhere the persecution may be traced from province to province and from city to city in the mournful and poignant documents known as the Passions of the Martyrs. Naturally it varied in intensity according to local conditions and according to the personal predilections of the magistrates.

Where the populace was fiercely anti-Christian or where the pagan priests were zealous, there the Christians suffered severely. Their churches would be razed to the ground and the prisons would be full. Some of the weaker brethren would recant; others would hide themselves or quit the district; others again would suffer martyrdom. In more fortunate districts, where public opinion was with the Christians, the churches might not be destroyed, though they stood empty and silent.

The fiercest persecution seems to have taken place in Asia Minor. There had been a partial revolt of the troops at Antioch, easily suppressed by the Antiochenes themselves, but Diocletian apparently connected it in some way with the Christians and let his hand fall heavily upon them. Just at this time, moreover, in the neighbouring kingdom of Armenia, Saint Gregory the Illuminator was preaching the gospel with marvelous success, and the Christians of Cappadocia, just over the border, paid the penalty for the uneasiness which this ferment caused to their rulers. We hear, for example, in Phrygia of a whole Christian community being extirpated. Magistrates, senators, and people—Christians all—had taken refuge in their principal church, to which the troops set fire. Eusebius, in his History of the Church, paints a lamentable picture of the persecution which he himself witnessed in Palestine and Syria, and, in his Life of Constantine, he says a that even the barbarians across the frontier were so touched by the sufferings of the Christian fugitives that they gave them shelter. Athanasius, too, declares that he often heard survivors of the persecution say that many pagans risked the loss of their goods and the chance of imprisonment in order to hide Christians from the officers of the law. There is no question of exaggeration. The most horrible tortures were invented; the most barbarous and degrading punishments were devised. The victim who was simply ordered to be decapitated or drowned was highly favored. In a very large number of cases death was delayed as long as possible. The sufferer, after being tortured on the rack, or having eyes or tongue torn out, or foot or hand struck off, was taken back to prison to recover for a second examination.

Even when the victim was dead the law frequently pursued the corpse with its futile vengeance. It was no uncommon thing for a body to be thrown to the dogs, or to be chopped into fragments and cast into the sea, or to be burnt and the ashes flung upon running water. He was counted a merciful judge who allowed the friends of the martyr to bear away the body to decent burial and lay it in the grave. At Augsburg, when the magistrate heard that the mother and three servants of a converted courtesan, named Afra, had placed her body in a tomb, he ordered all four to be enclosed in one grave with the corpse and burnt alive.

It is, of course, quite impossible to compute the number of the victims, but it was unquestionably very large. We do not, perhaps, hear of as many bishops and priests being put to death as might have been expected, but if the extreme rigor of the law had been enforced the Empire would have been turned into a shambles. The fact is, as we have said, that very much depended upon the personal character of the Governors and the local magistrates. In some places altars were put up in the law courts and no one was allowed either to bring or defend a suit without offering sacrifice. In other towns they were erected in the market squares and by the side of the public fountains, so that one could neither buy nor sell, nor even draw water, without being challenged to do homage to the gods. Some Governors, such as Datianus in Spain, Theotecnus in Galatia, Urbanus of Palestine, and Hierocles of Bithynia and Egypt, were noted for the ferocity with which they carried out the edicts; others— and, when the evidence is carefully examined, the humane judges seem to have formed the majority—presided with reluctance at these lamentable trials. Many exhausted every means in their power to convert the prisoners back to the old religion, partly from motives of humanity, and partly, no doubt, because their success in this respect gained them the notice and favor of their superiors.

We hear of magistrates who ordered the attendants of the court to place by force a few grains of incense in the hands of the prisoner and make him sprinkle it upon the altar, or to thrust into his mouth a portion of the sacrificial meat. The victim would protest against his involuntary defilement, but the magistrate would declare that the offering had been made. Often, the judge sought to bribe the accused into apostasy. "If you obey the Governor", St. Victor of Galatia was told, "you shall have the title of Friend of Caesar and a post in the palace". Theotecnus promised Theodotus of Ancyra "the favor of the Emperors, the highest municipal dignities, and the priesthood of Apollo". The bribe was great, but it was withstood. The steadfast confessor gloried in replying to every fresh taunt, entreaty, or bribe, "I am a Christian." It was to him the only, as well as the highest argument.

Sometimes the kindest-hearted judges were driven to exasperation by their total inability to make the slightest impression upon the Christians.

"Do abandon your foolish boasting", said Maximus, the Governor of Cilicia, to Andronicus, "and listen to me as you would listen to your father. Those who have played the madman before you have gained nothing by it. Pay honor to our Princes and our fathers and submit yourself to the gods".

"You do well", came the reply, "to call them your fathers, for you are the sons of Satan, the sons of the Devil, whose works you perform".

A few more remarks passed between judge and prisoner and then Maximus lost his temper.

"I will make you die by inches", he exclaimed.

"I despise", retorted Andronicus, "your threats and your menaces".

While an old man of sixty-five was being led to the torture, a friendly centurion said to him: "Have pity on yourself and sacrifice".

"Get thee from me, minister of Satan", was the reply. The main feeling uppermost in the mind of the confessor was one of exultation that he had been found worthy to suffer. Such a spirit could neither be bent nor broken.

Of active disloyalty to the Emperor there is absolutely no trace. Many Christian soldiers boasted of their long and honorable service in the army; civilians were willing to pay unto Caesar the things that were Caesar's. But Christ was their King. "There is but one God", cried Alpheus and Zaccheus at Caesarea, "and only one King and Lord, who is Jesus Christ". To the pagan judge this was not merely blasphemy against the gods, but treason against the Emperor. Sometimes, but not often, the martyr's feelings got the better of him and he cursed the Emperor. "May you be punished", cried the dauntless Andronicus to Maximus, when the officers of the court had thrust between his lips the bread and meat of sacrifice, "may you be punished, bloody tyrant, you and they who have given you the power to defile me with your impious sacrifices. One day you will know what you have done to the servants of God".

"Accursed scoundrel", said the judge, "dare you curse the Emperors who have given the world such long and profound peace?"

"I have cursed them and I will curse them", replied Andronicus, "these public scourges, these drinkers of blood, who have turned the world upside down. May the immortal hand of God tolerate them no longer and punish their cruel amusements, that they may learn and know the evil they have done to God's servants".

No doubt, most Christians agreed with the sentiments expressed by Andronicus, but they rarely gave expression to them.

"I have obeyed the Emperors all the years of my life", said Bishop Philippus of Heraclea, "and, when their commands are just, I hasten to obey. For the Holy Scripture has ordered me to render to God what is due to God and to Caesar what is due to Caesar. I have kept this commandment without flaw down to the present time, and it only remains for me to give preference to the things of heaven over the attractions of this world. Remember what I have already said several times, that I am a Christian and that I refuse to sacrifice to your gods".

Nothing could be more dignified or explicit. It is the Emperor-God and his fellow deities of Olympus, not the Emperor, to whom the Christian refuses homage. During a trial at Catania in Sicily the judge, Calvisianus, said to a Christian: "Unhappy man, adore the gods, render homage to Mars, Apollo, and Esculapius".

The answer came without a second's hesitation: "I adore the Father, Son, and Holy Spirit—the Holy Trinity—beyond whom there is no God. Perish the gods who have not made heaven and earth and all that they contain. I am a Christian".

From first to last, in Spain as in Africa, in Italy as in Sicily, this is the alpha and the omega of the Christian position: "Christianus sum".

To what extent was the martyrdom self-inflicted? How far did the Christians pile with their own hands the faggots round the stakes to which they were tied? It is significant that some churches found it necessary to condemn the extraordinary exaltation of spirit which drove men and women to force themselves upon the notice of the authorities and led them to regard flight from danger as culpable weakness. They not only did not encourage but strictly forbade the overthrowing of pagan statues or altars by zealous Christians anxious to testify to their faith. They did not wish, that is to say, to provoke certain reprisals. Yet, in spite of all their efforts, martyrdom was constantly courted by rash and excitable natures in the frenzy of religious fanaticism, like that which impelled Theodorus of Amasia in Pontus to set fire to a temple of Cybele in the middle of the city and then boast openly of the deed. Often, however, such martyrs were mere children. Such was Eulalia of Merida, a girl of twelve, whose parents, suspecting her intention, had taken her into the country to be out of harm's way. She escaped their vigilance, returned to the city, and, standing before the tribunal of the judge, proclaimed herself a Christian. The judge, instead of bidding the officials remove the child, began to argue with her, and the argument ended in Eulalia spitting in his face and overturning the statue which had been brought for her to worship. Then came torture and the stake, a martyred saint, and in later centuries a stately church, flower festivals, and a charming poem from the Christian poet, Prudentius. But even his graceful verses do not reconcile us to the pitiful futility of such child-martyrdom as that of Eulalia of Merida or Agnes of Rome.

Or take, again, the pathetic inscription found at Testur, in Northern Africa;

"Sande Tres ; Maxima,

Donatilla Et Secunda,

Bona Peella".

These were three martyrs of Thuburbo. Two of them, Maxima and Donatilla, had been denounced to the judge by another woman. Secunda, a child of twelve, saw her friends from a window in her father's house, as they were being dragged off to prison. "Do not abandon me, my sisters," she cried. They tried to wave her back. She insisted. They warned her of the cruel fate which was certain to await her; Secunda declared her confidence in Him who comforts and consoles the little ones. In the end they let her accompany them. All three were sentenced to be torn by the wild beasts of the amphitheatre, but when they stood up to face that cruel death, a wild bear came and lay at their feet. The judge, Anulinus, then ordered them to be decapitated. Such is the story that lies behind those simple and touching words, "Secunda, Bona Puella".

Nor were young men backward in their zeal for the martyr's crown. Eusebius tells us of a band of eight Christian youths at Caesarea, who confronted the Governor, Urbanus, in a body shouting: "We are Christians", and of another youth named Aphianus, who, while reading the Scriptures, heard the voice of the heralds summoning the people to sacrifice. He at once made his way to the Governor's house, and, just as Urbanus was in the act of offering libation, Aphianus caught his arm and upbraided him for his idolatry. He simply flung his life away.

In this connection may be mentioned the five martyred statuary workers belonging to a Pannonian marble quarry. They had been converted by the exhortations of Bishop Cyril, of Antioch, who had been condemned to labor in their quarry, and, once having become Christians, their calling gave them great searching of heart. Did not the Scriptures forbid them to make idols or graven images of false gods? When, therefore, they refused to undertake a statue of Esculapius, they were challenged as Christians, and sentenced to death. Yet they had not thought it wrong to carve figures of Victory and Cupid, and they seem to have executed without scruple a marble group showing the sun in a chariot, doubtless satisfying themselves that these were merely decorative pieces, which did not necessarily involve the idea of worship. But they preferred to die rather than make a god for a temple, even though that god were the gentle Esculapius, the Healer.

We might dwell at much greater length upon this absorbing subject of the persecution of Diocletian, and draw upon the Passions of the Saints for further examples of the marvelous fortitude with which so many of the Christians endured the most fiendish tortures for the sake of their faith. "I only ask one favor", said the intrepid Asterius: "it is that you will not leave unlacerated a single part of my body". In the presence of such splendid fidelity and such unswerving faith, which made even the weakest strong and able to endure, one sees why the eventual triumph of the Church was certain and assured. One can also understand why the memory and the relics of the martyrs were preserved with such passionate devotion; why their graves were considered holy and credited with powers of healing; and why, too, the names of their persecutors were remembered with such furious hatred. It may be too much to expect the early chroniclers of the Church to be fair to those who framed and those who put into execution the edicts of persecution, but we, at least, after so many centuries, and after so many persecutions framed and directed by the Churches themselves, must try to look at the question from both sides and take note of the absolute refusal of the Christian Church to consent to the slightest compromise in its attitude of hostility to the religious system which it had already dangerously undermined.

It is not easy from a study of the Passions of the Saints to draw any sweeping generalizations as to what the public at large thought of the torture and execution of Christians. We get a glimpse, indeed, of the ferocity of the populace at Rome when Maximian went thither to celebrate the Ludi Cereales in 304. The "Passion of St. Savinus" shows an excited crowd gathered in the Circus Maximus, roaring for blood and repeating twelve times over the savage cry: "Away with the Christians and our happiness is complete. By the head of Augustus let not a Christian survive." Then, when they caught sight of Hermogenianus, the city prefect, they called ten times over to the Emperor: "May you conquer, Augustus! Ask the prefect what it is we are shouting." Such a scene was natural enough in the Circus of Rome; was it typical of the Empire? Doubtless in all the great cities, such as Alexandria, Antioch, Ephesus, Carthage, the 'baser sort' would be quite ready to shout: Away with the Christians". But it is to be remembered that we find no trace anywhere in this persecution of a massacre on the scale of that of St. Bartholomew or the Sicilian Vespers. On the contrary, we see that though the prisons were full, the relations of the Christians were usually allowed to visit them, take them food, and listen to their exhortations. Pamphilus of Caesarea, who was in jail for two years, not only received his friends during that period, but was able to go on making copies of the Scriptures!

We rarely hear of the courts being packed with anti-Christian crowds, or of the judges being incited by popular clamor to pass the death sentence. The reports of the trials show us silent, orderly courts, with the judges anxious not so much to condemn to death as to make a convert. If Diocletian had wanted blood he could have had it in rivers, not in streams. But he did not. He wished to eradicate what he believed to be an impious, mischievous, and, from the point of view of the State's security, a dangerous superstition. There was no talk of persecuting for the sake of saving the souls of heretics; that lamentable theory was reserved for a later day. Diocletian persecuted for what he considered to be the good of the State. He lived to witness the full extent of his failure, and to realize the appalling crime which he had committed against humanity, amid the general overthrow of the political system which he had so laboriously set up.

THE ABDICATION OF DIOCLETIAN AND THE SUCCESSION OF CONSTANTINE

ON the 1st of May, in the year 305, Diocletian, by an act of unexampled abnegation, resigned the purple and retired into private life. The renunciation was publicly performed, not in Rome, for Rome had ceased to be the centre of the political world, but on a broad plain in Bithynia, three miles from Nicomedia, which long had been the Emperor's favorite residence. In the centre of the plain rose a little hill, upon which stood a column surmounted by a statue of Jupiter. There, years before, Diocletian had with his own hands invested Galerius with the symbols of power; there he was now to perform the last act of a ruler by nominating those whom he thought most fit to succeed him. A large platform had been constructed; the soldiers of the legions had been ordered to assemble in soldier's meeting and listen to their chief's farewell. Diocletian took leave of them in few words. He was old, he said, and infirm. He craved for rest after a life of toil. The Empire needed stronger and more youthful hands than his. His work was done. It was time for him to go.

The two Augusti were laying down their powers simultaneously, for Maximian was performing a similar act of renunciation at Milan. The two Caesars, Constantius and Galerius, would thus automatically move up into the empty places and become Augusti in their stead. It had been necessary, therefore, to select two new Caesars, and these Diocletian was about to present to the loyalty of the legions. We are told that the secret had been well kept, and that the soldiers waited with suppressed excitement until Diocletian suddenly announced that his choice had fallen upon Severus, one of his trusted generals, and upon Maximin Daza, a nephew of Galerius. Severus had already been sent to Milan to be invested by Maximian; Maximin was present on the tribunal and was then and there robed in the purple. The ceremony over, Diocletian—a private citizen once more, though he still retained the title of Augustus—drove back to Nicomedia and at once set out for Salona, on the Adriatic, where he had built a sumptuous palace for his retirement.

The scene which we have depicted is described most fully and most graphically by a historian whose testimony, unfortunately, is entirely suspect in matters of detail. The author of The Deaths of the Persecutors—it is very doubtful whether Lactantius, to whom the work has long been attributed, really wrote it, but for the sake of convenience of reference we may credit him with it—is at once the most untrustworthy and the most vigorous and attractive writer of the period. His object throughout is to blacken the characters of the Emperors who persecuted the Christian Church, and he does not scruple to distort their actions, pervert their motives, and even invent, with well calculated malice, stories to their discredit. Lactantius knows, or pretends to know, all that takes place even in the most secret recesses of the palace; he recounts all that passes at the most confidential conferences; and with consummate artistry he throws in circumstantial details and touches of local colour which give an appearance of truth, but are really the most convincing proofs of falsehood. Lactantius represents the abdication of Diocletian as the act of an old man, shattered in health, and even in mind, by a distressing malady sent by Heaven as the just punishment of his crimes. He depicts him cowering in tears before the impatient insolence of Galerius, now peremptorily clamoring for the succession with threats of civil war. They discuss who shall be the new Caesars.

"Whom shall we appoint?" asks Diocletian.

"Severus" says Galerius.

"What?" says the other, "that drunken sot of a dancer who turns night into day and day into night?"

"He is worthy" replies Galerius, "for he has proved a faithful general, and I have sent him to Maximian to be invested"

"Well, well" says the old man, "who is the second choice?"

"He is here" says Galerius, indicating his nephew, a young semi-barbarian named Maximin Daza.

"Why, who is this you offer me?"

"He is my kinsman" is the reply. Then said Diocletian, with a groan:

"These are not fit men to whom to entrust the care of the State"

"I have proved them" said Galerius.

"Well, you must look to it" rejoins Diocletian, "you who are about to assume the reins of the Empire. I have toiled enough. While I ruled, I took care that the State stood safe. If any harm now befalls, the fault is not mine".

Such is a characteristic specimen of Lactantius's history, and so, when he comes to describe the ceremony of abdication, he makes Galerius draw Maximin Daza to the front of the group of imperial officials by whom Diocletian is surrounded, and represents the soldiers as staring in surprise at their new Caesar, as at one whom they had never seen before. Yet a favorite nephew of Galerius can scarcely have been a stranger to the troops of Nicomedia. Galerius not only—according to Lactantius—drew forward Maximin Daza, but at the same time rudely thrust back into the throng the son of Constantius, the senior of the two new Augusti. This was young Constantine, the future Emperor, who for some years past had been living at the Court of Diocletian.

But it was no broken down Emperor in his dotage, passing, according to the spasms of his malady, from sanity to insanity, who resigned the throne on the plain of Nicomedia. Diocletian was but fifty-nine years of age. He had just recovered, it is true, from a very severe illness, which, even on the testimony of Lactantius, had caused "grief in the palace, sadness and tears among his guards, and anxious suspense throughout the whole State". But his brain was never clearer than when he took final leave of his troops. His abdication was the culminating point of his policy. He had planned it twenty years before. He had kept it before his eyes throughout a long and busy reign. It was the completion of, the finishing touch to his great political system. It would have been perfectly easy for Diocletian to forswear himself. Probably very few of his contemporaries believed that he would fulfill his promise to abdicate after twenty years of reign. Kings talk of the allurements of retirement, but they usually cling to power as tenaciously as to life. The first Augustus had delighted to mystify his Ministers of State by speaking of restoring the Republic. He died an Emperor. Diocletian, alone of the Roman Emperors, laid down the sceptre when he was at the height of his glory. It was a hazardous experiment, but he was faithful to his principles. He thought it best for the world that its master should not grow old and feeble on the throne.

Constantine, of whom we have just caught a glimpse at the abdication of Diocletian, was born either in 273 or 274. The uncertainty attaching to the year of his birth attaches even more to its place. No one now believes that he was born in Britain—a pleasing fiction which was invented by English monks, who delighted to represent his mother Helena as the daughter of a British King, though they were quite at a loss where to locate his kingdom. The only foundation for this was a passage in one of the Panegyrists, who said that Constantine had bestowed lustre upon Britain "illic oriundo". But the words are now taken as referring to his accession and not to his birth. He was certainly proclaimed Emperor in Britain, and might thus be said to have "sprung thence". Constantine's birth-place seems to have been either Naissus, a city in Upper Moesia, or Drepanum, a city near Nicomedia. The balance of evidence, though none of it is very trustworthy, inclines to the former.

His father was Constantius Chlorus, afterwards Caesar and Augustus, but at the time of Constantine's birth merely a promising officer in the Roman army. Constantius belonged to one of the leading families of Moesia and his mother was a niece of the capable and soldierly Claudius, the conqueror of the Goths. Claudius had only been dead four years when Constantine was born, and we may suppose that it was his influence which had set Constantius in the way of rapid promotion. He had formed one of those secondary marriages which were recognized by Roman law, when the wife was not of the same social standing as the husband. Helena is said to have been the daughter of an innkeeper of Drepanum, and Constantine's enemies lost no opportunity of dwelling upon the obscurity of his ancestry upon his mother's side. But that he was born in wedlock is beyond question. Had the relationship between Constantius and Helena been an irregular one, there would have been no need for Maximian to insist on a divorce when he ratified Constantius's elevation to the purple by giving him the hand of his daughter, Theodora.

Of Constantine's early years we know nothing, though we may suppose that they were spent in the eastern half of the Empire. Constantius served with the eastern legions in the campaigns which preceded the accession of Diocletian in 284, and it is as a young officer in the entourage of that Emperor that Constantine makes his earliest appearance in history. Eusebius tells us that he first saw the future champion of Christianity in the train of Diocletian during one of the latter's visits to Palestine. He recalls his vivid remembrance of the young Prince standing at the Emperor's right hand and attracting the gaze of all beholders by the beauty of his person and the imposing air which betokened his consciousness of having been born to rule. Eusebius adds that while Constantine's physical strength extorted the respectful admiration of his younger associates, his remarkable qualities of prudence and wisdom aroused the jealousy and excited the apprehensions of his chiefs. However, the recollections of the Bishop of Caesarea, with half a century of interval, are somewhat suspect, and we need see no more than a high-spirited, handsome, and keen-witted Prince in Eusebius's "paragon of bodily strength, physical beauty, and mental distinction". As for Diocletian's jealous fears, they are best refuted by the fact that Constantine was promoted to be a tribune of the first rank and saw considerable military service. The foolish stories that his superiors set him to fight a gigantic Sarmatian in single combat, and dared him to contend against ferocious wild beasts, in the hope that his pride and courage might be his undoing, may be dismissed as childish. If Diocletian had feared Constantine, Constantine would never have survived his residence in the palace.

It is certainly remarkable that we should know so little, not only of the youth but of the early manhood of Constantine, who was at least in his thirty first year when Diocletian retired into private life. Why had he spent all those years in the East instead of sharing with his father the dangers and glories of his Gallic and British campaigns? The answer is doubtless to be found in the fact that it was no part of Diocletian's system for the son to succeed the father. Constantius's loyalty was never in doubt, but Constantine, if Zosimus can be trusted, had already given evidence of consuming ambition to rule. However that may be, it is obvious that his position became much more hazardous when Galerius succeeded Diocletian as supreme ruler in the palace of Nicomedia. One can understand Galerius wondering whether the capable young Prince, who slept under his roof, was destined to cross his path, and the anxiety of Constantius, conscious of declining strength, that his long-absent son should join him. Constantine himself might well be uneasy, and scheme to quit a place where he could not hope' to satisfy his natural ambitions.

We need not doubt, therefore, that Constantius repeatedly sent messages to Galerius asking that his son might come to him, or that the son was eager to comply.

Lactantius, who does his best to make history romantic and exciting, describes the eventual escape of Constantine in one of his most graphic chapters. He shows us Galerius in his palace reluctantly signing an order which authorized Constantine to travel post across the Continent of Europe. He only consented to do so, we are told, because he could find no pretext for further delay, and he gave the order to Constantine late in the afternoon, on the understanding that he should see him again in the morning to receive his final instructions. Yet all the time, says Lactantius, Galerius was scheming to find some excuse for keeping him in Nicomedia, or contemplated sending a message to Severus, asking him to delay Constantine when he reached the border of northern Italy. Galerius then took dinner, retired for the night, and slept so well and deliberately that he did not wake until the following midday. He then sent for Constantine to come to his apartment. But Constantine was already gone, scouring the roads as fast as the post horses could carry him, and so anxious to increase the distance between himself and Galerius that he caused the tired beasts to be hamstrung at every stage. He had waited for Galerius to retire and had then slipped away, lest the Emperor should change his mind. Galerius was furious when he found that he had been outwitted. He ordered pursuit. His servants came back to tell him that the fugitive had swept the stables clear of horses.

And then Galerius could scarce restrain his tears.

It is a story which does infinite credit to Lactantius's feeling for strong melodramatic situation. No picturesque detail is omitted—the setting sun, the tyrant plotting vengeance over dinner, his resolve to sleep long, his baffled triumph, the escaping hero, and the butchery of the horses. Yet we question if there is more than a shred of truth in the whole story. Galerius would not have given Constantine the sealed order overnight had he intended to take it back the next morning. A word to the officer of the watch in the palace and to the officer on duty at the city gate would have prevented Constantine from quitting Nicomedia. The imperial post service must have been very much under horsed if the Emperor's servants could not find mounts for the effective pursuit of a single fugitive. Galerius may very well have been unwilling for Constantine to go, and Constantine doubtless covered the early stages of his long journey at express speed, in order to minimize the chance of recall, but the lurid details of Lactantius are probably simply the outcome of his own lively imagination.

Constantine seems to have found his father at the port of Gessoriacum (Boulogne), just waiting for a favorable wind to carry him across the Channel into Britain. Constantius was ill, and welcomed with great joy the son whom he had not seen for many years. We do not know what time elapsed before Constantius died at York,—apparently it was after the conclusion of a campaign in Scotland,—but before he died he commended to Constantine the welfare of his young half-brothers and half-sisters, the eldest of whom was no more than thirteen years of age, and he also evidently commended Constantine himself to the loyalty of his legions. The Emperor, we are informed both by Lactantius and by the author of the Seventh Panegyric, died with a mind at rest because he was sure of his heir and successor—Jupiter himself, says the pagan orator, stretched out his right hand and welcomed him among the gods. Clearly, the ground had been well prepared, for no sooner was the breath out of Constantius's body than the troops saluted Constantine with the title of Augustus. Aurelius Victor adds the interesting detail that he had no stouter supporter than Erocus, a Germanic King, who was serving as an auxiliary in the Roman army. Constantine was nothing loth, though, as usual in such circumstances, he may have feigned a reluctance which he did not feel. His panegyrist, indeed, represents him as putting spurs to his horse to enable him to shake off the robe which the soldiers sought to throw over his shoulders, and suggests that it had been Constantine's intention to write "to the senior Princes" and consult their wishes as to the choice of a successor. Had he done so, he knew very well that Galerius would have sent over to Britain some trusted lieutenant of his own to take command and Constantine would have received peremptory orders to return. Instead of that, Constantine assumed the insignia of an Emperor, and wrote to Galerius announcing his elevation. Galerius, it is said, hesitated long as to the course he should adopt. That the news angered him we may be sure. Apart from all personal considerations, this choice of an Emperor by an army on active service was a return to the bad old days of military rule, from which Diocletian had rescued the Empire, and was a clear warning that the new system had not been established on a permanent basis. The only alternative, however, before Galerius was acceptance or war. For the latter he was hardly prepared, and moreover, there was no reply to the argument that Constantius had been senior Augustus, and, therefore, had been fully entitled to have his word in the appointment of a successor. Galerius gave way. He accepted the laurelled bust which Constantine had sent to him and, instead of throwing it into the fire with the officer who had brought it—which, according to Lactantius, had been his first impulse, —he sent the messenger back with a purple robe to his master as a sign that he frankly admitted his claims to partnership in the Empire.

But while he acknowledged Constantine as Caesar, he refused him the full title of Augustus, which he bestowed upon the Caesar Severus. This has been represented as an act of petty spite. In reality, it was simply the automatic working of the system of Diocletian. The latest winner of imperial dignity naturally took the fourth place. Constantine accepted the check without demur. He had not spent so many years by the side of Diocletian and Galerius without discovering that if it came to war, it was the master of the best army who was sure to be the winner and survivor, whether his title were Caesar or Augustus. Thus, in July, 306, Constantine commenced his eventful reign as the Cesar of the West, overlord of Gaul, Spain, and Britain, and commander of the Army of the Rhine, and, for the next six years, down to his invasion of Italy in 312, he spent most of his time in the Gallic provinces, where he gained the reputation of being a capable soldier and a generous Prince.

Gaul was slowly recovering from chaos and ruin. During the anarchy which had preceded the accession of Diocletian, she had lain at the mercy of the Germanic tribes across the Rhine. The Roman watch on the river had been almost abandoned; the legions and the garrisons had been so weakened as to be powerless to keep the invader in check. The Gallic provinces were, in the striking words of the Panegyrist, "maddened by their injuries of the years gone by". The result had been the peasant rising of the Bagauds, ruthlessly suppressed by Maximian in 285, but the desperate condition of the country may be inferred from the fact that Diocletian and Maximian felt compelled to recognize the pretensions of Carausius in the province of Britain, which, for some years, was practically severed from the Empire. And, moreover, the peace of Gaul, which Maximian laboriously restored, was punctuated by invasion from the Germans across the Rhine. In the Panegyric of Mamertinus there occurs a curious passage, which shows with what eyes the Romans regarded that river. The orator is eulogizing Maximian in his most fulsome strain for restoring tranquillity, and then says: "Was there ever an Emperor before our day who did not congratulate himself that the Gallic provinces were protected by the Rhine? When did the Rhine shrink in its channel after a long spell of fine weather without making us shiver with fear? When did it ever swell to a flood without giving us an extra sense of security?" In other words, the danger of invasion rose and fell with the rising and falling of the Rhine. But now, continues the Panegyrist, thanks to Maximian, all our fears are gone. The Rhine may dry up and shrink until it can scarce roll the smooth pebbles in its limpid shallows, and none will be afraid. As far as I can see beyond the Rhine, all is Roman". Rarely has a court rhetorician uttered a more audacious lie.

There was no quality of permanence in the Gallic peace. Constantius took advantage of a temporary lull to recover Britain, but in 301 he was again fighting the invading Germans and Franks, winning victories which had to be repeated in the following summer, and making good the dearth of laborers on the devastated lands of Gaul by the captives he had taken in battle. There is a remarkable passage in the Fifth Panegyric in which the author refers to the long columns of captives which he had seen on the march in Gaul, men, women, and children on their way to the desert regions assigned to them, there to bring back to fertility by their labor as slaves the very countryside which in their freedom they had pillaged and laid waste. He recalled the familiar sight of these savage barbarians tamed to surprising quiescence, and waiting in the public places of the Eduan cities until they were sold off to their new masters. Gaul had suffered so long from these roving ruffians from over the Rhine that the orator broke out into a pan of exultation at the thought that the once dreaded Chamavan or Frisian now tilled his estates for him, and that the vagabond freebooter had become an agricultural laborer, who drove his stock to the Gallic markets and cheapened the price of commodities by increasing the sources of supply.

Full allowance must be made for exaggeration. The tribes, which are described as having been extirpated, reappear later on in the same numbers as before, and there was security only so long as the Emperor and his legions were on the spot. When Constantius crossed to Britain on the expedition which terminated with his death, the Franks took advantage of his absence to "violate the peace". The words would seem to imply that there had been a treaty between Constantius and the Kings Ascaricus and Regaisus. They crossed the Rhine and Constantine, the new Cesar, hastened back from Britain to confront them. Where the battle took place is not known, but both Kings were captured and, together with a multitude of their followers, flung to the wild beasts in the amphitheatre at Treves. Constantine, who prided himself upon his clemency to a Roman foe, whose sensitive soul was harrowed when even a wicked enemy perished, inflicted a fearful punishment.

"Those slain in battle were beyond numbers; very many more were taken prisoners. All their flocks were carried off or butchered; all their villages burnt with fire; all their young men, who were too treacherous to be admitted into the Roman army, and too brutal to act as slaves, were thrown to the wild beasts, and fatigued the ravening creatures because there were so many of them to kill".

Those atrocious sentences—written in praise, not in condemnation—assuredly throw some light upon the "perpetual hatreds and inextinguishable rage" of the Franks. The common herd, says the rhetorician, may be slaughtered by the hundred without their becoming aware of the slaughter; it saves time and trouble to slay the leaders of an enemy whom you wish to conquer. The effect for the moment was decisive, even if we refuse to believe that the castles and strong places, set at intervals along the banks of the Rhine, were henceforth regarded rather as ornaments to the frontier than as a source of protection. The bridge, too, which Constantine built at Cologne, was likewise built for business and not, as the orator suggests, for the glory of the Empire and the beauty of the landscape. When we read of the war galleys, which ceaselessly patrolled the waters of the Rhine, and of the soldiery stationed along its banks from source to mouth, we may judge how anxiously the watch was kept, how nervously alert the Caesar or Augustus of the West required to be to guard the frontier, and how profound a respect he entertained for the free German whom he called barbarian.

CONSTANTINE AND HIS COLLEAGUES

WHILE Constantine thus peacefully succeeded his father in the command of Gaul, Spain, and Britain, Italy was the scene of continued disturbance and of a successful usurpation. We have seen how Severus, an officer of the eastern army and a trusted friend of Galerius, had been chosen to take over the command which Maximian so unwillingly laid down at Milan. He was proclaimed Cesar, with Italy and Africa for his portion, and the administration passed into his hands. But he preferred, apparently, to remain on the Illyrian border rather than show himself in Rome, and, in his absence, Maxentius, a son of Maximian, took the opportunity of claiming the heritage of which he considered himself to have been robbed.

No single historian has had a good word to say for Maxentius, who is described by Lactantius as "a man of depraved mind, so consumed with pride and stubbornness that he paid no deference or respect either to his father or his father-in-law and was in consequence hated by both." He had married a daughter of Galerius, but had been thrust on one side at the choosing of the new Caesars, and Severus and Maximin Daza had been preferred to him. He owed his elevation to the purple to a successful mutiny on the part of the Praetorians at Rome, and to the general discontent of the Roman population. It is evident that Rome watched with anger and jealousy the loss of her old exclusive and imperial position. The Emperors no longer resided on the Palatine, and ignored and disdained the city on the Tiber. Diocletian had preferred Nicomedia; Maximian had fixed his Court at Milan. The imperial trappings at Rome were becoming a mockery. When, in addition to neglect, it was ordered that Italy should no longer be exempt from the census, and that the sacred Saturnian soil should submit to the exactions of the tax-gatherer, public opinion was ripe for revolt.

Lactantius affects to see in the extension of the census to Rome a crowning example of Galerius's rapacity. He speaks of the Emperor "devouring the whole world", and declares that his madness carried him to such outrageous lengths that he would not suffer even the Roman people to escape bondage. But Galerius was thoroughly justified in the step he took. The immunity of Rome from taxation had been a monstrous piece of fiscal injustice to the rest of the world, designed merely to flatter the pride and purse of the Roman citizen. Galerius, moreover, had disbanded some of the Praetorians—who were at once the Household Troops and the permanent garrison of the capital; but now that the Emperor and the Court had quitted Rome, their raison d'être was gone. The vast expenditure on their pay and their barracks was money thrown away. Galerius, therefore, abolished the Praetorian camps. Such an act would give clear warning that the absence of the Emperors was not merely temporary, but permanent, that the shifting of the capital had been due not merely to personal predilections, but to abiding political reasons.

That the Praetorians themselves received the order with sullen anger may well be understood. For three centuries they had been the corps of elite of the Roman army, enjoying special pay and special advantages. They had made and unmade Emperors. They had repeatedly held the fortunes of the Empire in their hands. The traditions of their regiments fostered pride and arrogance, for they had seen little active service in their long history, and the severest conflicts they had had to face were tumults in the imperial city. Now their privileges were destroyed by a stroke of the pen, and needing but little instigation to rebellion, they offered the purple to Maxentius, who gladly accepted it. Nor, it is said, were the people unfavorable to his cause, for Maxentius's agents had already been busy among them, and so, after Abellius, the prefect of the city, had been murdered, Maxentius made himself master of Rome without a struggle. His position, however, was very precarious. He had practically no army and he knew that neither Galerius nor Severus would recognize his pretensions. The latter had already taken over the command of the armies of Maximian, and was the nominee of Galerius, who at once incited his colleague to march upon Rome. Maxentius saw that his only chance of success was to corrupt his father's old legions, and with this object in view he sent a purple robe to Maximian, urging him to resume his place and title of Augustus. Maximian agreed with alacrity. He had been spending his enforced leisure not in amateur gardening and contentment, like his colleague at Salona, but in his Campanian villa, chafing at his lost dignity. Hence he eagerly responded to the summons of his son and resumed the purple, not so much as Maxentius's' supporter, but as the senior acting Augustus.

Severus marched straight down the Italian peninsula and laid siege to Rome, only to find himself deserted by his soldiers. According to Zosimus, the troops which first played him false were a Moorish contingent fresh from Africa. Then, when the treachery spread, Severus hastily retired on Ravenna, where he could maintain touch with Galerius in Illyria, and was there besieged by Maximian and Maxentius. Doubtless, if he had waited, Galerius would have sent him reinforcements or come in person to his assistance, for his own prestige was deeply involved in that of Severus. But the latter seems to have allowed himself to be enticed out of his strong refuge by the plausible overtures of his rivals. He set out for Rome, prepared to resign the throne on condition of receiving honorable treatment, but on reaching a spot named "The Three Taverns," on the Appian Road, he was seized and thrown into chains. The only consideration he received from his captors was that they allowed him to choose his own way of relieving them of his presence. He opened his veins. So gentle a death in those violent times was considered "good."

This victory over Severus, gained with such astonishing ease, speaks well for the popularity of Maximian with his old soldiers. Galerius prepared to avenge the defeat and murder of his friend and invaded Italy at the head of a large army. He too, like Severus, marched down the peninsula, but he got no nearer to Rome than Narnia, sixty miles distant. There he halted, despite the fact that no opposition was being offered to his advance. Why? The reason is undoubtedly to be found in the attitude of Constantine, who had mobilized his army upon the Gallic frontier and was waiting on events. There was no love lost between Constantine and

Galerius. If Constantine crossed the Alps and followed down on the track of Galerius, the latter would find himself between two fires. Galerius is represented by Zosimus as being suspicious of the loyalty of his troops; it is more probable that he decided to retreat as soon as he heard that Constantine had thrown in his lot with Maximian and Maxentius. Maximian had been sedulously trying to secure alliances for himself and his son. He had made overtures to the recluse of Salona. But Diocletian had turned a deaf ear. Even if he had hankered after power again, he would hardly have declared himself in opposition to the ruler of Illyria, while he was dwelling within reach of Galerius. With Constantine, however, Maximian had better success. He gave him his daughter Fausta in marriage and incited him to attack Galerius, who at once drew his troops off into Illyria, after laying waste the Transpadane region with fire and sword.

Some very curious stories are told in connection with this expedition of Galerius. Lactantius declares that he invaded Italy with the intention of extinguishing the Senate and butchering the people of Rome; that he found the gates of all the cities shut against him; and discovered that he had not brought sufficient troops with him to attempt a siege of the capital. "He had never seen Rome", says Lactantius naively, "and thought it was not much bigger than the cities with which he was familiar".

Galerius was, it is true, a rough soldier of the camp, but it is ludicrous to suppose that he was not fully cognizant of the topography and the fortifications of Rome. Then we are told that some of the legions were afflicted with scruples at the idea of being called to fight for a father-in-law against his son-in-law—as though there were prohibited degrees in hatreds—and shrank as Roman soldiers from the thought of moving to the assault of Rome. And, as a finishing touch to this most extraordinary canvas, Lactantius paints into it the figure of Galerius kneeling at the feet of his soldiers, praying them not to betray him, and offering them large rewards. We do not recognize Galerius in such a guise. Again, an unknown historian, of whose work only a few fragments survive, says that when Galerius reached Narnia he opened communications with Maximian and proposed to treat for peace, but that his overtures were contemptuously spurned. This does not violate the probabilities like the reckless malevolence of Lactantius, but, after all, the simplest explanation is the one which we have given above. Galerius halted and then retired when he heard that Constantine had come to an understanding with Maximian, had married his daughter, and was waiting and watching on the Gallic border. No pursuit seems to have been attempted.

Maximian and Maxentius were thus left in undisputed possession of Italy. They were clearly in alliance with Constantine, but their relations with one another were exceedingly anomalous. Both are represented in equally odious colours. Eutropius describes the father as "embittered and brutal, faithless, troublesome, and utterly devoid of good manners"; Aurelius Victor says of the son that no one ever liked him, not even his own father. Indeed, the scandal-mongers of the day denied the parentage of Maxentius and said that he was the son of some low-born Syrian and had been foisted upon Maximian by his wife as her own child. Public opinion, however, was inclined to throw the blame of the rupture, which speedily took place between Maximian and Maxentius, upon the older man, who is depicted as a restless and mischievous intriguer. In Rome, at any rate, the army looked to the son as its chief, and as there was but one army, there was no room for two Emperors. Lactantius tells the story that Maximian called a great mass meeting of citizens and soldiers, dilated at length upon the evils of the situation, and then, turning to his son, declared that he was the cause of all the trouble and snatched the purple from his shoulders. But Maximian had the mortification of seeing Maxentius sheltered instead of slaughtered by the soldiers, and it was he himself who was driven with ignominy from the city, like a second Tarquin the Proud.

Whether these circumstantial details are to be accepted or not, there is no doubt as to the sequel. Maximian was expelled from Rome and Italy, and began a series of wanderings which were only to end with his death. He seems first of all to have fled into Gaul and thrown himself upon the protection of his son-in-law, Constantine, and then to have opened up negotiations with Galerius, who must naturally have desired to establish some modus vivendi between all the rival Emperors. Galerius called a conference at Carnuntum on the Danube and invited the presence of Diocletian. Maximian was there; so too was Licinius, an old companion-in-arms of Galerius and his most trusted lieutenant. Of the debates which took place no word has survived. But the fact that Diocletian was invited to attend is clear proof that Galerius regarded him with the profound respect that was due to the senior Augustus and the founder of the system which had broken down so badly. Galerius wished the old man to suggest a way out of the impasse which had been reached, to devise some plan whereby his dilapidated fabric might still be patched up. Even in his retirement the practical wisdom of Diocletian was gladly recognized, and three years later we find one of the Panegyrists sounding his praises in the presence of Constantine. This shows that Diocletian and Constantine were on friendly terms, else Diocletian would only have been mentioned with abuse, or would have been passed over in significant silence. The passage deserves quotation:

"That divine statesman, who was the first to share his Empire with others and the first to lay it down, does not regret the step he took, nor thinks that he has lost what he voluntarily resigned; nay, he is truly blessed and happy, since, even in his retirement, such mighty Princes as you offer him the protection of your deep respect. He is upheld by a multiplicity of Empires; he rejoices in the cover of your shade".

Diocletian would not have been called to Carnuntum, or, if called, he would scarcely have undertaken so tedious a journey, had there not been affairs of the highest moment to be discussed. We know of only one certain result of this strange council of Emperors. It is that a new Augustus was created by Galerius without passing through the intermediate stage of being a Caesar. He was found in Licinius, to whom was assigned the administration of Illyria with the command of the Danubian legions, and the status of second rank in the hierarchy of the Augusti, or rather of the Augusti in active life. Galerius, we may infer, was sensible of the approaching breakdown of his health and wished his friend Licinius to be ready to step into his place. Apparently, a genuine attempt was made to restore to something like its old position the system of Diocletian. Perhaps as reasonable a supposition as any is that it was decided at the conference that Diocletian and Maximian should again be relegated to the ranks of retired Augusti, that Galerius and Licinius should be the two active Augusti, and Constantine and Maximin the two Caesars. Maximian had unquestionably gone to Carnuntum with the hope of fishing in troubled waters and Lactantius' even attributes to him a wild scheme for assassinating Galerius. It is, at any rate, certain that he left the conference in a fury of disappointment. The ambitious and restless old man had received no encouragement to his hopes of again being supreme over part of the Empire.

But what then of Maxentius, who was in possession of Italy and Africa? If the theory we have propounded be right, he must have been studiously ignored and treated as a usurper, to be thrown out—just as Carausius had been—at a favorable opportunity. There is a passage in Lactantius which seems to corroborate this suggestion. That author says that Maximin Daza, the Caesar of Egypt and Syria and the old protégé of Galerius, heard with anger that Licinius had been promoted over his head to be Augustus and hold the second place in the charmed circle of Emperors. He sent angry remonstrances; Galerius returned a soft answer. Maximin assumed an even more aggressive bearing, urged more peremptorily than ever his superior right, and spurned Galerius's entreaties and commands. Then—Lactantius goes on to say—overborne by Maximin's stubborn obstinacy, Galerius offered a compromise, by naming himself and Licinius as Augusti and Maximin and Constantine as Sons of the Augusti, instead of simple Caesars.

But Maximin was obdurate and wrote saying that his soldiers had taken the law into their own hands and had already saluted him as Augustus. Galerius therefore, in the face of the accomplished fact, gave way and recognized not only Maximin but Constantine also as full Augusti. Such is the story of Lactantius. It will be noted that the name of Maxentius is not mentioned. He is treated as non-existent. There need be no surprise that nothing is said of Diocletian and Maximian, for they were ex-Augusti, so to speak, though still bearing the courtesy title. But if Maxentius had been recognized as one of the "Imperial Brothers" at the conference of Carnuntum, the omission of his name by Lactantius is exceedingly strange. From his account we should judge that the policy decided upon at Carnuntum was to restore the fourfold system of

Diocletian in the persons of Galerius, Licinius, Maximin, and Constantine, taking precedence in the order named. When Maximin refused to be content with his old title of Caesar or to accept the new one of Son of Augustus, and insisted on being acknowledged as Augustus, the system broke down anew. At the beginning of 308, there were no fewer than seven who bore the name of Augustus. And of these Diocletian alone had outlived his ambitions.

Maximian returned to Gaul, where he received cordial welcome from Constantine. He had resigned his pretensions not—as says Lactantius, cognizant as ever of the secret motives of his enemies—that he might the more easily deceive Constantine, but because it had been so decided at Carnuntum. He was thus a private citizen once more; he had neither army, nor official status, nothing beyond the prestige attaching to one who had, so to speak, "passed the chair." There can be little doubt that his second resignation was as reluctant as the first, but as he was at open enmity with his son, Maxentius, he had only Constantine to look to for protection and the means of livelihood. And Constantine, according to the author of the Seventh Panegyric, gave him all the honours due to his exalted rank. He assigned to him the place of honor on his right hand; put at his disposal the stables of the palace; and ordered his servants to pay to Maximian the same deference that they paid to himself. The orator declares that the gossip of the day spoke of Constantine as wearing the robe of office, while Maximian wielded its powers. Evidently Constantine had no fear that Maximian would play him false.

His confidence, however, soon received a rude shock. The Franks were restless and threatened invasion. Constantine marched north with his army, leaving Maximian at Arles. He did not take his entire forces with him, for a considerable number remained in the south of Gaul—no doubt to guard the frontier against danger from Maxentius, though Lactantius explains it otherwise. Maximian waited till sufficient time had elapsed for Constantine to be well across the Rhine, and then began to spread rumours of his having been defeated and slain in battle. For the third time, therefore, he assumed the purple, seized the State treasuries, and took command of the legions, offering them a large donative, and appealing to their old loyalty. The usurpation was entirely successful for the moment, but when Constantine heard of the treachery he hurried back, leaving the affairs of the frontier to settle themselves.

Constantine knew the military value of mobility, and his soldiers eagerly made his quarrel their own. There is an amusing passage in the Seventh Panegyric in which the orator says that the troops showed their devotion by refusing the offer of special travelling-money on the ground that it would hamper them on the march. Their generous pay, they said, was more than sufficient, though no Roman army before this time had ever been known to refuse money. Then he describes how they marched from the Rhine to the Aar without rest, yet with unwearied bodies; how at Châlons they were placed on board river boats, but found the current too sluggish for their impetuous eagerness to come to conclusions with the traitor, and cried out that they were standing still; and how, even when they entered the rapid current of the Rhone, its pace scarcely satisfied their ardor.

Such, according to the Court rhetorician, was the enthusiasm of the soldiers for their young leader. When, at length, Arles was reached, it was found that Maximian had fled to Marseilles and had shut himself up within that strongly fortified town. His power had crumbled away. The legions, which had sworn allegiance to him, withdrew it again as soon as they found that he had lied to them of Constantine's death; even the soldiers he had with him in Marseilles only waited for the appearance of Constantine before the walls to open the gates. The picture which Lactantius draws of Constantine reproaching Maximian for his ingratitude while the latter—from the summit of the wall—heaps curses on his head, or the companion picture of the anonymous rhetorician, who shows us the scaling ladders falling short of the top of the battlements and the devoted soldiers climbing up on their comrades' backs, are vivid but unconvincing. What emerges from their doubtful narratives is that Marseilles was captured without a siege, and that Maximian fell into the hands of his justly angry son-in-law, who stripped him of his titles but vouchsafed to him his life.

Was Maximian in league with his son, Maxentius, in this usurpation? Had they made up their old quarrel in order to turn their united weapons against Constantine? There were those who thought so at the time, as

Lactantius says, the theory being that the old man only pretended violent enmity towards his son in order to carry out his treacherous designs against Constantine and the other Emperors.

Lactantius himself denies this supposition bluntly and then goes on to say that Maximian's real motive was to get rid both of Maxentius and the rest, and restore Diocletian and himself to power. Even for Lactantius, this is an extraordinarily wild theory. It runs counter to all that we know of Diocletian's wishes during his retirement, and it speaks of the "extinction of Maxentius and the rest" as though it only needed an order to a centurion and the deed was done. It is much more probable that Maximian had actually re-entered into negotiations with Maxentius and had offered, as the price of reconciliation, the support of the legions which he had treacherously won from Constantine. The impetuous haste with which Constantine flew back from the Rhine indicates that the crisis was one of extreme gravity.

Maximian did not long survive his degradation. That he died a violent death is certain; the circumstances attending it are in doubt. Lactantius gives a minute narrative which would carry greater conviction if the details had not been so manifestly borrowed from the chronicles of the East. He says that Maximian, tiring of his humiliating position, engaged in new plots against Constantine, and tempted Fausta, his daughter, to betray her husband by the promise of a worthier spouse. Her part in the conspiracy was to secure the removal of the guards from Constantine's sleeping apartment. Fausta laid the whole scheme before her husband, who ordered one of his eunuchs to sleep in the royal chamber. Maximian, rising in the dead of night, told the sentries that he had dreamed an important dream which he wished at once to communicate to his son-in-law and thus gained entrance to the room. Drawing his sword, he cut off the eunuch's head and rushed out boasting that he had slain Constantine—only to be confronted by Constantine himself at the head of a troop of armed men. The corpse was brought out; the self-convicted murderer stood "speechless as Marpesian flint". Constantine upbraided him with his treachery, gave him permission to choose his own mode of dying, and Maximian hanged himself, "drawing"—as Virgil had said— "from the lofty beam the noose of shameful death"

Such is the story of Lactantius; it could scarcely be more circumstantial. But if this had been the manner of Maximian's death, it is hardly possible that the other historians would have passed it by in silence. Eusebius, in his Ecclesiastical History, simply says that Maximian strangled himself; Aurelius Victor that he justly perished. The author of the Seventh Panegyric declares that, though Constantine offered him his life, Maximian deemed himself unworthy of the boon and committed suicide. Eutropius, evidently borrowing from Lactantius, remarks that Maximian paid the penalty for his crimes. There is little doubt, therefore, that Constantine ordered his execution and gave him choice of death, just as Maxentius had given similar choice to Severus. Officially it would be announced that Maximian had committed suicide. At the time, public opinion was shocked by the manner of his death, though it was generally conceded that his life was justly forfeit.

THE INVASION OF ITALY

THE tragic end of his old colleague must have raised many disquieting thoughts in the mind of Diocletian, already beginning to be anxious lest his successors should think that he was living too long. While Galerius flourished he was sure of a protector, but Galerius died in 311. In the eighteenth year of his rule he had been stricken with an incurable and loathsome malady, into the details of which Lactantius enters with a morbid but lively enjoyment, affecting to see in the torture of the dying Emperor the visitation of an angry Providence. He describes minutely the progress of the cancer and the "appalling odour of the festering wound which spread not only through the palace but through the city". He shows us the unhappy patient raising piercing cries and calling for mercy from the God of the Christians whom he had persecuted, vowing under the stress of physical anguish that he would make reparation; and, finally, when at the very point of death, dictating the edict which stayed the persecution and gave the Christians full liberty to worship in their own way. It will be more convenient to discuss in another place this remarkable document, the forerunner, so to speak, of the famous Edict of Milan. It was promulgated at Nicomedia on the thirtieth of April, 311, and a few days later Galerius's torments were mercifully ended by death.

The death of Galerius gave another blow to the already tottering system of Diocletian. It had been his intention to retire, as Diocletian had done, at the end of his twentieth year of sovereignty, and make way for a younger man, and there can be little doubt that he would have been as good as his word. Galerius has not received fair treatment at the hands of posterity. Lactantius, his bitter enemy, describes him as a violent ruffian and a hectoring bully, an object of terror and fear to all around him in word, deed, and aspect. Lactantius belittles the importance of his victory over Narses, the Persian King, by saying that the Persian army marched encumbered with baggage and that victory was easily won. He makes Galerius the leading spirit of the Persecution; represents him as having goaded Diocletian into signing the fatal edicts; accuses him of having fired the palace at Nicomedia in order to work on the terrors of his chief; charges him with having invented new and horrible tortures; and declares that he never dined or supped without whetting his appetite with the sight of human blood. No one would gather from Lactantius that Galerius was a fine soldier, a hard-working and capable Emperor, and a loyal successor to a great political chief. Eutropius does him no more than justice when he describes him as a man of high principle and a consummate general. Aurelius Victor fills in the light and shade. Galerius was, he says, a Prince worthy of all praise; just if unpolished and untutored; of handsome presence; and an accomplished and fortunate general. He had risen from the ranks; in his young days he had been a herd boy, and the name of Armentarius clung to him through life. This rough and ready Pannonian spent too energetic and busy a career to have time for culture. He came from a province where, in the forceful phrase of one of the Panegyrists, "life was all hard knocks and fighting

Galerius had already nominated Licinius as his successor, but Licinius was far away in Pannonia and did not cross over at once into Asia to take command of Galerius's army—no doubt because it was not safe for him to leave his post. In the meantime, Maximin Daza, the Augustus of Syria and Egypt, had been preparing to march on Nicomedia as soon as Galerius breathed his last, for he claimed, as we have seen, that by seniority of rule he had a better right than Licinius to the title of senior Augustus. While, therefore, Licinius remained in Europe, Maximin Daza advanced from Syria across the Taurus and entered Bithynia, where, to curry favour with the people, he abolished the census. It was expected that the two Emperors would fight out their quarrel, but an accommodation was arrived at, and they agreed that the Hellespont should form the boundary between them. Maximin, by his promptitude, had thus materially increased his sovereignty, and, at the beginning of 312, the eastern half of the Empire was divided between Licinius and Maximin Daza, while Constantine ruled in Great Britain, Spain, and Gaul, and Maxentius was master of Italy and Africa.

Whether or not his position had been recognized by the other Emperors at the conference of Carnuntum, Maxentius had remained in undisturbed possession of Italy since the hurried retreat of the invading army of Galerius. In Africa, indeed, a general named Alexander, who, according to Zosimus, was a Phrygian by descent, and timid and advanced in years, raised the standard of revolt. Maxentius commissioned one of his lieutenants to attack the usurper and Alexander was captured and strangled. There would have been nothing to distinguish this insurrection from any other, had it not been for the ruthless severity with which the African cities were treated by the conqueror. Carthage and Cirta were pillaged and sacked; the countryside was laid desolate; many of the leading citizens were executed; still more were reduced to beggary. The ruin of Africa was so complete that it excited against Maxentius the public opinion of the Roman world. He had begun his reign, as will be remembered, as the special champion of the Praetorians and of the privileges of Rome, but he soon lost his early popularity, and rapidly developed into a cruel and bloodthirsty tyrant. His profligacy was shameless and excessive, even for those licentious times. Eusebius tells the story of how Sophronia, the Christian wife of the city prefect, stabbed herself in order to escape his embraces, when the imperial messengers came to summon her to the palace.

If Maxentius had been accused of all the vices only on the authority of the Christian authors and the official panegyrists of Constantine, their statements might have been received with some suspicion—for a fallen Roman Emperor had no friends. Zosimus, however, is almost as severe upon him as Lactantius, and Julian, in the Banquet of the Caesars, excludes him from the feast as one utterly unworthy of a place in honorable society. According to Aurelius Victor, he was the first to start the practice of exacting from the senators large sums of money in the guise of free gifts on the flimsiest pretexts of public necessity, or as payment for the bestowal of office or civil distinction. Moreover, knowing that, sooner or later, he would find himself at war with one or other of his brother Augusti, Maxentius amassed great stores of corn and wealth and took no heed of a morrow which he knew that he might not live to witness. He despoiled the temples,—says the author of the Ninth Panegyric,—butchered the Senate, and starved the people of Rome. The

Praetorians—who had placed and kept him on the throne—ruled the city. Zosimus tells the curious story of how, in the course of a great fire in Rome, the Temple of Fortune was burned down and one of the soldiers looking on spoke blasphemous and disrespectful words of the goddess. Immediately the mob attacked him. His comrades went to his assistance and a serious riot ensued, during which the Praetorians would have massacred the citizens had they not been with difficulty restrained. All the authorities, indeed, agree that a perfect reign of terror prevailed at Rome after Maxentius's victory over Alexander in Africa, while Maxentius himself is depicted as a second Commodus or Nero.

One of the most vivid pictures of the tyrant is given in the Panegyric already quoted. The orator speaks of Maxentius as a "stupid and worthless wild-beast skulking for ever within the walls of the palace and not daring to leave the precincts. Fancy, he exclaims, an indoor Emperor, who considers that he has made a journey and achieved an expedition if he has so much as visited the Gardens of Sallust! Whenever he addressed his soldiers, he would boast that, though he had colleagues in the Empire, he alone was the real Emperor; for he ruled while they kept the frontiers safe and did his fighting for him. And then he would dismiss them with the three words: "Fruimini! Dissipate! Prodigite!". Such an invitation to drunkenness, riot, and debauch would not be unwelcome to the swaggering Praetorians and to the numerous bands of mercenaries which Maxentius had collected from all parts of the world.

We ought not, perhaps, to take this scathing invective quite literally. For all his vices, Maxentius was probably not quite the hopeless debauchee he is represented to have been. It is at least worth remark that it was this Emperor, of whom no one has a charitable word to say, who restored to the Christians at Rome the church buildings and property which had been confiscated to the State by the edicts of Diocletian and Galerius. Neither Eusebius nor Lactantius mentions this, but the fact is clear from a passage in St. Augustine, who says that the first act of the Roman Christians on regaining possession of their cemetery was to bring back the body of Bishop Eusebius, who had died in exile in Sicily. Nor did Maxentius's political attitude towards the other Augusti betray indications of incompetence or want of will. He was ambitious—a trait common to most Roman Emperors and certainly shared by all his colleagues. There was no cohesion among the four Augusti; there was no one much superior to the others in influence and prestige. Constantine and Maxentius feared and suspected each other in the West, just as Licinius and Maximin Daza feared and suspected each other in the East. When the two latter agreed that the Hellespont should divide their territories, Licinius, who had lost Asia Minor by the bargain, made overtures of alliance to Constantine. It was arranged that Licinius should marry Constantia, the sister of the Augustus of Gaul. Naturally, therefore, Maximin Daza turned towards Maxentius and sent envoys asking for alliance and friendship. Lactantius adds the curious phrase that Maximin's letter was couched in a tone of familiarity and says that Maxentius was as eager to accept as Maximin had been to offer. He hailed it, we are told, as a god-sent help, for he had already declared war against Constantine on the pretext of avenging his father's murder.

The outbreak of this war, which was fraught with such momentous consequences to the whole course of civilization, found the Empire strangely divided. The Emperor of Italy and Africa was allied with the Emperor of Egypt, Syria, and Asia Minor, against the rulers of the armies of the Danube and the Rhine. We shall see that the alliance was—at any rate, in result—defensive rather than offensive. Licinius and Maximin never moved; they simply neutralized one another, though the advantage clearly lay with Constantine and Licinius, for Maxentius was absolutely isolated, so far as receiving help on the landward side was concerned. We need not look far to find the real cause of quarrel between Constantine and Maxentius, whatever pretexts were assigned. Maxentius would never have risked his Empire for the sake of a father whom he detested; nor would Constantine have jeopardized his throne in order to avenge an insult. Each aspired to rule over the entire West; neither would acquiesce in the pretensions of the other. Both had been actively preparing for a struggle which became inevitable when neither took any radical steps to avoid it. We have already seen that Constantine kept the larger part of the army of Gaul stationed in the south near Arelate and Lugdunum, in order to watch the Alpine passes; we shall find that Maxentius had also posted his main armies in the north of Italy from Susa on the one side, where he was threatened by Constantine, to Venice on the other, where he was on guard against Licinius. There is a curious reference in one of the authorities to a plan formed by Maxentius of invading Gaul through Rhaetia,—no doubt because Constantine had made the Alpine passes practically unassailable,—while Lactantius tells us that he had drawn every available man from Africa to swell his armies in Italy.

Constantine acted with the extreme rapidity for which he was already famous. He hurried his army down from the Rhine, and was through the passes and attacking the walled city of Susa before Maxentius had certain knowledge of his movements. That he was embarking on an exceedingly hazardous expedition seems to have been recognized by himself and his captains. The author of the Ninth Panegyric says quite bluntly that his principal officers not only muttered their fears in secret, but expressed them openly, and adds that his councillors and haruspices warned him to desist. A similar campaign had cost Severus his life and had been found too hazardous even by Galerius. Superiority of numbers lay not with him, but with his rival. Constantine was gravely handicapped by the fact that he had to safeguard the Rhine behind him against the Germanic tribes, which he knew would seize the first opportunity to pass the river. Zosimus gives a detailed account of the numbers which the rivals placed in the field. Maxentius, he says, had 170,000 foot and 18,000 horse under his command, including 80,000 levies from Rome and Italy, and 40,000 from Carthage and Africa. Con-stantine, on the other hand, even after vigorous recruiting in Britain and Gaul, could only muster 90,000 foot and 8000 horse. The author of the Ninth Panegyric, in a casual phrase, says that Constantine could hardly employ a fourth of his Gallic army against the 100,000 men in the ranks of Maxentius, on account of the dangers of the Rhine. Ancient authorities, however, arc never trustworthy where numbers are concerned; we only know that Maxentius had by far the larger force, and that Constantine's army of invasion was probably under 40,000 strong. Whether the numerical supremacy of the former was not counterbalanced by the necessity under which Maxentius laboured of guarding against Licinius, is a question to which the historians have paid no heed.

Marching along the chief military highroad from Lugdunum to Italy, which crossed the Alps at Mont Cenis, Constantine suddenly appeared before the walls of Susa, a strongly garrisoned post, and took it by storm, escalading the walls and burning the gates. The town caught fire; Constantine set his soldiers to put out the flames, a more difficult task, says Nazarius, than had been the actual assault. From Susa the victor advanced to Turin, which opened its gates to him after the cavalry of Maxentius had been routed in the plains. These were troops clad in ponderous but cleverly jointed armour, and the weight of their onslaught was calculated to crush either horse or foot upon which it was directed. But Constantine disposed his forces so as to avoid their charge and render their weight useless, and when these horsemen fled for shelter to Turin they found the gates closed against them and perished almost to a man. Milan, by far the most important city in the Transpadane region, next received Constantine, who entered amid the plaudits of the citizens, and charmed the eyes of the Milanese ladies, says the Panegyrist, without causing them anxieties for their virtue. Milan, indeed, welcomed him with open arms; other cities sent deputations similar to the one which, according to the epitomist Zonaras, had already reached him from Rome itself, praying him to come as its liberator. It seemed, indeed, that he had already won not only the Transpadane region, but Rome itself.

Constantine, however, had still to meet and overthrow the chief armies of Maxentius in the north of Italy. These were under the command of Ruricius Pompeianus, a general as stubborn as he was loyal, and of well-tried capacity. Pompeianus held Verona in force. He had thrown out a large body of cavalry towards Brescia to reconnoitre and check Constantine's advance, but these were routed with some slaughter and retired in confusion. If we may interpret the presence of Pompeianus at Verona as indicating that Maxentius had feared attack by Licinius more than by Constantine, this would explain the comparative absence of troops in Lombardy and the concentration in Venetia, though it is strange that we do not hear of Licinius taking any steps to assist his ally. Verona was a strongly fortified city resting upon the Adige, which encircled its walls for three-quarters of their circumference. Constantine managed to effect a crossing at some distance from the city and laid siege in regular fashion. Pompeianus tried several ineffectual sorties, and then, secretly escaping through the lines, he brought up the rest of his army to offer pitched battle or compel Constantine to raise the siege. A fierce engagement followed. We are told that Constantine had drawn up his men in double lines, when, noticing that the enemy outnumbered him and threatened to overlap either flank, he ordered his troops to extend and present a wider front. He distinguished himself that day by pressing into the thickest of the fight, "like a mountain torrent in spate that tears away by their roots the trees on its banks and rolls down rocks and stones." The orator depicts for us the scene as Constantine's lieutenants and captains receive him on his return from the fray, panting with his exertion and with blood dripping from his hands. With tears in their eyes, they chide him for his rashness in imperiling the hopes of the world. "It does not beseem an Emperor", they say, "to strike down an enemy with his own sword. It does not become him to sweat with the toil of battle". In simpler language, Constantine fought bravely at the head of his men and won the day. Pompeianus was slain; Verona opened her gates, and so many prisoners fell into the hands of the conqueror that Constantine made his armourers forge chains and manacles from the iron of the captives' swords. In accordance with his usual policy, he conciliated the favor of those whom he had defeated by sparing the city from pillage, and sheaved an equal clemency to Aquileia and the other cities of Venetia, all of which speedily submitted on the capitulation of Verona.

With the entire north of Italy thus wrested from Maxentius, Constantine could turn his face towards Rome. He encountered no opposition on the march. Maxentius did not even contest the passage of the Apennines; the Umbrian passes were left open; and if the historians are to be trusted— and they speak with unanimity on the point—the Italian Emperor simply waited for his doom to come upon him, as Nero had done, and made no really serious effort to defend his throne. This slave in the purple, as the author of the Ninth Panegyric calls him, cowered trembling in his palace, paralyzed with fear because lie had been deserted by the Divine Intelligence and the Eternal Majesty of Rome, which had transferred themselves from the tyrant to the side of his rival. We are told, indeed, that a few days before the appearance of Constantine, Maxentius quitted the palace with his wife and son and took up his abode in a private house, not being able to endure the terrible dreams that came to him by night and the spectres of the victims which haunted his crime-stained halls.

Constantine moved swiftly down from the north of Italy along the Flaminian Way, and in less than two months after the fall of Verona, he was at Saxa Rubra, only nine miles from Rome, with an army eager for battle and confident of victory. There he found the troops of Maxentius drawn up in battle array, but posted in a position which none but a fool or a madman would have selected. The probabilities are that Maxentius could not trust the citizens of Rome and therefore dared not stand a siege within the ramparts of Aurelian. Then, having decided to offer battle, he allowed his army to cross the Tiber and take up ground whence, if defeated, their only roads of escape lay over the narrow Milvian Bridge and a flimsy bridge of boats, one probably on either flank.

It is said that Maxentius had not intended to be present in person when the issue was decided. He was holding festival within the city, celebrating his birthday with the usual games and pretending that the proximity of Constantine caused him no alarm. The populace began to taunt him with cowardice, and uttered the ominous shout that Constantine was invincible. Maxentius's fears grew as the clamour swelled in volume. He hurriedly called for the Sibylline Books and ordered them to be consulted. These gave answer that on that very day the enemy of the Romans should perish—a characteristically safe reply. Such ambiguity of diction had usually portended the death of the consulting Prince, but Lactantius says that the hopes with which the words inspired Maxentius led him to put on his armour and ride out of Rome.

The issue was decided at the first encounter. Constantine charged at the head of his Gallic horse—now accustomed to and certain of victory—into the cavalry of Maxentius, which broke and ran in disorder from the field. Only the Praetorians made a gallant and stubborn resistance and fell where they had stood, knowing that it was they who had raised Maxentius to the throne and that their destruction was involved in his. While these fought valiantly with the courage of despair, their comrades were crowding in panic towards the already choked bridges. At the Milvian Bridge the passage was jammed, and the pursuers wrought great execution. The pontoon bridge collapsed, owing to the treachery of those who had cut or loosened its supports. All the reports agree that there was a sickening slaughter, and that hundreds were drowned in the Tiber in their vain effort to escape. Among the victims was Maxentius himself. He was either thrust into the river by the press of frenzied fugitives or was drowned in trying to scale the high bank on the opposite shore, when weighed down by his heavy armour. His corpse was recovered later from the stream, which the Panegyrists hailed in ecstatic terms as the co-savior of Rome with Constantine and the partner of his triumph.

The victor entered Rome. He had won the prize which he sought—the mastery of the West—and, like scores of Roman conquerors before him, he marched through the famous streets. His triumphal procession was graced, says Nazarius, not by captive chiefs or barbarians in chains, but by senators who now tasted the joy of freedom again, and by consulars whose prison doors had been opened by Constantine's victory—in a word, by a Free Rome. Only the head of Maxentius, whose features still wore the savage, threatening look which even death itself had not been able to obliterate, was carried on the point of a spear behind Constantine amid the jeers and insults of the crowd. Another Panegyrist gives us a very lively picture of the throngs as they waited for the Emperor to pass, describing how they crowded at the rear of the procession and swept up to the palace, almost venturing to cross the sacred threshold itself, and how, when Constantine appeared in the streets on the succeeding days, they sought to unhorse his carriage and draw it along with their hands. One of the conqueror's first acts was to extirpate the family of his fallen rival. Maxentius's elder son, Romulus, who for a short time had borne the name of Cesar, was already dead; the younger son, and probably the wife too, were now quietly removed. There were other victims, who had committed themselves too deeply to Maxentius' fortunes to escape. Rome, says Nazarius, was reconstituted afresh on a lasting basis by the complete destruction of those who might have given trouble. But still the victims were comparatively few, so few, in the estimation of public opinion, that the victory was regarded as a bloodless one, and Constantine's clemency was the theme and admiration of all. When the people clamoured for more victims — doubtless the most hated instruments of Maxentius's tyranny—and when the informer pressed forward to offer his deadly services, Constantine refused to listen. He was resolved to let bygones be bygones. The laws of the period immediately succeeding his victory, as they appear in the Theodosian Code, amply confirm what might otherwise be the suspect eulogies of the Panegyrists. A general act of amnesty was passed, and the ghastly head of Maxentius was sent to Africa to allay the terrors of the population and convince them that their op-pressor would trouble them no more. There, it is to be supposed, it found a final burial-place.

Another early act of Constantine was to disband the Praetorians, thus carrying out the intention and decrees of Galerius. The survivors of these long-famous regiments were marched out of Rome away from the Circus, the Theatre of Pompeius, and the Baths, and were set to do their share in the guarding of the Rhine and the Danube. Whether they bore the change as voluntarily as the Panegyrist suggests is doubtful, and we may question whether they so soon forgot in their rude cantonments the fleshpots and deliciae of the capital. But the expulsion was final. The Praetorians ceased to exist. Rome may have been glad to see the empty barracks, for the Praetorians had been hated and feared. But the vacant quarters also spoke eloquently of the fact that Rome was no longer the mistress of the world. The domina gentium, the regina terrarum, without her Praetorians, was a thing unthinkable.

Constantine only stayed two months in Rome, but in that short time, says Nazarius, he cured all the maladies which the six years' savage tyranny of Maxentius had brought upon the city. He restored to their confiscated estates all who had been exiled or deprived of their property during the recent reign of terror. He showed himself easy of approach; his ears were the most patient of listeners; he charmed all by his kindliness, dignity, and good humor. To the Senate he showed unwonted deference. Diocletian, during his solitary visit to Rome just prior to his retirement, had treated the senators with brusqueness, and hardly concealed his contempt for their mouldy dignities. Constantine preferred to conciliate them. According to Nazarius, he invested with senatorial rank a number of representative provincials, so that the Senate once more became a dignified body in reality as well as in name, now that it consisted of the flower of the whole world. Probably this signifies little more than that Constantine filled up the vacancies with respectable nom-inees, spoke the Senate fair, and swore to maintain its ancient rights and privileges.

The Emperor certainly entertained no such quixotic idea as that of giving the Senate a vestige of real governing power or a share in the administration of the Empire. In return for his consideration, the Senate bestowed upon him the title of Senior Augustus, and a golden statue, adorned, according to the Ninth Panegyrist, with the attributes of a god, while all Italy subscribed for the shield and the crown.

The Senate also instituted games and festivals in honor of Constantine's victory, and voted him the triumphal arch which still survives as one of the most imposing ruins of Imperial Rome and a lasting monument to the outrageous vandalism which stripped the Arch of Titus of its sculptures to grace the memorial of his successor. Under the central arch on the one side is the dedication, "To the Liberator of the City", on the other, "To the Founder of Our Repose". Above stands the famous inscription in which the Senate and people of Rome dedicate this triumphal arch to Constantine "because, at the suggestion of the divinity, and at the prompting of his own magnanimity, he and his army had vindicated the Republic by striking down the tyrant and all his satellites at a single blow". "At the suggestion of the divinity!" The words lead us naturally to discuss the conversion of Constantine and the Vision of the Cross.

THE VISION OF THE CROSS AND THE EDICT OF MILAN

IT was during the course of the successful invasion of Italy, which culminated in the battle of the Milvian Bridge and the capture of Rome, that there took place—or was said to have taken place—the famous vision of the cross, surrounded by the swords, "Conquer by This," which accompanied the triumph of Constantine's arms. There are two main authorities for the legend, Eusebius and Lactantius, both, of course, Christians and uncompromising champions of Constantine, with whom they were in close personal contact. A third, though he makes no mention of the cross, is Nazarius, the author of the Tenth Panegyric. The variations which subsequent writers introduce into the story relate merely to details, or are obvious embroideries upon an original legend, such, for example, as the statement of Philostorgius that the words of promise around the cross were written in stars. We need not trouble, therefore, with the much later versions of Sozomen, Socrates, Gregory of Nazianzen, and Nicephorus it will be enough to study the more or less contemporary statements of Eusebius, Lactantius, and Nazarius. And of these by far the fullest and most important is that of Eusebius, Bishop of Caesarea, who explicitly declares that he is repeating the story as it was told to him by Constantine himself.

Eusebius shows us the Emperor of Gaul anxiously debating within his own mind whether his forces were equal to the dangerous enterprise upon which he had embarked. Maxentius had a formidable army. He had also labored to bring over to his side the powers of heaven and hell. Constantine's information from Rome apprised him that Maxentius was assiduously employing all the black arts of magic and wizardry to gain the favour of the gods. And Constantine grew uneasy and apprehensive, for no one then disbelieved in the efficacy of magic, and he considered whether he might not counterbalance this undue advantage which Maxentius was obtaining by securing the protecting services of some equally potent deity. Such is the only possible meaning of Eusebius's words, "He thought in his own mind what sort of god he ought to secure as ally",—words which seem strange in the twentieth century, but were natural enough in the fourth. And then, says his biographer, the idea occurred to him that though his predecessors in the purple had believed in a multiplicity of gods, the great majority of them had perished miserably. The gods, at whose altars they had offered rich sacrifice and plenteous libation, had deserted them in their hour of trouble, and had looked on unmoved while they and their families were exterminated from off the face of the earth, leaving scarcely so much as a name or a recollection behind them. The gods had cheated them and lured them to their doom with suave promises of treacherous oracles. Whereas, on the other hand, his father, Constantius, had believed in but one god, and had marvelously prospered throughout his life, helped and protected by this single deity who had showered every blessing upon his head. From such a contrast, what other deduction could be drawn than that the god of Constantius was the deity for Constantius's son to honor? Constantine resolved that it would be folly to waste time or thought upon deities who were of no account. He would worship no other god than the god of his father.

Such, according to Eusebius, is the first phase of the Emperor's conversion, a conviction not of sin, but of the folly of worshipping gods who cannot or will not do anything for their votaries. But this god of his father, this single unnamed divinity, who was it? Was it one of the gods of the Roman Pantheon, Jupiter, or Apollo, or Hercules, whose special protection Constantine had claimed for himself, as Augustus had claimed that of Apollo, and Diocletian that of Jupiter? Or was it the vague spirit of deity itself, the Theo of the Greek philosophers, the divinitas of the cultured Roman, whose delicacy was offended by the grossness of the exceedingly human passions of the Roman gods and goddesses? Obviously, it must be the latter, and Eusebius tell us that Constantine offered up a prayer to this god of his father, beseeching him, "to declare himself who he was," and to stretch forth his right hand' to help. "To declare himself who he was!". That had ever been the stumbling-block in the way of the acceptance by the masses of the immaterial principles propounded by the philosophers. Constantine must have a god with a name, and he must have a sign from heaven in visible proof. Many have asked for such a sign just as importunately as Constantine, but without success. To him it was vouchsafed.

The answer came one afternoon, when the sun had just passed its zenith and was beginning to decline. Lifting his eyes, the Emperor saw in the heavens just above the sun the figure of a cross, a cross of radiant light, and attached to it was the inscription, "Conquer by This". Eusebius admits that if anyone else had told the story it would not have been easy to believe it, but it was told to him by the Emperor himself, who had confirmed his words with a royal oath. How then was it possible to doubt? Constantine was awe-struck at the vision, which Eusebius expressly declares was seen also by the entire army. All that afternoon the Emperor pondered long upon the significance of the words, and night fell while he was still asking himself what they could mean. Then, as he slept, Christ appeared to him in a dream, bearing with Him the sign that had flamed in the sky, and bade the sleeper make a copy of it and use it as a talisman whenever he gave battle. As soon as dawn broke, Constantine summoned his friends and told them of the message he had received. Workers in gold and precious stones were hastily sent for, and, sitting in the midst of them, Constantine carefully described the outline of the vision and bade them execute a replica of it in their most precious materials. This was the famous Labarum, fashioned from a long gilded spear and a transverse bar. Above was a crown of gold, with jewels encircling the monogram of Christ, and from the bar depended a rich purple cloth, heavily embroidered with gold, blazing with jewels, and bearing the busts of Constantine and his sons. It suggested the Cross just as much but no more than did the ordinary cavalry standards of the Roman armies; the sacred monogram alone indicated the supreme change which had come over the Emperor, who, in answer to his prayer, had thus found that the single Deity which his father, Constantius, had worshipped was none other than Christ, the God of the Christians. For the Emperor, desiring to know more of the Cross and the Christ, summoned certain Christian teachers in his camp to explain these things more fully to him, and they told him that "Christ was God, the only begotten Son of the one true God, and that the vision he had seen was the symbol of immortality and of the victory which Christ had won over death". Such, according to Eusebius, was the conversion of Constantine, and such was the Emperor's own account of the circumstances which led up to it. This was the official story, as it might have appeared in a Roman Court Circular at the time when Eusebius wrote.

But when did Eusebius write The Life of Constantine, from which we have taken this narrative? Not until Constantine himself was dead, not, that is to say, until after 337; fully a quarter of a century after the event described. The date is important. In twenty-five years a story may be transfigured out of all knowledge through constant repetition by the narrator, to say nothing of the changes it suffers if it passes in active circulation from mouth to mouth. Has this been the fate of the story of the Vision of the Cross? The Life of Constantine was not the first volume of contemporary history published by Eusebius. He had already written a History of the Church, which he issued to the world in 326. What, then, had the author to say in that year about this marvellous vision? Nothing. There is not a word about the flaming cross, or the coming of Christ to Constantine in a dream, or the fashioning of the Labarum. All Eusebius says, in his History, of the conversion of Constantine, is that the Emperor "piously called to his aid the God of Heaven and his son Jesus Christ". It is a strange silence. If the heavenly cross had been seen by the whole army; if the current version of the story had been the same in 326 as it was in 337, it is at least difficult to understand why Eusebius omitted all mention of an event which must have been the talk of the whole Roman world and must have made the heart of every Christian exult. Such manifest signs from Heaven were scarcely so common in the opening of the fourth century that an ecclesiastical historian would think any allusion to it unnecessary. The argument from silence is never absolutely conclusive, but the reticence of Eusebius in 326 at least warrants a strong suspicion that the legend had not then crystallized itself into its final shape.

Of even greater importance are the extraordinary discrepancies between the versions of Eusebius and Lactantius. Lactantius wrote his treatise On the Deaths of the Persecutors very shortly after the battle of the Milvian Bridge, and it has a special value, therefore, as containing the earliest account of the vision. The author, who was the tutor of the Emperor's son, Crispus, must have known all there was to be known of the incident, for he lived in the closest intimacy with the court circle. We should confidently expect, therefore, that the author who retails verbatim the conversation of Diocletian and Galerius in the penetralia of the palace of Nicomedia would be fully aware of what took place in full view of Constantine's army.

What then is the version of Lactantius? It is that just before the battle of the Milvian Bridge, Constantine was warned in a dream to have the divine sign of the cross inscribed on the shields of his soldiers before leading them to the attack. He did as he was bidden, and the letter X, with one of the bars slightly bent—thus, -r- —to form the sacred monogram, was placed upon his legionaries' shields. Such is the legend in its earliest guise. There is not a word about Constantine's anxiety and searching of soul. The event is placed, not at the opening of the campaign, as Eusebius would seem to suggest though he does not expressly say so, but on the eve of the decisive battle. There is nothing about the cross flaming in the afternoon sky, nothing of the inscription, "Conquer by This", nothing of the entire army being witness of the portent. Constantine simply has a dream and is warned to place the initial of Christ on his soldiers' shields. It is not even said who gave the warning; there is not a hint that it was Christ Himself—as in the story of Eusebius—who appeared to Constantine; there is no mention of the Labarum. Obviously, Lactantius was aware of no triumphant answer to Constantine's prayer for a sign. According to him, the Emperor was merely warned in a dream that victory would reward him if he dedicated his weapons to the honor and service of Christ.

We come back, therefore, to the official version of Eusebius somewhat shaken in our belief of its literal accuracy. Let us note, too, the extreme vagueness of the time and the place where the incident is reported to have taken place, and remember that one who had dwelt with Diocletian and Galerius when they signed the edicts of persecution could not possibly have been ignorant of the principles of Christianity, which was no longer the religion of an obscure sect. We need not, indeed, find any difficulty in accepting the first part of the story of Eusebius in so far as it represents Constantine anxiously enquiring after divine protection. It has been urged, very shrewdly, that the story would have been idealized if it had been altogether invented. Constantine was afraid that he had rashly committed himself and that Maxentius had already secured the favor of the Roman gods. His objective, too, was Rome, still regarded with superstitious dread and reverence throughout the world, and reverenced all the more, no doubt, in proportion as distance lent enchantment to the view. What then more natural than that he should take for granted that, if ever the gods of Rome had interfered in mortal affairs, they would do so now on behalf of Maxentius, who had been raised to empire as Rome's champion? Constantine was not one of those rarer and choicer spirits, who seek truth for its own sake without regard for material advantage. Conversion in his case did not mean some sudden or even gradual change permanently altering his outlook upon life, and refining and transmuting personal character. It merely meant worshipping at another shrine, entering another temple, reciting another formula. His ruling motive was ambition. He would worship the god who should bring victory to his arms. The intensity of his conviction was to be measured by the extent of his success and by the height to which he carried his fortunes.

But what of the second part of the story—the vision of the cross flaming in the sky in full view of Constantine and his army? Even those who admit miracles into critical history allow that the evidence for this one is exceedingly inconclusive. We need not doubt that Eusebius related the story just as it was told to him by Constantine, though the Bishop, if there were choice versions, would unhesitatingly accept the one which contained most of the miraculous and the abnormal. Nor does the oath which Constantine swore in support of his story add anything to its credibility. It was his habit to swear an oath when he wished to be emphatic. Are we, then, to consider that the whole legend was an invention of the Emperor's from beginning to end? In this connection it is important to take into account the narrative of Nazarius, a rhetorician who delivered a formal panegyric upon Constantine on the anniversary of his tenth year of rule, and took the opportunity of reviewing the whole campaign against Maxentius. Nazarius was a pagan; what then was (the pagan version, if any, of the miracle described by Eusebius and the Emperor? Did the pagans attribute divine assistance to Constantine throughout this critical campaign? The answer is unmistakable. They did so most unequivocally. Nazarius tells us that all Gaul was talking with awe and wonder of the marvels which had taken place, how the soldiers of Constantine had seen in the sky celestial armies marching in battle array and had been dazzled by their flashing shields and glittering armour. Not only had the dull eyes of earthly men for once availed to look upon heavenly brightness; Constantine's soldiery had also heard the shouts of these armies in the sky, "We seek Constantine; we are marching to the aid of Constantine". Clearly the pagan as well as the Christian world insisted upon attributing divine assistance to Constantine and had its own version of how that succor came. Nazarius's explanation was simple. According to him, it was Constantius Chlorus, the deified Emperor, who was leading up the hosts of heaven, and such miraculous intervention was due to the supreme virtue of the father, which had descended to the son.

The question at once arises whether this is merely a pagan version of the Christian legend. Unable to deny the miracle, did the pagans, in order to rob the Christians of this wonderful testimony to the truth of their religion, invent the story of Constantius and the heavenly hosts? Such a theory is absolutely untenable. It leaves out of sight the all-important fact that public opinion in the fourth century—as indeed for many centuries both before and after—was not only willing to believe in supernatural intervention at moments of great crisis, but actually insisted that there should be such intervention. The greater the crisis, the more entirely reasonable it was that some deity or deities should make their influence especially felt and turn the scale to one side or the other. Every Roman believed that Castor and Pollux had fought for Rome in the supreme struggle against Hannibal. Julius believed that the favour of Venus Genetrix, the special patroness of the Julian House, had helped him to win the battle of Pharsalus. Augustus was just as certain that Apollo had fought on his side at Philippi and at Actium. It was easy—and modest — for the winner to believe in his protecting deity's strength of arm.

One curious phrase employed by Nazarius is worth noting. It is that in which he claims that the special interference of Heaven on behalf of Constantine was not merely an extraordinary and gratifying tribute to the Emperor's virtues, but that it was no more than his due. In short, the crisis was so tremendous that Heaven would have stood convicted of a strange failure to see events in their just proportion if it had not done "some great thing", and wrought some corresponding wonder. Such was the idea at the back of Nazarius's mind; we suspect that it was not wanting in the mind of Eusebius or of Constantine. We may put the matter paradoxically and say that a miracle in those days was not much considered unless it was a very great one. People who were accustomed to see—or to think that they saw—statues sweating blood, and to hear words proceeding from lips of bronze or marble, and were accustomed to treat such untoward events merely as portents denoting that something unusual was about to happen, must have been difficult people to surprise. Naturally, therefore, legends grew more and more marvelous with repetition after the event. The oftener a man told such a story the less appeal it would make to his own wonder, unless he fortified it with some new incident. But to impress one's auditors it is above all things necessary to be impressed oneself. Hence the well-garnished narrative of Nazarius. The idea of armies marching along the sky was common enough. Any one can imagine he sees the glint of weapons as the sun strikes the clouds. But this does not satisfy the professional rhetorician. He bids us see the proud look in the faces of the heavenly hosts, and distinguish the cries with which they move to battle. But if Nazarius is suspect, why not Eusebius and Constantine? Unless, indeed, there is to be one standard for pagan and another for Christian miracles!

But was there some unusual manifestation in the sky which was the common basis of the stories of Eusebius and Nazarius? It is not unreasonable to suppose so. Scientists say that the natural phenomenon known as the parhelion not infrequently assumes the shape of a cross, and Dean Stanley, while discussing this possible explanation in his Lectures on the Eastern Church, instanced the extraordinary impression made upon the minds of the vulgar by the aurora borealis of November, 1848. He recalled how, throughout France, the people thought they saw in the sky the letters L. N.—the initials of Louis Napoleon—and took them as a clear indication from Heaven of how they ought to vote at the impending Presidential election, and as an omen of the result. That was the interpretation in France. In Rome—where the people knew and cared nothing for Louis Napoleon—no one saw the Napoleonic initials. The lurid gleam in the sky was there thought to be the blood of the murdered Rossi, which had risen to heaven and was calling for vengeance. In Oporto, on the other hand, the conscience-stricken populace thought the fire was coming down from heaven to punish them for their profligacy. If such varying interpretations of a natural if rare phenomenon were possible in the middle of the nineteenth century, what interpretation was not possible in the fourth? The world was profoundly superstitious. When people believe in manifest signs they usually see them. Some Polonius, gifted either with better vision or livelier imagination than his fellows, declares that he can distinguish clear and definite shapes amid the vague outline of the clouds; the report spreads; the legend grows. And when legends are found to serve a useful purpose the authorities lend them countenance, guarantee their accuracy, and even take to themselves the credit of their authorship. At the outbreak of the Russo-Japanese war a strange story came from St. Petersburg that the Russian moujiks were passing on from village to village the legend that St. George had been seen in the skies leading his hosts to the Far East against the infidel Japanese. Had Russian victories followed, what better "proof" of celestial aid could have been desired? But as disaster ensued, it is to be supposed that St. George remembered midway that he also had interests in the Anglo-Japanese alliance, and remained strictly neutral.

But though we may be justly skeptical of the circumstances attending the conversion of Constantine, there is no room to doubt the conversion itself. We do not believe that he fought the battle of the Milvian Bridge as the avowed champion of Christianity, but the probabilities are that he had made up his mind to become a Christian when he fought it. The miraculous vision in the heavens, the dream in the quiet of the night, the appearance of Christ by the bedside of the Emperor—as to these things we may keep an open mind, but the fashioning of the Labarum—the sacred standard which was preserved for so many centuries as the most precious of imperial heirlooms and was seen and described as late as the ninth century—this was the outward and visible proof of the change which had come over the Emperor. He had abandoned Apollo for Christ. The sun-god had been the favourite deity of his youth and early manhood, as it had been of Augustus Cesar, the founder of the Empire, and the originator of the close association between the worship of Apollo and the worship of the reigning Cesar. Constantine would not fail to note that many of the most gracious attributes of Apollo belonged also to Christ.

He soon manifested the sincerity of his conversion. After a short stay in Rome, he went north to Milan, where he gave the hand of his sister, Constantia, to his ally, Licinius. Diocletian was invited, but declined to make the journey. The two Emperors, no doubt, desired to secure the prestige of his moral support in their mutual hostility to the Emperor of the East, and the benefit of his counsel in their deliberations upon the state of the Empire. But even if Diocletian had been tempted to leave his cabbages to join in the marriage festivities and the political conference at Milan, we imagine that he would still have declined if he had been given any hint of the intentions of Constantine and Licinius with respect to the great question of religious toleration or persecution. He might have been candid enough to admit the failure of his policy, but he would still have shrunk from proclaiming it with his own lips. For, before the festivities at Milan were interrupted by the news that Maximin had thrown down the gage of battle, Constantine and Licinius issued in their joint names the famous Edict of Milan, which proclaimed for the first time in its absolute entirety the noble principle of complete religious toleration. Despite their length, it will be well to give in full the more important clauses. They are found in the text which has been happily preserved by Lactantius in the original Latin, while we also have the edict in Greek in the Ecclesiastical History of Eusebius . It runs as follows:

"Inasmuch as we, Constantine Augustus and Licinius Augustus, have met together at Milan on a joyful occasion, and have discussed all that appertains to the public advantage and safety, we have come to the conclusion that, among the steps likely to profit the majority of mankind and demanding immediate attention, nothing is more necessary than to regulate the worship of the Divinity.

"We have decided, therefore, to grant both to the Christians and to all others perfect freedom to practice the religion which each has thought best for himself, that so whatever Divinity resides in heaven may be placated, and rendered propitious to us and to all who have been placed under our authority. Consequently, we have thought this to be the policy demanded alike by healthy and sound reason—that no one, on any pretext whatever, should be denied freedom to choose his religion, whether he prefers the Christian religion or any other that seems most suited to him, in order that the Supreme Divinity, whose observance we obey with free minds, may in all things vouchsafe to us its usual favors and benevolences.

"Wherefore, it is expedient for your Excellency to know that we have resolved to abolish every one of the stipulations contained in all previous edicts sent to you with respect to the Christians, on the ground that they now seem to us to be unjust and alien from the spirit of our clemency.

"Henceforth, in perfect and absolute freedom, each and every person who chooses to belong to and practice the Christian religion shall be at liberty to do so without let or hindrance in any shape or form.

"We have thought it best to explain this to your Excellency in the fullest possible manner that you may know that we have accorded to these same Christians a free and absolutely unrestricted right to practice their own religion.

"And inasmuch as you see that we have granted this indulgence to the Christians, your Excellency will understand that a similarly free and unrestricted right, conformable to the peace of our times, is granted to all others equally to practice the religion of their choice. We have resolved upon this course that no one and no religion may seem to be robbed of the honor that is their due".

Then follow the most explicit instructions for the restoration to the Christians of the properties of which they had been robbed during the persecutions, though the robbery had been committed in accordance with imperial command. Whether a property had been simply confiscated, or sold, or given away, it was to be handed back without the slightest cost and without any delays or ambiguities. Purchasers who had bought such properties in good faith were to be indemnified from the public treasury by grace of the Emperor.

But the abiding interest of this celebrated edict lies in the general principles there clearly enunciated. Every man, without distinction of rank or nationality, is to have absolute freedom to choose and practice the religion which he deems most suited to his needs. The phrase is repeated with almost wearisome iteration, but the principle was novel and strange, and one can see the anxiety of the framers of this edict that there shall be no possible loophole for misunderstanding. Everybody is to have free choice; all previous anti-Christian enactments are annulled; not only is no compulsion to be employed against the Christian, he is not even to be troubled or annoyed. The novelty lay not so much in the toleration of the existence of Christianity, —both Constantine and Licinius had two years before signed the edict whereby Galerius put an end to the persecution,—but in its formal official recognition by the State.

What motives, then, are assigned by the Emperors for this notable change of policy? Certainly not humanity. Nothing is said of the terrors of the late persecutions and the horrible sufferings of the Christians— there is merely a bald reference to previous edicts which the Emperors consider "unjust and alien from the spirit of our clemency". There is no appeal to political necessity, such as the exhaustion of the world and its palpable need of rest. The motives assigned are purely religious. The Emperors proclaim religious toleration in order that they and their subjects may continue to receive the blessings of Heaven. One of them at least had just emerged victoriously from the manifold hazards of an invasion of Italy. Surely we can trace a reference to the battle of the Milvian Bridge and the overthrow of Maxentius in the mention of "the Divine favor towards us, which we have experienced in affairs of the highest moment". What Constantine and Licinius hope to secure is a continuance of the favor and benevolence of the Supreme Divinity, the patronage of the ruling powers of the sky. The phraseology is important. The name of God is not mentioned—only the vague Summa Divinitas, Divinus favor, and the still more curious and non-committal phrase, whatever Divinity resides in heaven. In Eusebius the same phrase appears in a form still more nebulous: Whatever Divinity there is and heavenly substance. A pagan philosopher, more than half skeptical as to the existence of a personal God, might well employ such language, but it reads strangely in an official edict.

But then this edict was to bear the joint names of Constantine and Licinius. Constantine might be a Christian, but Licinius was still a pagan, and Licinius was not his vassal, but his equal. He would certainly not have been prepared to set his name to an edict which pledged him to personal adherence to the Christian faith. Constantine, in the flush of triumph, would insist that the persecution of the Christians should cease, and that the Christian religion should be officially recognized. Licinius would raise no objection. But they would speedily find, when it came to drafting a joint edict, that the only religious ground common to them both was very limited in extent, and that the only way to preserve a semblance of unity was to employ the vaguest phraseology which each might interpret in his own fashion. If we can imagine the Pope and the Caliph drafting a joint appeal to mankind which necessitated the mention of the Higher Power, they would find themselves driven to use words as cloudy and indistinct as the Whatever Divinity there is and heavenly substance of Eusebius. No, it was not that Constantine's mind was in the transitional stage; it was rather that he had to find a common platform for himself and Licinius.

But to have converted Licinius at all to an official recognition of the Christians and complete toleration was a great achievement, for the principle, as we have said, was entirely new. M. Gaston Boissier, in discussing this point, recalls how even the broad-minded Plato had found no place in his ideal republic for those who disbelieved in the gods of their fatherland and of the city of their birth. Even if they kept their opinions to themselves and did not seek to disturb the faith of others, Plato insisted upon their being placed in a House of Correction—it is true he calls it a Sophronisterion, or House of Wisdom—for five years, where they were to listen to a sermon every day; while, if they were zealous propagandists of their pernicious doctrines, he proposed to keep them all their lives in horrible dungeons and deny their bodies after death the right of sepulture. How, one wonders, would Socrates have fared in such a state? No better, we fancy, than he fared in his own city of Athens. But, throughout antiquity, every lawgiver took the same view, that a good citizen must accept without question the gods of his native place who had been the gods of his fathers; and it was a simple step from that position to the stern refusal to allow a man, in the vigorous words of the Old Testament, to go a-whoring after other gods. "For I, thy God, am a jealous God". The God of the Jews was not more jealous than the gods of the Assyrians, the Egyptians, the Greeks, or the Romans would like to have been, had they had the same power of concise expression.

What was the theory of the State religion in Rome? Cicero tells us in a well-known passage in his treatise On the Laws, where he quotes the ancient formula, "Let no man have separate gods of his own: nor let people privately worship new gods or alien gods, unless they have been publicly admitted." Nothing could be more explicit. But theory and practice in Rome had a habit of becoming divorced from one another. It is a notorious fact that, as Rome's conquering eagles flew farther afield, the legions and the merchants who followed in their track brought all manner of strange gods back to the city, where every wandering Chaldean thaumaturgist, magician, or soothsayer found welcome and profit, and every stray goddess—especially if her rites had mysteries attached to them—received a comfortable home. In a word, Rome found new religions just as fascinating—for a season or two—as do the capitals of the modern world, and these new religions were certainly not "publicly admitted " by the Pontiff Maximus and the representatives of the State religion. Occasionally, usually after some outbreak of pestilence or because an Emperor was nervous at the presence of so many swarthy charlatans devoting themselves to the Black Arts, an order of expulsion would be issued and there would be a fluttering of the dove-cotes. But they came creeping back one by one, as the storm blew over. While, therefore, in theory the gods of Rome were jealous, in practice they were not so. The easy skepticism or eclecticism of the cultured Roman was conducive to tolerance. Cicero's famous sentence in the Pro Flacco, "Each state has its own religion, Laelius: we have ours", shows how little of the religious fanatic there was in the average Roman, who stole the gods of the people he conquered and made them his own, so that they might acquiesce in the Roman domination The Roman was tolerant enough in private life towards other people's religious convictions: all he asked was reciprocity, and that was precisely what the Christian would not and could not give him. If the Christian would have sacrificed at the altars of the State gods, the Roman would never have objected to his worship of Christ for his own private satisfaction. There lies the secret of the persecutions, and of the fierce anti-Christian hatreds.

Constantine and Licinius, by their edict of recognition and toleration, "publicly admitted" into the Roman worship the God of the Christians.

THE DOWNFALL OF LICINIUS

IT will be convenient in this chapter to present a connected narrative of the course of political events from the Edict of Milan in 313 down to the overthrow of Licinius by Constantine in 324. We have seen that Maximin Daza never moved a single soldier to help his ally, Maxentius, during Constantine's invasion of Italy, though he soon gave practical proof that his hostility had not abated by invading the territory of Licinius. The attack was clearly not expected. Licinius was still at Milan, and his troops had probably been drawn off into winter quarters, when the news came that Maximin had collected a powerful army in Syria, had marched through to Bithynia regardless of the sufferings of his legions and the havoc caused in the ranks by the severity of the season, and had succeeded in crossing the Bosphorus. Apparently, Maximin was besieging Byzantium before Licinius was ready to move from Italy to confront him.

Byzantium capitulated after a siege of eleven days and Heraclea did not offer a prolonged resist-ance. By this time, however, Licinius was getting within touch of the invader and preparations were made on both sides for a pitched battle. The numbers of Licinius's army were scarcely half those of his rival, but Maximin was completely routed on a plain called Serenus, near the city of Adrianople, and fled for his life, leaving his broken battalions to shift for themselves. Lactantius, in describing the engagement, represents it as having been a duel to the death between Christianity and paganism. He says that Maximin had vowed to eradicate the very name of the Christians if Jupiter favored his arms; while Licinius had been warned by an angel of God in a dream that, if he wished to make infallibly sure of victory, he and his army had only to recite a prayer to Almighty God which the angel would dictate to him.

Licinius at once sent for a secretary and the prayer was taken down. It ran as follows:

"God most High, we call upon Thee; Holy God, we call upon Thee. We commend to Thee all justice; we commend to Thee our safety; we commend to Thee our sovereignty. Through Thee we live; through Thee we gain victory and happiness. Most High and Holy God, hear our prayers. We stretch out our arms to Thee. Hear us, Most High and Holy God".

Such was the talismanic prayer of which the Emperor's secretary made hurried copies, distribu-ting them to the general officers and the tribunes of the legions, with instructions that the troops were at once to get the words off by heart. When the armies moved against one another in battle array, the legions of Licinius at a given signal laid down their shields, removed their helmets, and, lifting their hands to heaven, recited in unison these rhythmic sentences with their strangely effective repetitions. Lactantius tells us that the murmur of the prayer was borne upon the ears of the doomed army of the enemy. Then, after a brief colloquy between the rivals, in which Maximin refused to offer or agree to any concession, because he believed that the soldiers of Licinius would come over to him in a body, the armies charged and the standard of Maximin went down.

It is a striking story, and we may easily understand that Licinius, fresh from his meeting with Constantine and with vivid recollection of how valiantly this Summus Deus had fought for his ally against Maxentius, would be ready to believe beforehand in the efficacy of any supernatural warning conveyed by any supernatural "minister of grace". We may note, too, the splendid vagueness of the Deity invoked in the prayer. Lactantius, of course, claims that this Most High and Holy God is none other than the God of the Christians, but there was nothing to prevent the votary of Jupiter, of Apollo, of Mithra, of Baal, or of Balenus, from thinking that he was imploring the aid of his own familiar deity.

Maximin fled from the scene of carnage as though he had been pursued by all the Cabiri. Throwing aside his purple and assuming the garb of a slave—it is Lactantius, however, who is speaking—he crossed the Bosphorus, and, within twenty-four hours of quitting the field, reached once more the palace of Nicomedia—a distance of a hundred and sixty miles. Taking his wife and children with him, he hurried through the defiles of the Taurus, summoned to his side whatever troops he had left behind in Syria and Egypt, and awaited the oncoming of Licinius, who followed at leisure in his tracks. The end was not long delayed. Maximin's soldiers regarded his cause as lost, and despairing of clemency, he took his own life at Tarsus. His provinces passed without a struggle into the hands of Licinius, who butchered every surviving member of Maximin'' family.

Nor had the victor pity even for two ladies of imperial rank, whose misfortunes and sufferings excited the deepest compassion in that stony-hearted age. These were Prisca, the wife of Diocletian, and her daughter Valeria, the widow of the Emperor Galerius. On his death-bed Galerius had entrusted his wife to the care and the gratitude of Maximin, whom he had raised from obscurity to a throne. Maximin repaid his confidence by pressing Valeria to marry him and offering to divorce his own wife. Valeria returned an indignant and high-spirited refusal. She would never think of marriage, she said, while still wearing mourning for a husband whose ashes were not yet cold. It was monstrous that Maximin should seek to divorce a faithful wife, and, even if she assented to his proposal, she had clear warning of what was likely to be her own fate.

Finally, it was not becoming that the daughter of Diocletian and the widow of Galerius should stoop to a second marriage. Maximin took a bitter revenge. He reduced Valeria to penury, marked down all her friends for ruin, and finally drove her into exile with her mother, Prisca, who nobly shared the sufferings of the daughter whom she could not shield. Lactantius tells us that the two imperial ladies wandered miserably through the Syrian wastes, while Maximin took delight in spurning the overtures of the aged Diocletian, who sent repeated messages begging that his daughter might be allowed to go and live with him at Salona. Maximin refused even when Diocletian sent one of his relatives to remind him of past benefits, and the two unfortunate ladies knew no alleviation of their troubles. When the tyrant fell, they probably thought that the implacable hatred with which Maximin had pursued them would be their best recommendation to the favor of Licinius.

Again, however, they were disappointed, for Licinius, in his jealous anxiety to spare no one connected with the families of his predecessors in the purple, ordered the execution of Candidianus, a natural son of Galerius, who had been brought up by Valeria as her own child. In despair, therefore, the two ladies, who had boldly gone to Nicomedia, fled from the scene and "wandered for fifteen months, disguised as plebeians, through various provinces", until they had the misfortune to be recognized at Thessalonica.

They were at once beheaded and their bodies thrown into the sea, amid the pitying sympathy of a vast throng which dared not lift a hand to save them.

Constantine and Licinius now shared between them the whole of the Roman Empire. They were allies, but their alliance did not long stand the strain of their respective ambitions. Each had won an easy victory over his antagonist, and each was confident that his legions would suffice to win him undivided empire. We know very little of the pretexts assigned for the quarrel which culminated in the war of 316. Zosimus throws the blame upon Constantine, whom he accuses of not keeping faith and of trying to filch from Licinius some of his provinces. But as the sympathies of Zosimus were strongly pagan and as he invariably imputed the worst possible motive to Constantine, it is fairest and most reasonable to suppose that the two Emperors simply quarreled over the division of the Empire. Constantine had given the hand of his half-sister Anastasia to one of his generals, named Bassianus, whom he had raised to the dignity of a Cesar. But for some reason left unexplained—possibly because Constantine granted only the title, without the legions and the provinces, of a Cesar—Bassianus became discontented with his position and entered into an intrigue with Licinius. Constantine discovered the plot, put Bassianus to death, and demanded from Licinius the surrender of Senecio, a brother of the victim and a relative of Licinius. The demand was refused; some statues of Constantine were demolished by Licinius's orders at Emona (Laybach) and war ensued.

The armies met in the autumn of 316 near Cibalis, in Pannonia, between the rivers Drave and Save. Neither Emperor led into the field anything approaching the full strength he was able to muster; Licinius is said to have had only 35,000 men and Constantine no more than 20,000. From Zosimus's highly rhetorical account of the battle we gather that Constantine chose a position between a steep hill and an impassable morass, and repulsed the charge of the legions of Licinius. Then as he advanced into the plain in pursuit of the enemy, he was checked by some fresh troops which Licinius brought up, and a long and stubborn contest lasted until nightfall, when Constantine decided the fortunes of the day by an irresistible charge. Licinius is said to have lost 20,000 men in this encounter, more than fifty per cent of his entire force, and he beat a hurried retreat, leaving his camp to be plundered by the victor, whose own losses must also have been severe.

A few weeks later the battle was renewed on the plain of Mardia in Thrace. Licinius had evidently been strongly reinforced from Asia, for, though he was again defeated after a hotly contested battle, he was able to effect an orderly retreat and draw off his beaten troops without disorder—a rare thing in the annals of Roman warfare, where defeat usually involved destruction. Constantine is said to have owed his victory to his superior generalship and to the skill with which he timed a surprise attack of five thousand of his men upon the rear of the enemy. Yet we may be certain that he would not have consented to treat with Licinius for peace had he not had considerable cause for anxiety about the final issue of the campaign. However, his two victories, while not sufficiently decisive to enable him to dictate any terms he chose, at least gave him the authoritative word in the negotiations which ensued, and sealed the doom of the unfortunate Valens, whom Licinius had just appointed Cesar. When Licinius's envoy spoke of his two imperial masters, Licinius and Valens, Constantine retorted that he recognized but one, and bluntly stated that he had not endured tedious marches and won a succession of victories, only to share the prize with a contemptible slave. Licinius sacrificed his lieutenant without compunction and consented to hand over to Constantine Illyria and its legions, with the important provinces of Pannonia, Dalmatia, Moesia, and Dacia. The only foothold left him on the Continent of Europe, out of all that had previously been included in the eastern half of the Empire, was the province of Thrace.

At the same time, the two Emperors agreed to elevate their sons to the rank of Cesar. Constantine bestowed the dignity upon Crispus, the son of his first marriage with Minervina. Crispus was now in the promise of early manhood, and had proved his valour, and won his spurs in the recent campaign. Licinius gave the title to his son Licinianus, an infant no more than twenty months old. These appointments are important, for they show how completely the system of Diocletian had broken down. The Emperors appointed Caesars out of deference to the letter of that constitution, but they outrageously violated its spirit by appointing their own sons, and when the choice fell on an infant, insult was added to injury. It was plain warning to all the world that Constantine and Licinius meant to keep power in their own hands. When, a few years later, three sons were born to Constantine and Fausta in quick succession, the eldest, who was given the name of his father, was created Caesar shortly after his birth. No doubt the Empress—herself an Emperor's daughter— demanded that her son should enjoy equal rank with the son of the low-born Minervina, and the probabilities are that Constantine already looked forward to providing the young Princes with patrimonies carved out of the territory of Licinius. However, there was no actual rupture between the two Emperors until 323, though relations had long been strained.

We know comparatively little of what took place in the intervening years. They were not, however, years of unbroken peace. There was fighting both on the Danube and the Rhine. The Goths and the Sarmat, who had been taught such a severe lesson by Claudius and Aurelian that they had left the Danubian frontier undisturbed for half a century, again surged forward and swept over Moesia and Pannonia. We hear of several hard-fought battles along the course of the river, and then, when Constantine, at the head of his legions, had driven out the invader, he himself crossed the Danube and compelled the barbarians to assent to a peace whereby they pledged themselves to supply the Roman armies, when required, with forty thousand auxiliaries. The details of this campaign are exceedingly obscure and untrustworthy. The Panegyrists of the Emperor claimed that he had repeated the triumphs of Trajan. Constantine himself is represented by the mocking Julian as boasting that he was a greater general than Trajan, because it is a finer thing to win back what you have lost than to conquer something which was not yours before. The probabilities are that there took place one of those alarming barbarian movements from which the Roman Empire was never long secure, that Constantine beat it back successfully, and gained victories which were decisive enough at the moment, but in which there was no real finality, because no finality was possible. Probably it was the seriousness of these Gothic and Sarmatian campaigns which was chiefly responsible for the years of peace between Constantine and Licinius. Until the barbarian danger had been repelled, Constantine was perforce obliged to remain on tolerable terms with the Emperor of the East.

While the father was thus engaged on the Danube, the son was similarly employed on the Rhine. The young Cesar, Crispus, already entrusted with the administration of Gaul and Britain and the command of the Rhine legions, won a victory over the Alemanni in a winter campaign and distinguished himself by the skill and rapidity with which he executed a long forced march despite the icy rigors of a severe season. It is Nazarius, the Panegyrist, who refers in glowing sentences to this admirable performance—carried through, he says, with "incredibly youthful verve",—and praises Crispus to the skies as "the most noble Cesar of his august father." When that speech was delivered on the day of the Quinquennalia of the Cesars in 321, Constantine's ears did not yet grudge to listen to the eulogies of his gallant son.

But there is one omission from the speech which is exceedingly significant. It contains no mention of Licinius, and no one reading the oration would gather that there were two Emperors or that the Empire was divided. Evidently, Constantine and Licinius were no longer on good terms, and none knew better than the Panegyrists of the Court the art of suppressing the slightest word or reference that might bring a frown to the brow of their imperial auditor. But even two years before, in 319, the names of Licinius and the boy, Cesar Licinianus, had ceased to figure on the consular Fasti--a straw which pointed very clearly in which direction the wind was blowing.

Zosimus attributes the war to the ambition of Constantine; Eutropius roundly accuses him of having set his heart upon acquiring the sovereignty of the whole world. On the other hand, Eusebius depicts Constantine as a magnanimous monarch, the very pattern of humanity, long suffering of injury, and forgiving to the point of seventy times seven the ungrateful intrigues of the black-hearted Licinius. According to the Bishop of Caesarea, Constantine had been the benefactor of Licinius, who, conscious of his inferiority, plotted in secret until he was driven into open enmity. But it is very evident that the reason of Eusebius's enmity to Licinius was the anti-Christian policy into which the Emperor had drifted, as soon as he became estranged from Constantine. A more detailed description of Licinius's religious policy and of the new persecution which broke out in his provinces will be found in another chapter; here we need only point out Eusebius's anxiety to represent the cause of the quarrel between the Emperors as being in the main a religious one. He tells us that Licinius regarded as traitors to himself those who were friendly to his rival, and savagely attacked the bishops, who, as he judged, were his most bitter opponents. The phrase, not without reason, has given rise to the suspicion that the Christian bishops of the East were regarded as head centers of political disaffection, and Licinius evidently suspected them of preaching treason and acting as the agents of Constantine. We have not sufficient data to enable us to draw any sure inference, but the bishops could not help contrasting the liberality of Constantine to the Church, of which he was the open champion, with the reactionary policy of Licinius, which had at length culminated in active persecution.

But the dominant cause of this war is to be found in political ambitions rather than in religious passions, and if we must declare who of the two was the aggressor, it is difficult to escape throwing the blame upon Constantine. Licinius was advancing in years. Even if he had not outlived his ambitions, he can at least have had little taste for a campaign in which he put all to the venture. Constantine, on the other hand, was in the prime of life, and the master of a well tried, disciplined, and victorious army. The odds were on his side. He had all the legions which could be spared from the Rhine and the Danube, and all the auxiliaries from the Illyrian and Pannonian provinces—the best recruiting grounds in the Empire—to oppose to the legions of Syria and Egypt. Constantine doubtless seemed to the bishops to be entering the field as the champion of the Church, but the real prize which drew him on was universal dominion.

This time both Emperors exerted themselves to make tremendous preparations for the struggle. Zosimus describes how Constantine began a new naval harbor at Thessalonica to accommodate the two hundred war galleys and two thousand transports which he had ordered to be built in his dockyards. He mobilized, if Zosimus is to be trusted, 120,000 infantry and 10,000 marines and cavalry. Licinius, on the other hand, is said to have collected 150,000 foot and 15,000 horse. Whether these numbers are trustworthy or not, it is evident that the two Emperors did their best to throw every available man into the plain of Adrianople, where the two hosts were separated by the river Hebrus. Some days were spent in skirmishing and maneuvering; then on July 3, 323, a decisive action was brought on, which ended in the rout of the army of Licinius. Constantine, whose tactical dispositions seem to have been more skillful than those of Licinius, secretly detached a force of 5000 archers to occupy a position in the rear of the enemy, and these used their bows with overwhelming effect at a critical moment of the action, when Constantine himself, at the head of another detachment, succeeded in forcing a passage of the river. Constantine received a slight wound in the thigh, but he had the satisfaction of seeing the enemy driven from their fortified camp and betake themselves in hurried flight to the sheltering walls of Byzantium, leaving 34,000 dead and wounded on the field of battle.

Byzantium was a stronghold which had fallen be-fore Maximin after a siege of eleven days, but we may suppose that Licinius had looked well to its fortifications with a view to such an emergency as that in which he now found himself. He placed, however, his chief reliance in his fleet, which was nearly twice as numerous as that of Constantine. Licinius had assembled 35o ships of war, levied, in accordance with the practice of Rome, from the maritime countries of Asia and Egypt. No fewer than 130 came from Egypt and Libya, 110 from Phoenicia and Cyprus, and a similar quota from the ports of Cilicia, Ionia, and Bithynia. The galleys were probably in good fighting trim, but the service was not a willing one, and the fleet was as badly handled as it was badly stationed. Amandus, the admiral of Licinius, had kept his ships cooped up in the narrow Hellespont, thus acting weakly on the defensive instead of boldly seeking out the enemy. Constantine entrusted the chief command of his various squadrons to his son Crispus, whose only experience of naval matters had probably been obtained from the manoeuvres of the war galleys on the Rhine. But a Roman general was supposed to be able to take command on either element as circumstances required. In the present case Crispus more than justified his father's choice. He was ordered to attack and destroy Amandus, and the peremptoriness of the order was doubtless due to the difficulty of obtaining supplies for so large an army by land transport only. Two actions were fought on two successive days. In the first Amandus had both wind and current in his favor and made a drawn battle of it. The next day the wind had veered round to the south, and Crispus, closing with the enemy, destroyed 13o of their vessels and 5000 of their crews. The passage of the Hellespont was forced; Amandus with the remainder of his fleet fled back to the shelter of Byzantium, and the straits were open for the passage of Constantine's transports.

The Emperor pushed the siege with energy, and plied the walls so vigorously with his engines that Licinius, aware that the capitulation of Byzantium could not long be postponed, crossed over into Asia to escape being involved in its fate. Even then he was not utterly despondent of success, for he raised one of his lieutenants, Martinianus, to the dignity of Cesar or Augustus—a perilous distinction for any recipient with the short shrift of Valens before his eyes—and, collecting what troops he could, he set his fleet and army to oppose the crossing of Constantine when Byzantium had fallen. But holding as he did the command of the sea, the victor found no difficulty in effecting a landing at Chrysopolis, and Licinius's last gallant effort to drive back the invader was repulsed with a loss of 25,000 men. Eusebius, in an exceptionally foolish chapter, declares that Licinius harangued his troops before the battle, bidding them carefully keep out of the way of the sacred Labaruni, under which Constantine moved to never-failing victory, or, if they had the mischance to come near it in the press of battle, not to look heedlessly upon it. He then goes on to ascribe the victory not to the superior tactical dispositions of his chief or to the valour of his men, but simply and solely to the fact that Constantine was "clad in the breast-plate of reverence and had ranged over against the numbers of the enemy the salutary and life-giving sign, to inspire his foes with terror and shield himself from harm".

We suspect, indeed, that far too little justice has been done to the good generalship of Constantine, who, by his latest victory, brought to a close a brilliant and entirely successful campaign over an Emperor whose stubborn powers of resistance and dauntless energy even in defeat rendered him a most formidable opponent.

Licinius fell back upon Nicomedia. His army was gone. There was no time to beat up new recruits, for the conqueror was hard upon his heels. He had to choose, therefore, between suicide, submission, and flight. He would perhaps have best consulted his fame had he chosen the proud Roman way out of irreparable disaster and taken his life. Instead he begged that life might be spared him. The request would have been hopeless, and would probably never have been made, had he not possessed in his wife, Constantia, a very powerful advocate with her brother. Constantia's pleadings were effectual: Constantine consented to see his beaten antagonist, who came humbly into his presence, laid his purple at the victor's feet, and sued for life from the compassion of his master. It was a humiliating and an un-Roman scene. Constantine promised forgiveness, admitted the suppliant to the Imperial table, and then relegated him to Thessalonica to spend the remainder of his days in obscurity. Licinius did not long survive. Later historians, anxious to clear Constantine's character of every stain, accused Licinius of plotting against the generous Emperor who had spared him. Others declared that he fell in a soldiers' brawl: one even says that the Senate passed a decree devoting him to death. It is infinitely more probable that Constantine repented of his clemency. No Roman Emperor seems to have been able to endure for long the existence of a discrowned rival, however impotent to harm. Eutropius expressly states that Licinius was put to death in violation of the oath which Constantine had sworn to him. Eusebius says not a word of Licinius's life having been promised him; he only remarks: "Then Constantine, dealing with the accursed of GOD and his associates according to the rules of war, handed them over to fitting punishment." A pretty euphemism for an act of assassination!

So died Licinius, unregretted by any save the zealous advocates of paganism, in the city where he himself had put to death those two hapless ladies, Prisca and Valeria. The best character sketch of him is found in

Aurelius Victor, who describes him as grasping and avaricious, rough in manners and of excessively hasty temper, and a sworn foe to culture, which he used to say was a public poison and pest, notably the culture associated with the study and practice of the law. Himself of the humblest origin, he was a good friend to the small farmers' interests; while he was a martinet of the strictest type in all that related to the army. He detested the paraphernalia of a court, in which Constantine delighted, and Aurelius Victor says that he made a clean sweep of all eunuchs and chamberlains, whom he described as the moths and shrew-mice of the palace. Of his religious policy we shall speak elsewhere; of his reign there is little to be said. It has left no impress upon history, and Licinius is only remembered as the Emperor whose misfortune it was to stand in the way of Constantine and his ambitions. Constantine threw down his statues; revoked his edicts; and if he spared his young son, the Cesar Licinianus, the clemency was due to affection for the mother, not to pity for the child. Martinianus, the Emperor at most of a few weeks, had been put to death after the defeat of Chrysopolis, and Constantine reigned alone with his sons. The Roman Empire was united once more.

LAST DAYS OF PERSECUTION

IN a previous chapter we gave a brief account of the terrible sufferings inflicted upon the Church during the persecution which followed the edicts of Diocletian. They continued for many years almost without interruption, but with varying intensity. When, for example, Diocletian celebrated his Vicennalia a general amnesty was proclaimed which must have opened the prison doors to many thousands of Christians. Eusebius expressly states that the amnesty was for "all who were in prison the world over", and there is no hint that liberty was made conditional upon apostasy. None the less, it is certain that a great number of Christians were still kept in the cells—on the pretext that they were specially obnoxious to the civil power—by governors of strong anti-Christian bias. The sword of persecution was speedily resumed and wielded as vigorously as before down to the abdication of Diocletian and Maximian.

Then came another lull. With Constantius as the senior Augustus the persecution came to an end in the West, and even in the East there was an interval of peace. For Maximin, who was soon to develop into the most ferocious of all the persecutors,—so St. Jerome speaks of him in comparison with Decius and Diocletian,—gave a brief respite to the Christians in his provinces of Egypt, Cilicia, Palestine, and Syria.

"When I first visited the East", Maximin wrote, some years later, in referring to his accession, "I found that a great number of persons who might have been useful to the State had been exiled to various places by the judges. I ordered each one of these judges no longer to press hardly upon the provincials, but rather to exhort them by kindly words to return to the worship of the gods. While my orders were obeyed by the magistrates, no one in the countries of the East was exiled or ill-treated, but the provincials, won over by kindness, returned to the worship of the gods".

Direct contradiction is given to this boast as to the number of Christian apostates by the fact that, within a twelvemonth, the new Cesar grew tired of seeking to kill Christianity by kindness and revoked his recent rescript of leniency. Maximin developed into a furious bigot. He fell wholly under the influence of the more fanatical priests and became increasingly devoted to magic, divination, and the black arts. Lactantius declares that not a joint appeared at his table which had not been taken from some victim sacrificed by a priest at an altar and drenched with the wine of libation. Edict followed edict in rapid succession, until, in the middle of 306, what Eusebius describes as "a second declaration of war" was issued, which ordered every magistrate to compel all who lived within his jurisdiction to sacrifice to the gods on pain of being burnt alive. House to house visitations were set on foot that no creature might escape, and the common informer was encouraged by large rewards to be active in his detestable occupation. It would seem indeed as if the Christians in the provinces of Maximin suffered far more severely than any of their brethren. The most frightful bodily mutilations were practiced. Batches of Christians were sentenced to work in the porphyry mines of Egypt or the copper mines of Phaenos in Palestine, after being hamstrung and having their right eyes burnt out with hot irons. The evidence of Lactantius, who says that the confessors had their eyes dug out, their hands and feet amputated, and their nostrils and ears cut off, is corroborated by Eusebius and the authors of the Passions.

Palestine seems to have had two peculiarly brutal governors, Urbanus and Firmilianus. The latter in a single day presided at the execution of twelve Christians, pilgrims from Egypt on their way to succor the unfortunate convicts in the copper mines of Palestine, whose deplorable condition had awakened the active sympathy of the Christian East. These bands of pilgrims had to pass through Caesarea, where the officers of Firmilianus were on the watch for them, and as soon as they confessed that they were Christians they were haled before the tribunal, where their doom was certain. A distinguishing feature of the persecution in the provinces of Maximin was the frequency of outrages upon Christian women and the fortitude with which many of the victims committed suicide rather than suffer pollution. The story of St. Pelagia of Antioch is typical. Maximin sent some soldiers to conduct her to his palace. They found her alone in her house and announced their errand. With perfect composure this girl of fifteen asked permission to retire in order to change her dress, and then, mounting to the roof, threw herself down into the street below. Eusebius, himself an eye-witness of this persecution, gives many a vivid story of the fury of Maximin and his officials, and of the cold-blooded calculation with which he sought to draw new victims into the net of the law. In 308 he issued an edict ordering every city and village thoroughly to repair any temple which, for whatever reason, had been allowed to fall into ruins. He increased ten-fold the number of priesthoods, and insisted upon daily sacrifices. The magistrates were again strictly enjoined to compel men, women, children, and slaves alike to offer sacrifice and partake of the sacrificial food. All goods exposed for sale in the public markets were to be sprinkled with lustral water, and even at the entrance to the public baths, officials were to be placed to see that no one passed through the doors without throwing a few grains of incense on the altar. Maximin, in short, was a religious bigot, who combined with a zealous observance of pagan ritual a consuming hatred of Christianity.

There are not many records of what was taking place in the provinces of Galerius, while Maximin was thus terrorizing Syria and Egypt. But the Emperor had begun to see that the persecution, upon which he had entered with such zest some years before, was bound to end in failure. The terrible malady which attacked him in 310 would tend to confirm his forebodings. Like Antiochus Epiphanies, Herod the Great, and Herod Agrippa, Galerius became, before death released him from his agony, a putrescent and loathsome spectacle. His physicians could do nothing for him. Imploring deputations were sent to beg the aid of Apollo and Aesculapius. Apollo prescribed a remedy, but the application only left the patient worse, and Lactantius quotes with powerful effect the lines from Virgil which describe Laocoon in the toils of the serpents, raising horror-stricken cries to Heaven, like some wounded bull as it flies bellowing from the altar. Was it when broken by a year's constant anguish that Galerius exclaimed that he would restore the temple of God and make amends for his sin? Was he, as Lactantius says, "compelled to confess GOD?". Whether that be so or not, here is the remarkable edict which the shattered Emperor found strength to dictate. It deserves to be given in full:

"Among the measures which we have constantly taken for the well-being and advantage of the State, we had wished to regulate everything according to the ancient laws and public discipline of the Romans, and especially to provide that the Christians, who had abandoned the religion of their ancestors, should return to a better frame of mind.

"For, from whatever reason, these Christians were the victims of such willfulness and folly that they not only refused to follow the ancient customs, which very likely their own forefathers had instituted, but they made laws for themselves according to their fancy and caprice, and gathered together all kinds of people in different places.

"Eventually, when our commands had been published that they should conform to long established custom, many submitted from fear, and many more under the compulsion of punishment. But since the majority have obstinately held out and we see that they neither give the gods their worship and due, nor yet adore the God of the Christians, we have taken into consideration our unexampled clemency and followed the dictation of the invariable mercifulness, which we show to all men. We have, therefore, thought it best to extend even to these people our fullest indulgence and to give them eave once more to be Christians, and rebuild their fleeting places, provided that they do nothing contrary to discipline.

"In another letter we shall make clear to the magistrates the course which they should pursue. In return for our indulgence the Christians will, in duty bound, pray to their God for our safety, for their own, and for that of the State, that so the State may everywhere be safe and prosperous, and that they themselves may dwell in security in their homes".

This extraordinary edict was issued at Nicomedia on the last day of April, 311. It is as abject a confession of failure as could be expected from an Emperor. Galerius admits that the majority of Christians have stubbornly held to their faith in spite of bitter persecution, and now, as they are determined to sin against the light and follow their own caprice, more in sorrow than in anger, he will recognize their status as Christians and give them the right of assembly, provided they do not offend against public discipline. But the special interest of this edict lies in the Emperor's request that the Christians will pray for him, in the despairing hope that Christ may succeed, where Apollo has failed, in finding a remedy for his grievous case. Galerius was ready to clutch at any passing straw.

The edict bore the names of Galerius, of Constantine, and of Licinius. Maxentius, who at this time ruled Italy, was not recognized by Galerius, so the absence of his name causes no surprise. Maximin's name is also absent, but we find one of his prefects, Sabinus, addressing shortly afterwards a circular letter to all the Governors of Cilicia, Syria, and Egypt, in which the signal was given to stop the persecution. Like Galerius, Maximin declared that the sole object of the Emperors had been to lead all men back to a pious and regular life, and to restore to the gods those who had embraced alien rites contrary to the spirit of the institutions of Rome. Then the letter continued :

"But since the mad obstinacy of certain people has reached such a pitch that they are not to be shaken in their resolution either by the justice of the imperial command or by the fear of imminent punishment, and since, actuated by these motives, a very large number have brought themselves into positions of extreme peril, it has pleased their Majesties in their great pity and compassion to send this letter to your Excellency". Their instructions are that if any Christian has been apprehended, while observing the religion of his sect, you are to deliver him from all molestation and annoyance and not to inflict any penalty upon him, for a very long experience has convinced the Emperors that there is no method of turning these people from their madness.

"Your Excellency will therefore write to the magistrates, to the commander of the forces, and to the town provosts, in each city, that they may know for the future that they are not to interfere with the Christians anymore".

In other words, the prisons were to be emptied and the mad sectaries to be let alone. The bigot was obliged to bow, however reluctantly, to the wishes and commands of the senior Augustus, even though Galerius was a broken and dying man.

Nevertheless, within six months we find Maximin devising new schemes for troubling the Christians. Eusebius tells us with what joy the edict of toleration had been welcomed, with what triumph the Christians had quitted their prisons, and with what enthusiastic exultation the bands of Christian confessors, returning from the mines to their own towns and villages, were received by the Christian communities in the places through which they passed. Those whose testimony to their faith had not been so sure and clear, those who had bowed the knee to Baal under the shadow of torture and death, humbly approached their stouter-hearted brethren and implored their intercession. The Church rose from the persecution proudly and confidently, and with incredible speed renewed its suspended services and repaired its broken organization. Maximin issued an order forbidding Christians to assemble after dark in their cemeteries, as they had been in the habit of doing, in order to celebrate the victory of their martyrs over death. Such assemblies, the Emperor said, were subversive of morality: they were to be allowed no more. This must have warned the Christians how little reliance was to be placed in the promises of Maximin, and shortly afterwards they had another warning. Maximin made a tour through his provinces and in several cities received petitions in which he was urged to give an order for the absolute expulsion of all Christians. No doubt it was known that such a request would be well pleasing to Maximin, but at the same time it undoubtedly points to the existence of a strong anti-Christian feeling. At Antioch, which was under the governorship of Theotecnus, the petitioners, according to Eusebius, said that the expulsion of the Christians would be the greatest boon the Emperor could confer upon them, but the full text of one of these petitions has been found among the ruins of a small Lycian township of the name of Aricanda. It runs as follows:

"To the Saviours of the entire human race, to the august Caesars, Galerius Valerius Maximinus Flavius Valerius Constantinus, Valerius Licinianus Licinius, this petition is addressed by the people of the

Lycians and the Pamphylians.

"Inasmuch as the gods, your congeners, 0 divine Emperor, have always crowned with their manifest favors those who have their religion at heart and offer prayers to them for the perpetual safety of our invincible masters, we have thought it well to approach your immortal Majesty and to ask that the Christians, who for years have been impious and do not cease to be so, may be finally suppressed and transgress no longer, by their wicked and innovating cult, the respect that is owing to the gods.

"This result would be attained if their impious rites were forbidden and suppressed by your divine and eternal decree, and if they were compelled to practice the cult of the gods, your congeners, and pray to them on behalf of your eternal and incorruptible Majesty. This would clearly be to the advantage and profit of all your subjects".

Eusebius records two replies of the Emperor to petitions of this character. One is contained in a letter to his prefect, Sabinus, and relates to Nicomedia. The other is a document copied by Eusebius from a bronze tablet set up on a column in Tyre. Maximin expatiates at great length on the debt which men owe to the gods, and especially to Jupiter, the presiding deity of Tyre, for the ordered succession of the seasons, and for keeping within their appointed bounds the overwhelming forces of Nature. If there have been calamities and cataclysms, to what else, he asks, can they be attributed than to the "vain and pestilential errors of the villainous Christians?". Those who have apostatized and have been delivered from their blindness are like people who have escaped from a furious storm or have been cured of some deadly malady. To them life offers once more its bounteous blessings. Then the Emperor continues:

"But if they still persist in their detestable errors, they shall be banished, in accordance with your petition, far from your city and your territory, that so this city of Tyre, completely purified, as you most properly desire it to be, may yield itself wholly to the worship of the gods. But that you may know how agreeable your petition has been to us, and how, even without petition on your part, we are disposed to heap favors upon you, we grant you in advance any favor you shall ask, however great, in reward for your piety. Ask, therefore, and receive, and do so without hesitation. The benefit which shall accrue to your city will be a perpetual witness of your devotion to the gods".

Evidently the Christians had not yet come to the end of their troubles. Those who read this circular letter, for it seems to have been sent round from city to city, must have expected the persecution to break out anew at any moment. We do not know to what extent the edict was observed. If it had been generally acted upon, we should certainly have heard more of it, inasmuch as it must have entailed a widespread exodus from the provinces of Maximin. But of this there is no evidence. We imagine rather that this circular was merely a preliminary sharpening of the sword in order to keep the Christians in a due state of apprehension.

Maximin, however, continued his anti-Christian propaganda with unabated zeal, and with greater cunning and better devised system than before. His court at Antioch was the gathering place of all the priests, magicians, and thaumaturgists of the East, who found in him a generous patron. We hear of a new deity being invented by Theotecnus, or rather of an old deity being invested with new attributes. Zeus Philios, or Jupiter the Friendly was the name of this god, to whom a splendid statue was erected in Antioch, and to whose shrine a new priesthood, with new rites, was solemnly dedicated. The god was provided with an attendant oracle to speak in his name; what more natural than that the first response should order the banishment of all Christians from the city? Very noteworthy, too, was the reappearance of a vigorous anti-Christian literature. Maximin set on his pamphleteers to write libelous parodies of the Christian doctrines and encouraged the more serious controversialists on the pagan side to attack the Christian religion wherever it was most vulnerable. The most famous of these productions was one which bore the name of The Acts of Pilate and purported to be a relation by Pilate himself of the life and conduct of Christ. It was really an old pamphlet rewritten and brought up to date, full, as Eusebius says, of all conceivable blasphemy against Christ and reducing Him to the level of a common malefactor. Maximin welcomed it with delight. He had thousands of copies written and distributed; extracts were cut on brass and stone and posted up in conspicuous places; the work was appointed to be read frequently in public, and—what shows most of all the fury and cunning of Maximin—it was appointed to be used as a text-book in schools throughout Asia and Egypt. There was no more subtle method of training bigots and poisoning the minds of the younger generation amongst Christianity. Some of the Emperor's devices, however, were much more crude. For example, the military commandant of Damascus arrested half a dozen notorious women of the town and threatened them with torture if they did not confess that they were Christians, and that they had been present at ceremonies of the grossest impurity in the Christian assemblies. Maximin ordered the precious confession thus extorted to be set up in a prominent place in every township.

But the Emperor was not merely a furious bigot. There is evidence that he fully recognized the wonderful strength of the Christian ecclesiastical organization and contrasted it with the essential weakness of the pagan system. In this he anticipated the Emperor Julian. Paganism was anything but a church. Its framework was loose and disconnected. There were various colleges of priests, some of which were powerful and had branches throughout the Empire, but there was little connection between them save that of a common ritual. There was also little doctrine save in the special mysteries, where membership was preceded by formal initiation. Maximin sought to institute a pagan clergy based upon the Christian model, with a definite hierarchy from the highest to the lowest. There were already chief priests of the various provinces, who had borne for long the titles of Asiarch, Pontarch, Galatarch, and Ciliciarch in their respective provinces. Maximin developed their powers on the model of those of the Christian bishops, giving them authority over subordinates and entrusting them with the duty of seeing that the sacrifices were duly and regularly offered. He tried to raise the standard of the priesthood by choosing its members from the best families, by insisting on the priests wearing white flowing robes, by giving them a guard of soldiers and full powers of search and arrest.

Evidently, Maximin was something more than the lustful, bloodthirsty tyrant who appears in the pages of Lactantius and the ecclesiastical historians. He dealt the Church much shrewder—though not less ineffectual—blows than his colleagues in persecution. With such an Emperor another appeal to the faggot and the sword was inevitable, and the death of Galerius was the signal for a renewal of the persecution. This time Maximin struck directly at the most conspicuous figures in the Christian Church and counted among his victims Peter, the Patriarch of Alexandria, and three other Egyptian bishops—Methodus, Bishop of Tyre, Basiliscus, Bishop of Comana in Bithynia, and Silvanus, Bishop of Emesa in Phoenicia. In Egypt the persecution was so sharp that it drew Saint Antony from his hermit's cell in the desert to succor the unfortunate in Alexandria. He escaped with his life, probably because he was overlooked or disdained, or because the mighty influence which he was to exercise upon the Church had not yet declared itself. This persecution was followed by a terrible drought, famine, and pestilence. Eusebius, in a vigorous chapter, describes how parents were driven by hunger to sell not only their lands but also their children, how whole families were wiped out, how the pestilence seemed to mark down the rich for its special vengeance, and how in certain townships the inhabitants were driven to kill all the dogs within their walls that they might not feed on the bodies of the unburied dead. Amid these horrors the Christians alone remained calm. They alone displayed the supreme virtue of charity in tending the suffering and ministering to the dying. From the pagans themselves, says Eusebius, was wrung the unwilling admission that none but the Christians, in the sharp test of adversity, shelved real piety and genuine worship of God.

Maximin's reign, however, was fast drawing to a close. After becoming involved in a war with Tiridates of Armenia, from which he emerged with little credit to himself, he entered into an alliance with Maxentius, the ruler of Italy, against Constantine and Licinius, but did not invade the territory of the latter until Maxentius had already been overthrown. As we have seen, Maximin was utterly routed and, after a hurried flight to beyond the Taurus, he there, according to Eusebius gathered together his erstwhile trusted priests and soothsayers and slew them for the proved falsehood of their prophecy. More significant still, when he found that his doom was certain, he issued a last religious edict in the vain hope of appeasing the resentment of the Christians and their God. The document is worth giving in full:

"The Emperor Cesar Caius Valerius Maximinus, Germanicus,

Sarmaticus, pious, happy, invincible, august.

"We have always endeavored by all means in our power to secure the advantage of those who dwell in our provinces, and to contribute by our benefits at once to the prosperity of the State and to the well-being of every citizen. Nobody can be ignorant of this, and we are confident that each one who puts his memory to the test, is persuaded of its truth. We found, however, some time ago that, in virtue of the edict published by our divine parents, Diocletian and Maximian, ordering the destruction of the places where the Christians were in the habit of assembling, many excesses and acts of violence had been committed by our public servants and that the evil was being increasingly felt by our subjects every day, inasmuch as their goods were, under this pretext, unwarrantably seized. Consequently, we declared last year by letters addressed to the Governors of the Provinces that if any one wished to attach himself to this sect and practice this religion, he should be allowed to please himself without interference and no one should say him nay, and the Christians should enjoy complete liberty and be sheltered from all fear and all suspicion. However, we have not been able entirely to shut our eyes to the fact that certain of the magistrates misunderstood our instructions, with the result that our subjects distrusted our words and were nervous about resuming the religion of their choice. That is why, in order to do away with all disquietude and equivocation for the future, we have resolved to publish this edict, by which all are to understand that those who wish to follow this sect have full liberty to do so, and that, by the indulgence of our Majesty, each man may practice the religion he prefers or that to which he is accustomed. It is also permitted to them to rebuild the houses of the LORD. Moreover, so that there may be no mistake about the scope of our indulgence, we have been pleased to order that all houses and places, formerly belonging to the Christians, which have either been confiscated by the order of our divine parents, or occupied by any municipality, or sold or given away, shall return to their original ownership, so that all men may recognize our piety and our solicitude".

The bigot must have been brought very low and reduced to the last depths of despair before he set his seal to such a document as this. One can see that it was drawn up by Maximin with a copy of the Edict of

Milan before him, and that he hoped, by this tardy and clumsy recognition of the principle of absolute liberty of conscience for all men, to make the Christians forget his brutalities. Doubtless, the Christians of Cilicia and Syria looked to Constantine in far off Gaul as a model prince and emperor, and heard with joy of the steady advance of Constantine's ally, Licinius. The latter would come in their eyes in the guise of a liberator, and prayers for his success would be offered up in every Christian church of the persecuted East. Maximin sought to repurchase their loyalty: it was too late. His absurd pretext that his orders had been misunderstood by his provincial governors would deceive no one. He had been the shrewdest enemy with whom the Church had had to cope; his edict of recantation was read with chilly suspicion or cold contempt, which was changed into hymns of rejoicing when the Christians heard that the tyrant had poisoned himself and died in agony, while his conqueror, Licinius, had drowned the fallen Empress in the Orontes and put to death her children, a boy of eight and a girl of seven. Those who had suffered persecution for ten years may be pardoned their exultation that there was no one left alive to perpetuate the names of their persecutors.

Throughout this time the West had escaped very lightly. Even Maxentius had begun his reign by seeking to secure the good-will of the Christians. Eusebius, indeed, makes the incredible statement that in order to please and flatter the Roman people he pretended to embrace the Christian faith and "assumed the mask of piety." Probably all he did was to leave the Christians of Rome in peace. The chair of St. Peter had remained empty for four years after the death of Bishop Marcellinus. In 308 Marcellos was elected to fill it and the Church was organized afresh. But it was rent with internal dissensions. There was a large section which insisted that the brethren who had been found weak during the recent persecution should be received back into the fold without penance and reproach. Marcellus stood out for discipline; the quarrel became so exacerbated that Maxentius exiled the Bishop, who shortly afterwards died. A priest named Eusebius was then chosen Pontiff, but the schismatics elected a Pontiff of their own, Heraclius by name, and the rival partisans quarreled and fought in the streets. Maxentius, with strict impartiality, exiled both. The record of this schism is preserved in the curious epitaph composed by Pope Damasus for the tomb of Eusebius:

"Heraclius forbade the lapsed to bewail their sins; Eusebius taught them to repent and weep for their wrong-doing. The people were divided into factions, raging and furious: then came sedition, bloodshed, war, discord, strife. Forthwith both were driven away by the cruelty of the tyrant. While the Bishop preserved intact the bonds of peace, he endured his exile gladly on the Trinacrian shores, knowing that God was his judge, and so passed from this world and from life".

On the confession of Damasus himself, the state of the Roman Church warranted the interference of Maxentius if it resulted in "sedition, bloodshed, war, discord, and strife",' and the "cruelty of the tyrant" in this particular case is not proven. Eusebius died in Sicily in 310; in the following year Miltiades was elected Bishop, and Maxentius restored to the Roman Christians their churches and cemeteries, which for eight years had been in the hands of the civil authorities.

The overthrow of Maxentius by Constantine, the destruction of Maximin by Licinius, the publication of the Edict of Milan, and the apparent sincerity of the two Emperors in their anxiety to restore peace and security, were naturally hailed by the Christians throughout the Empire with the liveliest joy. On every side stately churches began to rise from the ground, and as the triumph of Christianity over its enemies was incontestable, converts came flocking in by the thousand to receive what Eusebius calls "the mysterious signs of the Savior's Passion". The only troublers of the Church were members of the Church herself, like the extravagant Donatists in Africa. The canons of the Council of Ancyra, which was held soon after the death of Maximin, show how the ecclesiastical authorities imposed varying penances upon those who had shrunk from their duty as soldiers of Christ in the recent persecution, varying, that is to say, according to the extent of their shortcomings. Some had apostatized and themselves turned persecutors; some had sacrificed at the first command; some had endured prison, but had shrunk from torture; some had suffered torture, but quailed before the stake; some had bribed the executioners only to make a show of torturing them; some had attended the sacrificial feasts, but had substituted other meats. The punishments range from ten years of probation and every degree of penance, down to a few months' deprivation of the comforts and communions of the Church.

New dangers, however, speedily threatened. Constantine and Licinius quarreled between themselves and, after two stubborn battles, agreed upon a fresh division of the world. For eight years, from 315 to 323, this partition lasted, but, as the Emperors again drifted apart, Licinius became more and more anti-Christian. His rivalry with Constantine accounts for the change. Licinius suspected Constantine of intriguing with his Christian subjects just as Constantine regarded the pagan element in his own provinces as the natural focus of disaffection against his rule. Licinius had no definite Christian beliefs; he had been the friend and nominee of Galerius; and, like Galerius, he never got rid of the suspicion that the Christian assemblies were a danger to the public security. The Christians had aided him against Maximin: he thought they would do the same for Constantine against himself. Eusebius likens him to a twisted snake, wriggling along and concealing its poisoned fangs, not daring to attack the Church openly for fear of Constantine, but dealing it constant and insidious blows.

The simile was well chosen. Licinius seems to have opened his campaign against the Christians by forbidding the bishops in his provinces to leave their dioceses and take part in their usual synods and councils. They were to remain at home, he said, and mind their own business and not plot treason against their Emperor under the pretext of perfecting the discipline of the Church. Another edict, which came with poor grace from a man whose own excesses were notorious, forbade Christian men and women to meet for common worship in their churches: they were to worship apart, so that their morals might not be exposed to danger. On the same pretext, bishops and priests were only allowed to give teaching and consolation to their own sex; Christian women must find women teachers and advisers. Eusebius tells us that these edicts excited universal ridicule. It was too late to revive the old stories of gross immorality taking place at the communion services, and there was fresh cause for mocking laughter when Licinius forbade the Christians to assemble in their churches within the towns and ordered them to go outside the gates and meet, if they must meet, in the open air. This was necessary, he said, on the grounds of public health; the atmosphere beyond the gates was purer. Licinius's theory of hygiene was perfectly sound; its application was ludicrous.

These were the first steps leading, as his subjects must have known only too well, straight to persecution. After a time Licinius threw over bodily the Edict of Milan. He purged his court and his army in the old way. The choice was sacrifice or dismissal, and some pretext was usually made to tack on to official dismissal a confiscation of goods. Licinius, says Eusebius, thirsted for gold like a very Tantalus. Aurelius Victor says he had all the mean, sordid avarice of a peasant. And the Christians, of course, were fair game. He pillaged their churches, robbed them of their goods, sentenced them to exile and to the mines, or ruined them just as effectually by insisting on their becoming magistrates. Bloodshed followed, and Licinius aimed his severest blows at the bishops. He accused them of omitting his name in their prayers for the welfare of the Emperor and the State, though they carefully remembered that of Constantine; and, if none were actually put to death, many suffered imprisonment, torture, and mutilation. The story of the martyrs and confessors in the Licinian persecution is very like that of those who suffered under Diocletian and Maximin. But the fate of the forty soldier martyrs of the Twelfth Legion deserves special mention. They had refused to sacrifice, and, by order of their general, were stripped naked and ordered to remain throughout a winter's night upon a frozen pond, exposed to the elements. At the side of the pond was a building, where the water for the town baths was heated. Apparently no guard was kept. The martyrs were free to make their way to the warmth and shelter if they wished it, but only at the price of apostasy. One of them, after enduring bravely for many hours, crawled towards the warmth, but died of exhaustion as soon as he had crossed the threshold. The sight so affected the pagan attendant of the bath that he flung off his clothes in uncontrollable emotion, and with the shout, "I too am a Christian", took the place of the weak brother who had just lost the martyr's crown. In the morning the forty were found dead and their bodies were burnt at the stake. It was said that one of them was found to be still breathing, and the executioners put him apart from the rest. His mother, afraid lest he should miss entering heaven by the side of his brave companions in glory, herself placed him in the cart to be borne to the stake.

Another moving story of the Licinian persecution is that of Gordius of Caesarea, in Cappadocia. He had fled from his home to live the life of a hermit among the mountains, when suddenly an impulse came upon him to return and testify to the truth. The people were all assembled in the Circus, intent upon some public spectacle, when an uncouth figure was seen to move slowly down the marble steps and then pass out into the centre of the arena. A hush fell upon the multitude, as the hermit was recognized and dragged before the tribunal of the Governor. "I have come", he said, "to show how little I think of your edicts and to confess my faith in Jesus Christ, and I have chosen this moment, 0 Governor, because I know your cruelty, which surpasses that of all other men". They put him to the torture: he delighted in his pain. "The more you torture me", he said, "the greater will be my reward. There is a bargain between God and us. Each pang and torment that we suffer here will be rewarded there by increased glory and happiness".

Licinius bad thus, like Maximin, made himself the champion of the old religion and the religious reactionaries. When in 323 war again broke out between himself and Constantine, it was as the professed enemy of Christianity and its God that he took the field. The war was a war of ambition on both sides, but it was also a war between the two religions. We have mentioned elsewhere the oath which Licinius took before the battle, when he vowed that if the gods gave him the victory he would extirpate root and branch the Christian religion. Fate gave him no opportunity to fulfill his promise. Defeated at Adrianople and at Chrysopolis, and then exiled to Thessalonica, Licinius had not many months to live. Before he died he saw his pagan councilors pay for their folly with their lives and heard the rejoicings of the Christians of the East at the fall of the last of their pagan persecutors. The Church at last had won her freedom and was to suffer at the hands of the State no more. Eusebius has fortunately preserved for us the text of the edict addressed by Constantine after his victory to the inhabitants of Palestine, recalling from exile, from the mines, and from servitude the Christian victims of the recent persecution, restoring their property to those who had suffered confiscation, offering to soldiers who had been expelled in disgrace from the army either a return to their old rank or the certificate of honorable discharge, and giving back to the churches without diminution the corporate possessions of which they had been robbed. Constantine not merely passed the sponge over the administrative acts of Licinius: he granted large subsidies to the bishops who had suffered at the hands of "the dragon", and himself wrote to "his dearest beloved brother", Eusebius of Cesarea, urging him to see that the bishops, elders, and deacons in his neighborhood were "active and enthusiastic in the work of the Church".

CONSTANTINE AND THE DONATISTS

IF Constantine hoped that by the Edict of Milan he had stilled the voice of religious controversy, he was speedily disillusioned. He was now to find the peace of the Church violently disturbed by those belonging to her communions, and the hatreds of Christians against one another almost as menacing to the tranquility of the imperial rule as had been the bitter strife of pagan and Christian. In the same year (313) he received an appeal from certain African bishops imploring him to appoint a commission of Galilean bishops to settle certain difficulties which had arisen in Africa. The Donatist schism, which was destined to last for more than a century, had begun.

Its rise may be traced in a few words. Northern Africa had long been the home of a perfervid religious fanaticism. Montanism and Novatianism had found there their most violent adherents, to whom there was something peculiarly attractive in extravagant protest against the laxity or the liberalism of the Church elsewhere, and in emphatic insistence on the narrowness of the way which leads to salvation. Those who set up the most impossible standard of attainment; those who demanded from the Christian the most absolute spotlessness of life; those who insisted most strenuously on the enormity of sin and made fewest allowances for the weakness of humanity—these were surest of being heard most gladly in northern Africa. During the persecution of Diocletian and Maximian many of the African Christians had ostentatiously courted martyrdom. According to Catholic authors, such martyrdom had been sought not only by saints, but by men of immoral and dissolute life, who thought to purge the stains of a sinful career by dying in the odor of sanctity. Others, again, while not prepared to die for the faith, were not unwilling to suffer imprisonment for it, inasmuch as their fellow-Christians looked well after the creature comforts of those who languished in gaol. Mensurius, Bishop of Carthage and Primate of Africa, strongly disapproved of these proceedings. He discountenanced the fanaticism, which he knew to be the besetting weakness of his people; refused to recognize as martyrs those who had provoked death; and checked, as far as possible, the indiscriminate charity of his flock. If his critics are to be believed, Mensurius had resort to a trick in order to save the Holy Books of his own cathedral and thus escape the choice of being a traditor or of suffering for conscience' sake. It was said that when the officers of the civil power demanded the Holy Books in his keeping, he handed over to them a number of heretical volumes, which were at once burnt, while the Sacred Scriptures were carefully concealed. It is not surprising, therefore, to find that Mensurius was charged with actual persecution of those Christians who had a sterner sense of duty than himself.

It is manifest, however, from what took place at a synod of bishops held in Cirta in 303 that many of the natural leaders of the African Church had quailed before the persecution of Diocletian. They had assembled, under the presidency of Secundus, Bishop of Tigisis and Primate of Numidia, in order to fill the vacant see of Cirta. Secundus opened the proceedings by inviting all present to clear themselves of the charge of having surrendered their Holy Books, and began to put the question directly to each in turn. Donatus of Mascula returned an evasive answer, and said that he was responsible only to God. Many pleaded that they had substituted other books for the Scriptures; Victor of Russicas alone confessed that he had handed over the Four Gospels. "Valentinianus, the Curator, himself compelled me to send them", he said; "pardon me this fault, even as God pardons me". Then came the turn of Purpurius, Bishop of Limata. Secundus accused him not of being a traditor, but of the murder of two of his nephews. Purpurius stormed with rage. He vowed that he would not be browbeaten, and declared that Secundus was no better than his fellows and had purchased his own immunity, like the rest of them, by surrendering the Scriptures. As for murdering his nephews, the charge was true. "I did kill them", he said, "and I kill all who stand in my way". This candid avowal seems to have occasioned no surprise among the members of this extraordinary synod; they were all too indignant with Secundus for raising inconvenient questions and pretending to a sanctity beyond his colleagues. Eventually, another nephew of Secundus threatened that they would all withdraw from his communion and make a schism, unless he let the matter drop. "What business is it of yours what each has done?" asked the outspoken nephew. "It is to God that each must tender his account". The president thereupon drew in his horns, pronounced the acquittal of the accused, and with a general murmur of Deo gratias, they proceeded to the election of a bishop. Their choice fell upon Sylvanus, himself a traditor, much, it is said, to the indignation of the people of Cirta, who raised cries of, "He is a traditor let another be elected. We want our bishop to be pure and upright". Sylvanus had surrendered, without even a show of compulsion, one of the sacred silver lamps from the altar of his church. It is more than possible that the report of the proceedings at this synod, which is found only in works written specifically—but by episcopal hands—against the Donatists, is highly exaggerated. Among the bishops present at Cirta were those who, a few years later, were the principal leaders of the Donatist schism. But, even when all allowances are made for party coloring, the picture it gives of the Numidian Church is far from flattering.

During the life of Mensurius overt schism was avoided, though the Church of Carthage was by no means untroubled. For even before the persecution broke out, a certain lady named Lucilla had fallen under the censure of the ecclesiastical authorities, and had left the fold in high dudgeon. She became the lady patroness of the malcontent Christians of Carthage and the prime mover in any ecclesiastical intrigue that was afoot. She had been wont, before taking the Eucharist, to kiss the doubtful relic of a martyr, and she had set greater store on the efficacy of this unregistered bone than on the virtues of the sacred chalice. It was not, of course, for relic worship that Cecilianus, the Archdeacon, rebuked her, for the early Church everywhere acknowledged its intercessional value, and it was the usual practice for an officiating priest, before celebrating, to kiss the relics that were placed on the high altar. Lucilla was reproved because her relic was not recognized by the Church. It was doubtful whether it had belonged to a martyr at all, and, in any case, its identity had not been duly authenticated. But before Mensurius could deal with this revolted daughter the tempest of persecution broke over

Africa. The angry and insulting epithets with which the Catholic historians have loaded Lucilla are perhaps the best testimony to her ability and influence. She was very rich and a born intriguante, and as she had what she considered to be a personal insult to avenge, she was as willing as she was competent to cause trouble and mischief.

Shortly before the overthrow of Maxentius, one of Mensurius's deacons issued a defamatory libel against the Emperor and then took sanctuary at Carthage. The Bishop refused to surrender him and was peremptorily summoned to Rome. Evidently expecting that the Emperor would condemn him and order the confiscation of the holy vessels of his church, Mensurius secretly handed them over to the custody of certain elders in whose honesty he thought he could place implicit reliance. But he took the precaution—a wise one, as it subsequently proved—to make an inventory, which he gave to an old woman, with instructions that if he did not return she was to hand it to his lawfully appointed successor. Mensurius then went to Rome, succeeded in convincing Maxentius of his innocence, but died on the way home, in 311 AD. As soon as the news of his death reached Carthage, the round of intrigue began. According to Optatus, two deacons named Botrus and Celestius, each hoping to secure his own elevation, hurried on the election, in which the Numidian bishops were not invited to take part. The passage is obscure, for Optatus goes on to say that the choice fell upon Cecilianus, who was elected "by the suffrages of the whole people", and was consecrated in due form by Felix, Bishop of Aptunga. When Cecilianus called upon the elders to restore the Church ornaments, they quitted the Church—the suggestion of the Catholic historian is that they had hoped to steal them—and attached themselves to the faction of Lucilla, together with Botrus and Celestius, whom St. Augustine roundly denounces as "impious and sacrilegious thieves". The schism was now complete. It had its origin, says Optatus, in the fury of a headstrong woman; it was nurtured by intrigue and drew its strength from jealous greed.

Cecilianus' position was speedily challenged. The malcontents appealed to the Numidian bishops, urging them to declare in synod whether the election was valid. Accordingly, the Numidian Primate, Secundus of Tigisis, came with seventy other bishops to the capital, where they were received with open arms by the opposition party. Cecilianus seated himself on his throne in the cathedral and waited for the bishops to appear. When they did not come he sent a message saying: "If any one has any accusation to bring against me, let him come to make good the charge." But the Numidian bishops preferred to meet elsewhere within closed doors and finally declared the election of Cecilianus invalid on the ground that he had been consecrated by a traditor. To this Cecilianus replied that, if they thought Felix of Aptunga had been a traditor, they had better consecrate him themselves, as though he were still a simple deacon—a sarcasm which roused the violent Purpurius to exclaim: "Let him come here to receive the laying on of hands, and we will strike off his head by way of penance". They then elected Majorinus, who had been one of Cecilianus' readers and was now a member of Lucilla's household. There were thus two rival bishops of Carthage. Those who supported Cecilianus called themselves the Catholic party; their rivals, until the death of Majorinus in 315, were known as the party of Majorinus, though their moving spirit seems to have been, first, Donatus, the Bishop of Casa Nigre, and, afterwards, Donatus, surnamed Magnus, who gave his name to the schism.

Though Africa was thus split into two camps, there is no evidence that Majorinus was recognized by any of the churches of Europe, Egypt, or Asia. These all looked to Cecilianus as the rightful bishop, and so, when Constantine, fresh from his victory over Maxentius, wrote to the African churches in 312 to announce his intention of making a handsome present of money to their clergy, it was to Cecilianus that the letter was addressed, and the schismatics were rebuked in the sharpest terms. The letter ran as follows:

"CONSTANTINE AUGUSTUS to CECILIANUS, BISHOP OF CARTHAGE.

"Inasmuch as it has pleased us to contribute something towards the necessary expenses of certain ministers of the lawful and most holy Catholic religion throughout all the provinces of Africa, Numidia, and both Mauretanias, I have sent letters to Ursus, the most noble governor of Africa, and have instructed him to see that three thousand purses are paid over to your Reverence. When, therefore, you have received the above mentioned sum, you will take care that the money is divided among the clergy already spoken of according to the instructions sent to you by Hosius. If you consider amount insufficient for the purpose of testifying my regard for all of you in Africa, you are to ask without delay Heraclidas, the procurator of the imperial domains, for whatever you may think necessary. For I have personally instructed him that whatever sum your Reverence asks for is to be paid without hesitation. And since I have heard that certain persons of ill-balanced mind are acting in such a manner as to corrupt the people of the most holy and Catholic Church with wicked and adulterous falsehoods, I would have you know that I have given verbal instructions to Anulinus, the proconsul, and to Patricius, the vicar of the prefects, to include among their other duties a sharp lookout in this matter, and, if this movement continues, not to neglect or ignore it. Consequently, if you find persons of this character persevering in their mad folly you will at once approach the above mentioned judges and lay the matter before them, that they may punish the culprits in accordance with my personal instructions.

May the divinity of the Supreme God preserve you for many years".

In conjunction with this must be taken the letter addressed by Constantine to Anulinus, the proconsul of Africa:

"Greetings to our best beloved Anulinus! Inasmuch as it is abundantly proven that the neglect of the religion which preserves the greatest reverence for divine majesty has reduced the State to the direst peril, while its careful and due observance has brought the most splendid prosperity to the Roman name and unspeakable felicity to all things mortal, thanks to divine goodness, we have resolved, best beloved Anulinus, that those, who with due righteousness of life and continual observance of the law, perform their ministry in this divine religion shall reap the reward of their labors. Wherefore, it is our wish that all who, in the province under your care and in the Catholic Church over which Cecilianus presides, minister to this most holy religion—those, viz., whom people are wont to call the clergy—shall be absolved from all public duties of any kind, lest, by some slip or grave mischance, they may be distracted from the duties they owe to the Supreme Divinity, and that they may do the better service to their own ritual without any disturbing influences. Inasmuch as these people display the deepest reverence for the Divine Will, it seems to me that they ought to receive the greatest reward the State can bestow".

These are two remarkable letters. They clearly prove that the schism in the African Church was making a stir outside Africa, and that the Emperor had been instructed in the main points at issue. The new convert had cast his all-powerful influence upon the Catholic side—an Emperor would naturally be biased against schism—and he was prepared to utilize the civil power in order to compel the return of the schismatics to obedience. So little observant was he of his own edict of toleration that he was prepared to use force to secure uniformity within the Church! Constantine, indeed, reveals himself not merely as a Christian, but as a Catholic Christian; his bounty is reserved for the Catholic clergy, and the immunity from public duties involving heavy expense is reserved similarly for them alone.

Nevertheless, the party of Majorinus petitioned the Emperor to appoint a commission of Gallican bishops to enquire into and report upon their quarrel with the Bishop of Carthage: "We appeal to you, Constantine, best of Emperors, since you come of a just stock, for your father was alone among his colleagues in not putting the persecution into force, and Gaul was thus spared that frightful crime. Strife has arisen between us and other African bishops, and we pray that your piety may lead you to grant us judges from Gaul".

This petition was forwarded by Anulinus, the proconsul, whose covering letter, dated April, describes the opponents of Cecilianus as being resolute in refusing obedience. The Emperor, who was in Gaul when the petition reached him, granted the desired commission and instructed the bishops of Cologne, Autun, and Aries to repair to Rome. Cecilianus was instructed to attend with the bishops belonging to his party; ten of the rival bishops attached to Majorinus were to appear in the character of accusers, and for judges there were to be Miltiades, Bishop of Rome, the three Gallican bishops, and fifteen other Italian bishops selected by Miltiades from all parts of the peninsula. They met in October in the palace of the Empress Fausta, on the Lateran. Constantine had already written a letter to Miltiades, in which he deplored the existence of such serious schism in the populous African provinces, which, he said, had spontaneously surrendered to him, under the influence of divine Providence, as a reward for his devotion to religion. He, therefore, looked to the bishops to find a reasonable solution.

At the first sitting the credentials of the accusers of Cecilianus were examined, and some were disqualified on the score of bad character. Then, when the witnesses were called, those who had been brought to Rome by Majorinus and Donatus avowed that they had nothing to say against Cecilianus. The case of the petitioners practically collapsed, for the judges refused to listen to unsubstantiated gossip and scandal, and Donatus in the end declined to attend the enquiry, fearing lest he should be condemned on his own admissions. Later on, a second list of charges was handed in, but was not supported by a single witness, and then finally the commission passed on to enquire into the proceedings of the Council of the seventy bishops who had declared the election of Cecilianus invalid. They had no difficulty in reaching a general decision.

The accusations against Cecilianus had clearly broken down and the verdict of Miltiades began in the following terms: "Inasmuch as it is shown that Cecilianus is not accused by those who came with Donatus, as they had promised to do, and Donatus has in no particular established his charges against him, I find that Cecilianus should be maintained in the communion of his church with all his privileges, intact". St. Augustine warmly eulogizes the admirable moderation displayed by Miltiades, who, in the hope of restoring unity, offered to send letters of communion to all who had been consecrated by Majorinus, proposing that where there were two rival bishops, the senior in time of consecration should be confirmed in the appointment, while another see should be found for the other. But the Donatists would listen to no compromise. They appealed again to the Emperor, who, with a very pardonable outburst of wrath, denounced the rabid and implacable hatreds of these turbulent Africans.

Knowing that the quarrel would be resumed in full blast if Cecilianus and Donatus returned to Africa, Constantine detained them both in Italy. Two Italian bishops, Eunomius and Olympius, were meanwhile sent to Carthage to act as peacemakers and explain to the African congregations which was the true Catholic Church. It was none other, they said, than the Church which was diffused throughout the whole world, and they insisted that the judgment of the nineteen bishops was one from which there could be no appeal. The Donatists, however, retorted that if the verdict of nineteen bishops was sacred, a verdict of seventy must be even more so. They resisted the overtures of their visitors, and thus, when Donatus and Cecilianus in turn reappeared on the scene, the fires of partisanship did not lack for fuel. It was no longer possible for the Donatists to press for a rehearing on the ground of the personal character of Cecilianus. They had had their chance in Rome to impugn the Primate's character, and had failed. They now shifted their ground and based their claim upon the fact that Felix of Aptunga, who had consecrated Cecilianus, was a traditor, and the consecration was, therefore, invalid.

But was Felix a traditor? This was a plain, straightforward question, involving no disputed point of doctrine. Constantine, therefore, wrote to Elianus, Anulinus's successor as proconsul of Africa, instructing him to hold a public enquiry into the life and character of Felix of Aptunga. Part of the official report has come down to us. Among the witnesses were those who had been the chief magistrates of Aptunga at the time of the persecution. These must all have been acutely conscious of the curiously anomalous position in which they stood. If they found that Felix bad delivered up the Holy Books and utensils of the church, their verdict would acquit him of having broken the law of Diocletian, but would convict him of being a traditor, and would, therefore, be most unwelcome to the reigning sovereign. If they decided that Felix was not a traditor, they would convict him of having broken the law of Diocletian and convict themselves of having been lax administrators. The favor of a living Prince, however, outweighed consideration for the edicts of the dead, and the finding of the court was that "no volumes of Holy Scripture had been discovered at Aptunga, or had been defiled, or burnt." It went on to say that Felix was not present in the city at the time and that he had not temporized with his conscience. He had been, in short, a godly bishop. The character of Felix was, therefore, entirely rehabilitated and the validity of the consecration of Cecilianus was unimpaired.

Then follows the Council of Arles in 314. With a forbearance rarely displayed by a Roman emperor to inveterate and unreasoning opposition, Constantine yielded to the clamor of the Donatists for a new council on a broader and more authoritative scale than the commission of Italian and Gallic bishops. But his disappointment and disgust are plainly to be seen in his letter to the proconsul of Africa. Constantine began by saying that he had fully expected that the decision of a commission of bishops "of the very highest probity and competence would have commanded universal respect. He found, however, that the enemies of Cecilianus were as dogged and obstinate as ever, for they declared that the bishops had simply shut themselves up in a room and judged the case according to their personal predilections. They clamored for another council: he would grant them one which was to meet at Arles. Elianus, therefore, was to see that the public posting service throughout Africa and Mauretania was placed at the disposal of Cecilianus and his party and of Donatus and his party, that they might travel with dispatch and cross into Spain by the quickest passage. Then the letter continued :

"You will provide each separate Bishop with imperial letters entitling him to necessaries en route that he may arrive at Arles by the first of August, and you will also give all the bishops to understand that, before they leave their dioceses, they must make arrangements whereby, during their absence, reasonable discipline may be preserved and no chance revolt against authority or private altercations arise, for these bring the Church into great disgrace. On the other matters at issue, I wish the enquiry to be full and complete, and an end to be reached, as I hope it may be, when all those who are known to be at variance meet together in person. The quarrel may thus come to its natural and timely conclusion. For as I am well assured that you ae a worshipper of the supreme God, I confess to your Excellency that I consider it by no means lawful for me to ignore disputes and quarrels of such a nature as may excite the supreme Divinity to wrath, not only against the human race but against myself personally, into whose charge the Divinity by its Divine will has committed the governance of all that is on earth. In its just indignation, it might decree some ill against me. And then only can I feel really and absolutely secure, and hope for an unfailing supply of all the richest blessings that flow from the instant goodness of Almighty God, when I shall see all mankind reverencing most Holy God in brotherly singleness of worship and in the lawful rites of our Catholic religion".

Not only did Constantine write in this evidently sincere strain to the proconsul of Africa; he also sent personal letters to the bishops whose presence he desired. Eusebius has preserved the text of one of these, which was addressed to Chrestus, Bishop of Syracuse, in which the Emperor instructs him not to fail to reach Arles by August 1st, and bids him secure a public vehicle from Latronianus, the Governor of Sicily, and bring with him two presbyters of the second rank and three personal servants. In obedience to Constantine's wishes the bishops assembled at Arles by the appointed day. It is not known how many were present. On the fullest list of those who signed the canons there agreed to are found the names of thirty-three bishops, thirteen presbyters, twenty-three deacons, two readers, seven exorcists, and four representatives of the Bishop of Rome. But from the extreme importance attached to the council in later times it is certain that many more attended, and the numbers have been variously estimated at from two to six hundred. Not a single Eastern bishop was present. It was a council of the West, representing the various provinces of Africa and Gaul, Spain, Britain, Italy, Sicily, and Sardinia, From Britain came Eborius of York, Restitutus of London, and Adelfius, the Bishop of a diocese which has been variously interpreted as that of Colchester, Lincoln, and Caerleon on Usk, with a presbyter named Sacerdos and a deacon called Arminius. The Bishop of Rome, Sylvester, sent two presbyters and two deacons.

The Council investigated with great minuteness the points raised by the Donatists, but it is clear from the report sent to Sylvester that the Donatists were no better supplied with evidence than they had been at Rome. They simply repeated the old, unsubstantiated charge against Cecilianus that, as deacon, he had forcibly prevented the members of the Church of Carthage from succoring their brethren in prison during the persecution of Diocletian, and the disproved accusation against the bishop who consecrated him that he had been a traditor. In a word, they had absolutely no case and the Council of Arles endorsed the verdict of the Council of Rome. The synodal letter to Sylvester began as follows:

"We, assembled in the city of Arles at the bidding of our most pious

Emperor, in the common bonds of charity and unity, and knitted together by the ties of the mother Catholic Church, salute you, most holy Pope, with all due reverence. We have endured to listen to the accusations of desperate men, who have wrought grave injury to our law and tradition, men whom the present authority of our God and the rule of truth have so utterly disowned that there was no reason in their speeches, no bounds to the charges they brought, and no evidence or proof. And so, in the judgment of God and the Mother Church, which has known and attests them, they stand either condemned or rejected. Would that you, dearest brother, had found it possible to take part in such a gathering. We verily believe that in that case a more severe sentence would have been passed upon them, while if your judgment had coincided with ours, the joy of our assembly would have been intensified. But since you found it impossible to leave the chosen place where the Apostles make their daily home, and where their blood testifies ceaselessly to the glory of God, we thought, dearest brother, that we ought not simply to take in hand the subject for the discussion of which we had been called together, but also to consider other matters on our own account, and, as we have come from diverse provinces, diverse are the topics on which it seemed good to us to take counsel".

The letter then enumerates the canons to which the signatories had agreed and transmits them with the remark that as the Bishop of Rome's dioceses were wider than those of any other bishop, he was the most suitable person to press the acceptance of these canons upon the Church.

It does not fall within the province of this book to discuss these twenty-two canons; it will suffice to indicate the more important in the briefest outline. The first suggested that Easter should be celebrated on the same day throughout the whole world; the second insisted on the clergy residing in the places to which they were ordained; the third threatened with excommunication deserters from the army in times of peace. Of special importance in connection with the questions raised by the Donatists were the canons which prohibited the rebaptism of heretics if they had been baptized in the name of the Holy Trinity; which recognized the validity of baptism conferred by heretics, if conferred in the proper form; which ordered that a new bishop should be consecrated by seven, or at least three, bishops and never by a single one; which removed from the ministry all those who were clearly proved to have been traditores or to have denounced their brother clergy, though, if these had ordained any others to the ministry, the validity of the ordination was not to be challenged. Worthy also of note is the canon removing from the communion of the faithful all those engaged in any calling connected with the arena or the stage, such as charioteers, jockeys, actors, pantomimists, and the like, as long as they continue in professions which, in the eyes of the Church, tend to the subversion of public morals; the canon which excommunicated those of the clergy who practiced usury, and the canon exhorting those whose wives had been unfaithful not to marry again, as they were legally entitled to do, during the lifetime of their guilty partners.

If the Council of Arles was exceptionally fruitful in respect of new rules passed for the improvement of ecclesiastical discipline, it proved an entire failure in its primary object, that of putting an end to the Donatist schism. The African malcontents still refused to acknowledge Cecilianus and had the effrontery to appeal to Constantine for yet another investigation. As the bishops of the West were obstinately prejudiced against them, they desired the Emperor to be gracious enough to take charge of the enquiry himself. Constantine did not conceal his anger in the important letter which he addressed to the bishops at Arles, thanking them for their labors and giving them leave to return to their homes. He wrote:

"Certainly I cannot describe or enumerate the blessings which God in His heavenly bounty has bestowed upon me, His servant. I rejoice exceedingly, therefore, that after this most just enquiry you have recalled to better hope and future those whom the malignity of the Devil seemed to have seduced away by his miserable persuasion from the clearest light of the Catholic law. 0 truly conquering Providence of Christ, our Savior, solicitous even for these who have deserted and turned their weapons against the truth, and joined themselves to the heathen. Yet even now, if they will truly believe and obey His most holy law, they will be able to see what forethought has been taken in their behalf by the will of God. And I hoped, most holy brethren, to find such a disposition even in the stubbornest breasts. For not without just cause will the clemency of Christ depart from those, in whom it shines with a light so clear that we may perceive they are regarded with loathing by the Divine Providence. Such men must be bereft of reason, since with incredible arrogance they persuade themselves of the truth of things, of which it is neither meet to speak nor hear others speak, abandoning the righteous decisions which have been laid down. So persistent and ineradicable is their malignity. How often already have they shamelessly approached me, only to be crushed with the fitting response! Now they clamor for a judgment from me, who myself await the judgment of Christ. For I say that, as far as the truth is concerned, a judgment delivered by priests ought to be considered as valid as though Christ Himself were present and delivering judgment. For priests can form no thought or judgment, unless what they are taught to utter by the admonitory voice of Christ. What, then, can these malignant creatures be thinking of, creatures of the Devil, as I have truly said? They seek the things of this world, abandoning the things of Heaven. What sheer, rabid madness possesses them, that they have entered an appeal, as is wont to be done in mundane lawsuits? What do these detractors of the law think of Christ their Savior, if they refuse to acknowledge the judgment of Heaven and demand judgment from me? They are proven traitors; they have themselves convicted themselves of their crimes, without need of closer enquiry into them. Do you, however, dearest brothers, return to your own homes, and be ye mindful of me that our Savior may ever have mercy upon me".

It is not a little difficult to understand why an Emperor who wrote such a letter as the above should have again acceded to the Donatist demand for a rehearing. Possibly the Donatists had powerful friends at court of whom we know nothing, some member, it may be, of the Imperial Family, or perhaps the case against them was not so one-sided as the Catholic authorities agree in representing. At any rate, Constantine summoned Cecilianus to appear before him in Rome. Here is the letter which he wrote to the Donatist bishops to apprise them of his determination:

"A few days ago I had decided to accede to your request and permit you to return to Africa, that the case which you think you have established against Cecilianus might be fully investigated and brought to a proper conclusion. But, after long and careful consideration, I have deemed the following arrangement best. Knowing, as I do, that certain of you are of a decidedly turbulent nature and obstinately reject a right verdict and the reasoning of absolute truth, it might conceivably happen, if the case were heard in Africa, that the conclusion reached would not be a fitting one, or in accordance with the dictates of truth. In that event, owing to our exceeding obstinacy, something might occur which would greatly displease the Heavenly Divinity and do serious injury to my reputation, which I desire ever to maintain unimpaired. I have decided therefore, as I have said, that it is better for Cecilianus to come here and I think he will speedily arrive. But I pledge you my word that if, in his presence, you shall succeed in proving a single one of the crimes and misdeeds which you lay to his charge, it shall have as much weight with me as if you had proved every accusation you bring forward. May God Almighty keep you safe for ever".

At the same time Constantine wrote to Probianus, the successor of Elianus in the governorship of Africa, instructing him to send under guard to Italy certain witnesses who had been imprisoned for forging documents purporting to show that Felix of Aptunga was a traditor. Cecilianus failed to appear at the appointed time, for some reason which is unknown to St. Augustine, who gives a brief account of the sequence of events. The Donatists demanded that judgment should be given against the absent bishop by default, but Constantine refused and ordered them to follow him to Milan, where affairs of state necessitated his presence. If Augustine is to be trusted, the Emperor secured the attendance of the Donatists by clapping them under guard. This time Cecilianus did not fail his patron. Constantine, who was strongly averse from taking upon himself to revise, as it were, the judgments passed by so many bishops in council, deprecated their possible resentment by assuring them that his sole desire was to close the mouths of the Donatists.

After hearing the case all over again, Constantine pronounced judgment on Nov. 16, 316. St. Augustine says that the Emperor's letters prove his diligence, caution, and forethought. The praise may be deserved, but it is evident that he had made up his mind beforehand. He reaffirmed the absolute innocence of Cecilianus and the shamelessness of his accusers. In an interesting fragment of a letter written by the Emperor to Eumalius, one of his vicars, occurs this sentence: "I saw in Cecilianus a man of spotless innocence, one who observed the proper duties of religion and served it as he ought, nor did it appear that guilt could be found in him, as had been charged against him in his absence by the malice of his enemies". The publication of the Emperor's verdict was followed by an edict prescribing penalties against the schismatics. St. Augustine speaks of a "most severe law against the party of Donatus", and, from other scattered references, we learn that their churches were confiscated and that they were fined for non-obedience. The author of the Edict of Milan, who had promised absolute freedom of conscience to all, was so soon obliged to invoke the arm of the temporal authority for the correction of religious disunion!

But the Donatists, whose only raison d'être was their passionate insistence upon the obligation of the Christian to make no compromise with conscience, however sharp the edge of the persecutor's sword, were obviously not the kind of people to be overawed by so mild a punishment as confiscation of property. The Emperor's edicts were fruitless, and in 320, only four years later, we find Constantine trying a change of policy and recommending the African bishops to see once more what toleration would do. Active repression only made martyrs, and martyrdom was the goal of the fanatical Donatist's ambition. Hence the terms in which the Emperor addresses the Catholic Church of Africa. After enumerating the repeated efforts he has made in order to restore unity, and dwelling upon the deliberate and abandoned wickedness of those who have rendered his intervention nugatory, he continues:

"We must hope, therefore, that Almighty God may show pity and gentleness to his people, as this schism is the work of a few. For it is to God that we should look for a remedy, since all good vows and deeds are required. But until the healing comes from above, it behooves us to moderate our councils, to practice patience, and to bear with the virtue of calmness any assault or attack which the depravity of these people prompts them to deliver. Let there be no paying back injury with injury:

for it is only the fool who takes into his usurping hands the vengeance which he ought to reserve for God. Our faith should be strong enough to feel full confidence that, whatever we have to endure from the fury of men like these, will avail with God with all the grace of martyrdom. For what is it in this world to conquer in the name of God, unless it be to bear with fortitude the disordered attack of men who trouble the peaceful followers of the law! If you observe my will, you will speedily find that, thanks to the supreme power, the designs of the presumptuous standard-bearers of this wretched faction will languish, and all men will recognize that they ought not to listen to the persuasion of a few and perish everlastingly, when, by the grace of penitence, they may correct their errors and be restored to eternal life".

Patience, leniency, and toleration, however, were as futile as force in dealing with the Donatists, who bluntly told the Emperor that his protégé, Cecilianus, was a "worthless rascal", and refused to obey his injunctions. Donatus, surnamed the Great in order to distinguish him from the other Donatus, who had been Bishop of Casa Nigre, had by this time succeeded to the leadership of the schism on the death of Majorinus, and the extraordinary ascendency which he obtained over his followers, in spite of the powerful Imperial influence which was always at the support of Cecilianus, warrants the belief that he was a man of marked ability. Learned, eloquent, and irreproachable in private life, he is said to have ruled his party with an imperious hand, and to have treated his bishops like lackeys. Yet his authority was so unbounded and unquestioned that his followers swore by his name and grey hairs, and, at his death, ascribed to him the honours paid only to martyrs.

Under his leadership the Donatists rapidly increased in numbers. They were schismatics rather than heretics. They had no great distinctive tenet; what they seem to have insisted upon chiefly was absolute purity within the Church and freedom from worldly taint. That was their ideal, as it has been the ideal of many other wild sectaries since their day. They claimed special revelations of the Divine Will; they insisted upon rebaptizing their converts, compelling even holy virgins to take fresh vows on joining their communion, which they boasted was that of the one true Church. Such a sect naturally attracted to itself all the fanatical extremists of Africa and all those who had any grievance against the Catholic authorities. It became the refuge of the revolutionary, the bankrupt, and the criminal, and thus, inside the Donatist movement proper, there grew up a kind of anarchist movement against property, which had little or no connection with religious principles.

Constantine, during the remainder of his reign, practically ignored the African Church. He had done what he could and he wiped his hands of it. There soon arose an extravagant sect which took the name of Circumcelliones, from their practice of begging food from cell to cell, or cottage to cottage. They renounced the ordinary routine of daily life. Forming themselves into bands, and styling themselves the Champions of the Lord, they roamed through the countryside, which they kept in a state of abject terror. St. Augustine, in a well-known passage, declares that when their shout of "Praise be to God!" was heard, it was more dreaded than the roar of a lion. They were armed with wooden clubs, which they named "Israels", and these they did not scruple to use upon the Catholics, whose churches they entered and plundered, committing the most violent excesses, though they were pledged to celibacy. Gibbon justly compares them to the Camisards of Languedoc at the commencement of the 18th century, and others have likened them to the Syrian Assassins at the time of the Crusades and the Jewish Sicarii of Palestine during the first century of the Christian era. They formed, it seems, a sort of Christian Jacquerie, possessed in their wilder moments with a frantic passion for martyrdom and imploring those whom they met to kill them. The best of them were fit only for a madhouse; the worst were fit only for a gaol. Probably they had little connection with the respectable Donatists in the cities, whose organization was precisely the same as that of the Catholics, and their operations were mainly restricted to the thinly populated districts on the borders of the desert.

On one occasion, however, Constantine was obliged to interfere. The Donatists in Cirta,—the capital of Numidia,—which had been renamed Constantina in honour of the Emperor, had forcibly seized the church of the Catholics, that had been built at Constantine's command. The Catholics, therefore, appealed to the Emperor, and knowing that he was pledged to a policy of non-interference, they did not ask for punishment against the Donatists, or even for the restoration of the church in question, but simply that a new site might be given them out of public moneys. The Emperor granted their request, ordering that the building as well as the site should be paid for by the State, and granting immunity from all public offices to the Catholic clergy of the town. In his letter Constantine does not mince his language with respect to the Donatists.

"They are adherents", he says, "of the Devil, who is their father; they are insane, traitors, irreligious, profane, ranged against God and enemies of the Holy Church. Would to Heaven!", he concludes, "that these heretics or schismatics might have regard even now for their own salvation, and, brushing aside the darkness, turn their eyes to see the true light, leaving the Devil, and flying for refuge, late though it be, to the one and true God, who is the judge of all! But since they are set upon remaining in their wickedness and wish to die in their iniquities, our warning and our previous long continued exhortations must suffice. For if they had been willing to obey our commandments, they would now be free from all evil".

Evidently the Emperor was thoroughly weary of the whole controversy, and disgusted at such unreasoning contumacy. The same feelings find powerful expression in the letters and manifestoes of St. Augustine, a century later, when the great Bishop of Hippo constituted himself the champion of the Catholic Church and played the foremost part in the stormy debates which preceded the final disappearance of the Donatist schism, after the Council of Carthage in 410. Then the momentous decision was reached that all bishops who, after three appeals to them to return to the Church, still refused submission, should be brought back to the Catholic fold by force. The point in dispute was still just what it had been in the days of Constantine, whether a Christian Church could be considered worthy of the name if it had admitted faithless and unworthy members, or if the ministers had been ordained by bishops who had temporized with their consciences and fallen short of the loftiest ideal of duty. That was the great underlying principle at stake in the Donatist controversy, though, as in all such controversies, the personal element was paramount when the schism began, and was still the cause of the bitterness and fury with which the quarrel was conducted long after the intrigues of Lucilla and the personal animosities between Cecilianus and the Numidian bishops had ceased to be of interest or moment to the living Church. And it is interesting to note that while it was the Donatists themselves who had made the first appeal unto Caesar by asking Constantine to judge between them and Ctecilianus, in St. Augustine's day the Donatists hotly denied the capacity of the State to take cognizance of spiritual things. What, they asked, has an Emperor to do with the Church?

THE ARIAN CONTROVERSY

IF Constantine beheld with impatience the irreconcilable fury of the Donatists, who refused either to respect his wishes for Christian unity or to obey the bishops of the Western Church; if he angrily washed his hands of their stubborn factiousness and committed them in despair to the judgment of God, we may imagine with what bitterness of soul he beheld the gathering of the storm of violent controversy which is associated with the two great names of Arius and Athanasius. This was a controversy, and Arianism was a heresy, which, unlike the Donatist schism, were confined to no single province of the Empire, but spread like a flood over the Eastern Church, raising issues of tremendous importance, vital to the very existence of Christianity. It started in Alexandria. No birthplace could have been more appropriate to a system of theology which was professedly based upon pure reason than the great university city where East and West met, the home of Neo-Platonism, the inheritor of the Hellenic tradition, and the chief exponent of Hellenism, as understood and professed by Greeks who for centuries had been subject to and profoundly modified by Oriental ideas and thought.

We must deal very briefly with its origin. Arius was born in the third quarter of the third century, according to some accounts in Libya, according to others in Alexandria. He was ordained deacon by the Patriarch Peter and presbyter by Achillas, who appointed him to the church called Baucalis, the oldest and one of the most important of the city churches of Alexandria. Adus had been in schism in his earlier years. He had joined the party of Meletius, Bishop of Lycopolis, who was condemned by a synod of Egyptian bishops in 306 for insubordination and irregularity of conduct; but he had made submission to Achillas, and during the latter's short tenure of the see, Arius became a power in

Alexandria. We are told, indeed, that on the death of Achillas in 312 or 313 Arius was a candidate for the vacant throne, and Theodoretus states that he was greatly mortified at being passed over in favor of Alexander. But there is no indication of personal animosity or quarrel between the bishop and the parish priest until five or six years later. On the contrary, Alexander is said to have held Arius in high esteem, and the fame of the priest of Baucalis spread abroad through the city as that of an earnest worker, a strict and ascetic liver, and a powerful preacher who dealt boldly and frankly with the great principles of the faith. In person, Arius was of tall and striking presence, conspicuous wherever he moved by his sleeveless tunic and narrow cloak, and gifted with great conversational powers and charm of manner. He was also capable of infecting others with the enthusiasm which he felt himself. Arius has been described for us mainly by his enemies, who considered him a very anti-Christ, and attributed his remarkable success to the direct help of the Evil One. We may be sure that, like all the great religious leaders of the world,— among whom, heretic though he was, he deserves a place,—he was fanatically sincere and the doctrine which he preached was vital and fecund, even though the vitality and fecundity were those of error.

It was not, apparently, until the year 319 that serious disturbance began in the Christian circles of Alexandria. There would first of all be whispers that Arius was preaching strange doctrine and handling the great mysteries somewhat boldly and dogmatically. Many would doubt the wisdom of such outspokenness, quite apart from the question whether the doctrine taught was sound; others would exhibit the ordinary distrust of innovation; others would welcome this new kindling of theological interest from the mere pleasure of debate and controversy. We do not suppose that any one, not even Arius himself, foresaw—at any rate, at first—the extraordinary and lamentable consequences that were to follow from his teaching. The Patriarch Alexander has been blamed for not crushing the infant heresy at its birth, for not stopping the mouth of Arius be-fore the mischief was done. It is easy to be wise after the event. Doubtless Alexander did not ap-preciate the danger; possibly also he thought that if he waited, the movement would subside of itself. He may very well have believed that this popular preacher would lose his hold, that someone else would take his place as the fashionable clergyman of the hour, that the extravagance of his doctrines would speedily be forgotten. Moreover, Arius was a zealous priest, doing good work in his own way, and long experience has shown that it is wise for ecclesiastical superiors to give able men of marked power and originality considerable latitude in the expression of their views.

As time went on, however, it became clear that Alexander must intervene. Arius was now the enthusiastic advocate of theories which aimed at the very root of the Christian religion, inasmuch as they denied the essential Godhead of Christ. It was no longer a case of a daring thinker tentatively hinting at doctrines which were hardly in accord with established belief. Arius was devoting himself just to those points where he was at variance with his fellows, was insisting upon them in season and out of season, and was treating them as the very essence of Christianity. He had issued his challenge; Alexander was compelled to take it up. The Patriarch sent for him privately. He wished either to convince him of his error or to induce him to be silent. But the interview was of no avail. Arius simply preached the more. Alexander then summoned a meeting of the clergy of Alexandria, and brought forward for discussion the accepted doctrine of the Holy Trinity which Arius had challenged. Arius and his sympathizers were present and the controversy was so prolonged that the meeting had to be adjourned; when it reassembled, the Patriarch endeavored to bring the debate to a close by restating the doctrine of the Holy Trinity in a form which he hoped would be unanimously approved. But this merely precipitated an open rupture. For Arius immediately rose and denounced Alexander for falling into the heresy of Sabellianism and reducing the Second Person in the Trinity to a mere manifestation of the First.

It is to be remembered that the doctrine of the Holy Trinity—difficult as it is even now, after centuries of discussion, to state in terms that are free from all equivocation—must have been far more difficult to state then, before the Arian controversy had, so to speak, crystallized the exact meaning of the terms employed. It seems quite clear, moreover, from what subsequently took place, that Alexander was no match for Arius in dialectical subtlety and that Arius found it easy to twist his chief's unskillful arguments and expressions into bearing an interpretation which

Alexander had not intended. At any rate the inevitable result of the conference was that both sides parted in anger, and Arius continued as before to preach the doctrine that the Son of God was a creature. For this was the leading tenet of Arianism and the basis of the whole heresy, that the Son of God was a creature, the first of all creatures, it is true, and created before the angels and archangels, ineffably superior to all other creatures, yet still a creature and, as such, ineffably inferior to the Creator, God the Father Himself.

It does not fall within the scope of this book to discuss in detail the theological conceptions of Arius and the mysteries of the Holy Trinity. But it is necessary to say a few words about this new doctrine which was to shake the world, and to show how it came into being. Arius started from the Sonship of Christ, and argued thus: If Christ be really, and not simply metaphorically, the Son of God, and if the Divine Sonship is to be interpreted in the same way as the relationship between human father and son, then the Divine Father must have existed before the Divine Son. Therefore, there must have been a time when the Son did not exist. Therefore, the Son was a creature composed of an essence or being which had previously not been existent. And inasmuch as the Father was in essence eternal and ever existent, the Son could not be of the same essence as the Father. Such was the Arian theory stated in the fewest possible words. "Its essential propositions", as Canon Bright has said, "were these two, that the Son had not existed from eternity and that he differed from other creatures in degree and not in kind". There can be nothing more misleading than to represent the Arian controversy as a futile logomachy, a mere quarrel about words, about a single vowel even, as Gibbon has done in a famous passage. It was a vital controversy upon a vital dogma of the Christian Church.

Two years seem to have passed before Bishop Alexander, finding that Arius was growing bolder in declared opposition, felt compelled to make an attempt to enforce discipline within his diocese. The insubordinate priest of Baucalis had rejected the personal appeal of his bishop and disregarded the wishes of a majority of the Alexandrian clergy, and we may reasonably suppose that his polemics would grow all the more bitter as he became aware of the rapidly deepening estrangement. He would sharpen the edge of his sarcasm upon the logical obtuseness of his nominal superiors, for his appeal was always to reason and to logic. Given my premises, he would say, where is the flaw in my deductions, and wherein do my syllogisms break down? By the year 321 Arius was the typical rebellious priest, profoundly self-confident, rejoicing in controversy, dealing hard blows all around him, and prepared to stoop to any artifice in order to gain adherents. To win over the mob, he was ready to degrade his principles to the mob's understanding.

Alexander summoned a provincial synod of a hundred Egyptian and Libyan bishops to pronounce judgment upon the doctrines and the person of Arius. Attended by his principal supporters, Arius appeared before the synod and boldly stood to his guns. He maintained, that is to say, that God had not always been Father; that the Word was the creature and handiwork of the Father; that the Son was not like the Father according to substance and was neither the true Word nor the true Wisdom, having been created by the Word and Wisdom which are in God; that by His nature He was subject to change like all other rational creatures; that the Son does not perfectly know either the Father or His own essence, and that Jesus Christ is not true God. The majority of the bishops listened with horror as Arius thus unfolded his daring and, in their ears, blas-phemous creed. One of them at length put a searching test question. "If", he asked, "the Word of God is subject to change, would it have been possible for the Word to change, as Satan had changed, from goodness to wickedness?". "Yes", came the answer. Thereupon the synod promptly excommunicated Arius and his friends, including two bishops, Secundus of Ptolemais in the Pentapolis and Theonas of Marmorica, together with six priests and six deacons. The synod also anathematized his doctrines. The Arian heresy had formally begun.

Arius quitted Alexandria and betook himself to Palestine, where he and his companions received hospitable treatment at the hands of some of the bishops, notably Eusebius of Caesarea and Paulinus of Tyre. He bore himself very modestly, assuming the role not of a rebel against authority, but of one who had been deeply wronged, because he had been grievously misunderstood. He was no longer the turbulent priest, strong in the knowledge of his intellectual superiority over his bishop, but a minister of the Church who had been cast out from among the faithful and whose one absorbing desire was to be restored to communion. He did not ask his kindly hosts to associate themselves with him. Ile merely begged that they should use their good offices with Alexander to effect a reconciliation, and that they should not refuse to treat him as a true member of the Church. A few, like Macarius of Jerusalem, rejected his overtures, but a large number of bishops in the Province—if we may so term it—of the Patriarch of Antioch acceded to his wishes. No doubt Arius presented his case, when he was suing for recognition and favor, in a very different form from that in which he had presented it from the rostrum of his church at Baucalis. He was as subtle in his knowledge of the ways of the world as in his knowledge of the processes of logic. Nevertheless, he cannot possibly have disguised the main doctrine which he had preached for years—the doctrine, that is to say, that the Son was inferior to the Father and had been created by the Father out of a substance other than His own—and the fact that the champion of such a doctrine received recognition at the hands of so many bishops seems to prove that the Church had not yet formulated her belief in respect of this mystery with anything like precision; that theories similar to those advocated by Arius were rife throughout the East and were by no means repugnant to the general tendency of its thought.

Arianism would naturally, and did actually, make a most potent appeal to minds of very varying quality and calibre. It appealed, for example, to those Christians who had not quite succeeded in throwing off the influences of the paganism around them, a class obviously large and comprising within it alike the educated who were under the spell of the religious philosophy of the—Neo-Platonists, and the uneducated and illiterate who believed, or at any rate spoke as if they believed, in a multiplicity of gods. To minds, therefore, still insensibly thinking in terms of polytheism one can understand the attraction of the leading thought of Arianism, viz., one supreme, eternal, omnipotent God, God the Father, and a secondary God, God the Son, God and creature in one, and therefore the better fitted to be intermediary between the unapproachable God and fallen humanity. For how many long centuries had not the world believed in demi-gods as it had believed in gods? Arianism, on one side of its character, enabled men to cast a lingering look behind on an outworn creed which had not been wholly gross and which had not been too exacting for human frailty. Moreover, there were many texts in Holy Scripture which seemed in the most explicit language to cor-roborate the truth of Arius's teaching. "My Father is greater than I," so Christ had Himself said, and the obvious and literal meaning of the words seemed entirely inconsistent with any essential co-equality of Son and Father. The text, of course, is subject to another—if more recondite—interpretation, but the history of religion has shown that the origin of most sects has been due to people fastening upon individual texts and founding upon them doctrines both great and small.

Again,—and perhaps this was the strongest claim that Arianism could put forward—it appealed to men's pride and belief in the adequacy of their reason. Mankind has always hungered after a religious system based on reason, founded in reason; secure against all objectors, something four-square and solid against all possible assailants. Arianism claimed to provide such a system, and it unquestionably had the greater appearance—at any rate to a superficial view—of being based upon irrefutable argument. Canon Bright put the case very well where he wrote:

"Arianism would appeal to not a few minds by adopting a position virtually rationalistic, and by promising to secure a Christianity which should stand clear of philosophical objections, and Catholics would answer by insisting that the truths pertaining to the Divine Nature must be preeminently matter of adoring faith, that it was rash to speculate beyond the limit of revelation, and that the Arian position was itself open to criticism from reason's own point of view. Arians would call on Catholics to be logical, to admit the prior existence of the Father as involved in the very primary notion of fatherhood; to halt no more between a premise and a conclusion, to exchange their sentimental pietism for convictions sustainable by argument. And Catholics would bid them in turn remember the inevitably limited scope of human logic in regard to things divine and would point out the sublime uniqueness of the divine relation called Fatherhood".

If we consider the subsequent history of the Arian doctrine, its continual rebirth, the permanent appeal which, in at least some of its phases, it makes to certain types of intellect including some of the loftiest and shrewdest, there can be no reason for surprise that Arius met with so much recognition and sympathy, even among those who refused him their active and definite support. Alexander was both troubled and annoyed to find that so many of the Eastern bishops took Arius's part, and he sent round a circular letter of remonstrance which had the effect of arousing some of these kindly ecclesiastics to a sense of the danger which lurked in the Arian doctrine. But Arius was soon to find his ablest and most influential champion in the person of another Eusebius, Bishop of Nicomedia in Bithynia. This Eusebius had been Bishop of Berytus (Beyrout), and it has been thought that he owed his translation from that see to the more important one of Nicomedia to the influence of Constantia, sister of Constantine and wife of Licinius. He had, at any rate, been sufficiently astute to obtain the good-will of Constantine on the fall of his old patron and he stood well with the court circle.

He and Arius were old friends, for they had been fellow-pupils of the famous Lucian of Antioch. It has been suggested that Eusebius was rather the teacher than the pupil of Arius, but probably neither word expresses the true relationship. They were simply old friends who thought very much alike. Arius's letter to Eusebius asking for his help is one of the most interesting documents of the period. Arius writes with hot indignation of the persecution to which he has been subjected by Alexander, who, he says, had expelled him and his friends from Alexandria as impious atheists because they had refused to subscribe to the outrageous doctrines which the Bishop professed. He then gives in brief his version of Alexander's teaching and of his own, which he declares is that of Eusebius of Caesarea and all the Eastern bishops, with the exception of a few. "We are persecuted", he continues, "because we have said, the Son has a beginning, but God is without a beginning, and the Son is made of that which is not, and the Son is not part of God nor is he of any substance". It is the letter of a man angry at what he conceives to be the harsh treatment meted out to him, and it has the ring of honesty about it, for even , though it distorts the views put forward by Alexander, there never yet was a convinced theologian who stated his opponent's case precisely as that opponent would state it for himself.

We have not Eusebius's answer to this letter, the closing sentence of which begged him as "a true fellow-pupil of Lucian" not to fail him. But we know at least that it was favorable, for we next find Arius at Nicomedia itself, under the wing of the popular and powerful Bishop, who vigorously stood up for his friend. Eusebius wrote more than once to Alexander pleading the cause of the banished presbyter, and Arius himself also wrote to his old Bishop, restating his convictions and reopening the entire question in a temperate form. The tone of that letter certainly compares most favorably with that of the famous document which Alexander addressed to his namesake at Byzantium, warning him to be on guard against Arius and his friends. He can find no epithets strong enough in which to describe them. They are possessed of the Devil, who dwells in them and goads them to fury; they are jugglers and tricksters, clever conjurors with seductive words; they are brigands who have built lairs for themselves wherein day and night they curse Christ and the faithful; they are no better than the Jews or Greeks or pagans, whose good opinion they eagerly covet, joining them in scoffing at the Catholic doctrine and stirring up faction and persecution. The Bishop in his fury even declares that the Arians are threatening lawsuits against the Church at the instance of disorderly women whom they have led astray, and accuses them of seeking to make proselytes through the agency of the loose young women of the town. In short, they have torn the unbroken tunic of Christ. And so on throughout the letter.

The historians of the Church have done the cause of truth a poor service in concealing or glossing over the outrageous language employed by the Patriarch, whose violence raises the suspicion that he must have been conscious of the weakness of his own dialectical power in thus disqualifying his opponents and ruling them out of court as a set of frantic madmen. "What impious arrogance", he exclaims. "What measureless madness! What vainglorious melancholy! What a devilish spirit it is that indurates their unholy souls!". Even when every allowance is made, this method of conducting a controversy creates prejudice against the person employing it. It is, moreover, in the very sharpest contrast with the method employed by Arius, and with the tenor of the letter written by Eusebius of Nicomedia to Paulinus of Tyre, praying him to write to "My lord, Alexander". Eusebius hotly resented the tone of the

Patriarch's letter, and, summoning a synod of Bithynian bishops, laid the whole matter before them for discussion. Sympathizing with Arius, these bishops addressed a circular letter "to all the bishops throughout the Empire", begging them not to deny communion to the Arians and also to seek to induce Alexander to do the same. Alexander, however, stood out for unconditional surrender.

Arius returned to Palestine where three bishops permitted him to hold services for his followers, and the wordy war continued. Alexander drew up a long encyclical which he addressed "to all his fellow-workers of the universal Catholic Church", couched in language not quite so violent as that which he had employed in writing to the Bishop of Byzantium, yet denouncing the Arians in no measured terms as "lawless men and fighters against Christ, teaching an apostasy which one may rightly describe as preparing the way for anti-Christ". In it he attacks Eusebius of Nicomedia by name, accusing him of "believing that the welfare of the Church depended upon his nod", and of championing the cause of Arius not because he sincerely believed the Arian doctrine so much as in order to further his own ambitious interests. Evidently, this was not the first time that the two prelates had been at variance, and private animosities accentuated their doctrinal differences. The more closely the original authorities are studied, the more evident is the need for caution in accepting the traditional character sketches of Arius and Eusebius of Nicomedia. Alexander declares that he is prostrated with sorrow at the thought that Arius and his friends are eternally lost, after having once known the truth and denied it. But he adds, "I am not surprised. Did not Judas betray his Master after being a disciple?" We are skeptical of Alexander's sorrow. He closes his letter with a plea for the absolute excommunication of the Arians. Christians must have nothing to do with the enemies of Christ and the destroyers of souls. They must not even offer them the compliment of a morning salutation. To say "Good-morning" to an Arian was to hold communication with the lost. Such a manifesto merely added fuel to the fire, and the two parties drew farther and farther apart.

Nor was Arius idle. It must have been about this time that he composed the notorious poem, Thalia, in which he embodied his doctrines. He selected the metre of a pagan poet, Sotades of Crete, of whom we know nothing save that his verses had the reputation of being exceedingly licentious. Arius did this of deliberate purpose. His object was to popularize his doctrines. Sotades had a vogue; Arius desired one. What he did was precisely similar to what in our own time the Salvation Army has done in setting its hymns to the popular tunes and music-hall ditties of the day. This was at first a cause of scandal to many worthy people, who now admit the cleverness and admire the shrewdness of the idea. Similarly, Arius got people to sing his doctrines to the very tunes to which they had previously sung the indecencies of Sotades. He wrote ballads, so we are told by Philostorgius—the one Arian historian who has survived—for sailors, millers, and travellers. But it is certainly difficult to understand their popularity, judging from the isolated fragments which are quoted by Athanasius in his First Discourse Against the Arians (chap. XI). According to Athanasius, the Talia opened as follows :

"According to faith of God's elect, God's prudent ones, Holy children, rightly dividing, God's Holy Spirit receiving, Have I learned this from the partakers of wisdom, Accomplished, divinely taught, and wise in all things. Along their track have I been walking, with like opinions. I am very famous, the much suffering for God's glory, And taught of God, I have acquired wisdom and knowledge".

It is rather the unspeakable tediousness and frigidity of this exordium than its arrogant impiety that strike the modern reader. Athanasius then proceeds to quote examples of Arius's "repulsive and most impious mockeries". For example, "God was not always a Father; there was once a time when God was alone and was not yet a Father. But afterwards He became a Father". Or, "the Son was not always", or "the Word is not very God, but by participation in Grace, He, as all others, is God only in name". If these are good specimens of what Athanasius calls "the fables to be found in Arius's jocose composition", the standard of the jocose or the ridiculous must have altered greatly. Why such a poem should have been called the Thalia or "Merrymaking", it is hard to conceive.

Yet, one can understand how the ribald wits of Alexandria gladly seized upon this portentous controversy and twisted its prominent phrases into the catch-words of the day. There is a passage in Gregory of Nyssa bearing on this subject which has frequently been quoted.

"Every corner of Constantinople", he says, "was full of their discussions, the streets, the market-place, the shops of the money-changers and the victuallers. Ask a tradesman how many obols he wants for some article in his shop, and he replies with a disquisition on generated and ungenerated being. Ask the price of bread today, and the baker tells you. The Son is subordinate to the Father. Ask your servant if the bath is ready and he makes answer, The Son arose out of nothing. Great is the only Begotten, declared the Catholics, and the Arians rejoined, But greater is He that begot".

It was a subject that lent itself to irreverent jesting and cheap profanity. The baser sort of Arians appealed to boys to tell them whether there were one or two Ingenerates, and to women to say whether a son could exist before he was born. Even in the present day, any theological doctrine which has the misfortune to become the subject of excited popular debate is inevitably dragged through the mire by the ignorant partisanship and gross scurrilities of the contending factions. We may be sure that the "Ariomaniacs"—as they are called—were neither worse nor better than the champions of the Catholic side, and the result was tumult and disorder. In fact, says Eusebius of Caesarea, "in every city bishops were engaged in obstinate conflict with bishops, people rose against people, and almost, like the fabled Symplegades, came into violent collision with each other. Nay, some were so far transported beyond the bounds of reason as to be guilty of reckless and outrageous conduct and even to insult the statues of the Emperor."

Constantine felt obliged to intervene and addressed a long letter to Alexander and Arius, which he confided to the care of his spiritual adviser, Hosius, Bishop of Cordova, bidding him go to Alexandria in person and do what he could to mediate between the disputants. We need not give the text in full. Constantine began with his usual exordium. His consuming passion, he said, was for unity of religious opinion, as the precursor and best guarantee of peace. Deeply disappointed by Africa, he had hoped for better things from "the bosom of the East", whence had arisen the dawn of divine light. Then he continues :

"But Ah! glorious and Divine Providence, what a wound was inflicted not alone on my ears but on my heart, when I heard that divisions existed among yourselves, even more grievous than those of Africa, so that you, through whose agency I hoped to bring healing to others, need a remedy worse than they. And yet, after making careful enquiry into the origin of these discussions, I find that the cause is quite insignificant and entirely disproportionate to such a quarrel. I gather then that the present controversy originated as follows. For when you, Alexander, asked each of the presbyters what he thought about a certain passage in the Scriptures, or rather what he thought about a certain aspect of a foolish question, and you, Arius, without due consideration laid down propositions which never ought to have been conceived at all, or, if conceived, ought to have been buried in silence, dissension arose between you; communion was forbidden; and the most holy people, torn in twain, no longer preserved the unity of a common body".

The Emperor then exhorts them to let both the unguarded question and the inconsiderate answer be forgotten and forgiven. The subject, he says, never ought to have been broached, but there is always mischief found for idle hands to do and idle brains to think. The difference between you, he insists, has not arisen on any cardinal doctrine laid down in the Scriptures, nor has any new doctrine been introduced. "You hold one and the same view"; reunion, therefore, is easily possible. So little does the Emperor appreciate the importance of the questions at issue, that he goes on to quote the example of the pagan philosophers who agree to disagree on details, while holding the same general principles. How then, he asks, can it be right for brethren to behave towards one another like enemies because of mere trifling and verbal differences? "Such conduct is vulgar, childish, and petulant, ill-befitting priests of God and men of sense. It is a wile and temptation of the Devil. Let us have done with it. If we cannot all think alike on all topics, we can at least all be united on the great essentials. As far as regards divine Providence, let there be one faith and one understanding, one united opinion in reference to God." And then the letter concludes with the passionate outburst:

"Restore me then my quiet days and untroubled nights, that I may retain my joy in the pure light and, for the rest of my days, enjoy the gladness of a peaceful life. Else I needs must groan and be diffused wholly in tears, and know no comfort of mind till I die. For while the people of God, my fellow-servants, are thus torn asunder in unlawful and pernicious controversy, how can I be of tranquil mind?"

Some have seen in this letter proof of the Emperor's consummate wisdom, and have described its language as golden and the triumph of common sense. It seems to us a complete exposure of his profound ignorance of the subject in which he had interfered. It was easy to say that the question should not have been raised. Quieta non movere is an excellent motto in theology as in politics. But this was precisely one of those questions which, when once raised, are bound to go forward to an issue. The time was ripe for it. It suited the taste and temper of the age, and the resultant storm of controversy, so easily stirred up, was not easily allayed. For Constantine to tell Alexander and Arius that theirs was merely a verbal quarrel on an insignificant and non-essential point, or that they were really of one and the same mind, and held one and the same view on all essentials, was grotesquely absurd. The question at issue was none other than the Divine Nature of the Son of God. If theology is of any value or importance at all, it is impossible to conceive a more essential problem.

THE COUNCIL OF NICEA

CONSTANTINE'S letter was fruitless. Hosius sought to play the peacemaker in vain. Neither Alexander nor Arius desired peace except at the price of the other's submission, and neither was prepared to submit. Hosius, therefore, did not remain long in Alexandria, and, returning to Constantine, recommended him to summon a Council of the Church. The advice pleased the Emperor, who at once issued letters calling upon the bishops to assemble at Nicaea, in Bithynia, in the month of June, 325. The invitations were accepted with alacrity, for Constantine placed at the disposal of the bishops the posting system of the Empire, thus enabling them to travel comfortably, expeditiously, and at no cost to themselves.

"They were impelled", says Eusebius, "by the anticipation of a happy result to the conference, by the hope of enjoying present peace, and by the desire of beholding something new and strange in the person of so admirable an Emperor. And when they were all assembled, it appeared evident that the proceeding was the work of God, inasmuch as men, who had been most widely separated not merely in sentiment but by differences of country, place, and nation, were here brought together within the walls of a single city, forming as it were a vast garland of priests, composed of a variety of the choicest flowers".

The Council of Nicaea was the first of the great Ecumenical Councils of the Church. There had been nothing like it before; nor could there have been, for no pagan Emperor would have tolerated such an assembly. The exact number of those present is not known. Eusebius, with irritating and unnecessary vagueness, says that "the bishops exceeded two hundred and fifty, while the number of the presbyters and deacons in their train and the crowd of acolytes and other attendants was altogether beyond computation." There are sundry lists of names recorded by the ecclesiastical historians, but unfortunately all are incomplete. However, as a confident legend grew up within fifty years of the Council that the bishops were 318 in number, and as the Council itself became known as "the Council of the 318", we may accept that figure without much demur. Very few came from the West. Hosius of Cordova seems to have been the only representative of the Spanish Church, and Nacasius of Divio the only representative of Gaul. The Bishops of Arles, Autun, Lyons, Treves, Narbonne, Marseilles, Toulouse—all cities of first-class importance—were absent. Eustorgius came from Milan; Marcus from Calabria; Capito from Sicily. The aged Sylvester of Rome would have attended, had his physical infirmities permitted, but he sent two presbyters to speak for him, Vito and Vincentius. Bishop Donmus of Stridon represented Pannonia, and Theophilus the Goth came on behalf of the northern barbarians— probably to listen rather than to speak. Evidently, then, the composition of the Council was overwhelmingly Eastern. Greek, not Latin, was the language spoken, and certainly Greek, not Latin, was the heresy under discussion, for the Arian controversy could not have arisen in the western half of the Empire. For all practical purposes the Council of Nicaea was a well-attended synod of the Syrian and Egyptian Churches. The opinions there expounded were the opinions of the Christian schools of Antioch and Alexandria.

We may take the names of a few of the bishops as they pass through the gates of Nicaea, each accompanied by at least two presbyters and three slaves, riding on horseback or in carriages, with a train of baggage animals following. Alexander was there, bringing with him fourteen bishops from the valley of the Nile and five from Libya. The most conspicuous of these were Potammon of Heracleopolis and Paphnutius from the Thebaid, both of whom had lost an eye in the late persecution, while Paphnutius limped painfully, for he had been hamstrung. Eustathius, the Patriarch of Antioch, came at the head of the Syrian and Palestinian bishops, some of whom, like Eusebius of Caesarea, were gravely suspected of being unsound in the Faith and of having been influenced by the seductions of Arianism, while others, like Macarius of Jerusalem, were staunch supporters of Alexander. Another group hailed from the far Euphrates and Armenia—John of Persia, James of Nisibis in

Mesopotamia, Aitallaha of Edessa, and Paul of Neo-Caesarea, the tendons of whose wrists had been seared with hot irons. Another group came from near at hand, the bishops of what we now call Asia Minor, within the sphere of influence of the imperial city of Nicomedia and of its Bishop, Eusebius. He, too, was there with his friends, Theognis of Nicara, Menophantus of Ephesus, and Maris of Chalcedon, all committed to the cause and to the doctrines of Arius. Then there were a group of Thracian, Macedonian, and Greek bishops, a few from the islands, and Cecilianus from Carthage.

Arius, too, was present with his few faithful henchmen from Egypt, proudly self-confident as ever, but trusting mainly to the advocacy of Eusebius of Nicomedia and to the influence of the moderates, like Eusebius of Caesarea. But during the years that he had been absent from Alexandria a new protagonist had arisen among the ranks of his opponents. Alexander, so runs the legend, had one day seen from the windows of his house a group of boys playing at "church". Thinking that the imitation was too close to the reality and that the lads were carrying the game too far, the Bishop went out to check them and got into conversation with the boy who was taking the lead in their serious sport. Impressed by his earnestness, he took him into his house and trained him for the ministry. It was Athanasius, who now, as a young deacon of twenty-five, accompanied Alexander to Nicaea, having already by his cleverness and zeal gained a remarkable ascendency over the mind of his superior. This slip of a man—for he was of very slender build and insignificant stature—was to lay at Nicaea the sure foundations of his extraordinary and unparalleled fame as the champion of the Catholic Faith.

So the Council assembled in the June of 325 in the charming city of Nicaea, on the shores of the Ascanian lake. The intense interest which it aroused was not confined to those who were to take part in it, or even to the Christian population of the city and district. It spread, so we are expressly told, to those who still clung to the old religion. Debates on the nature of the Fatherhood of God and the Sonship of Christ would be almost as welcome and absorbing to a Neo-Platonist philosopher as to a Christian bishop. His pleasure in the intellectual exercise was marred by no anxiety lest it should result in disturbance of happy and settled belief. When Greek met Greek they began forthwith to argue, and so, without waiting for the Council formally to open, the early arrivals at Nicaea commenced their discussions with all corners on the question of the hour.

The story of one of these informal encounters is told by most of the ecclesiastical writers. A certain pagan philosopher was holding forth with great fluency and making mock of the Christian mysteries, to the amusement of a number of bystanders. Finally, his challenge of contradiction was accepted by "a simple old man, one of the confessors of the persecution", who knew nothing of dialectics. As he moved forward to answer the scoffer there was a burst of laughter from some of those present, while the Christians trembled lest their unskilled champion should be turned to ridicule by his practiced opponent. Their anxiety, however, was soon set at rest. "In the name of Jesus Christ, 0 philosopher, listen!", such was the old man's exordium, and the burden of his few unstudied words was to restate his "artless, unquestioning belief" in the cardinal truths of Christianity. There was no argument. "If you believe", he said, "tell me so". "I believe", said the philosopher, compelled, as he afterwards explained it, to become a Christian by some marvelous power. Such is the version of Sozomen; according to Socrates the old man said, "Christ and the apostles committed to us no dialectical art and no vain deception, but plain, bare doctrine, which is guarded by faith and good works." When we consider the endless floods of dialectical subtlety which were poured out during and after the Council of Nicaea by those engaged in the Arian controversy, it seems rather biting irony that a pagan philosopher should have been thus easily and rapidly converted from darkness to light.

It is certain, however, that many of the bishops collected at Nicaea belonged to the same class as this "simple old man", peasants who had had no theological training and owed their elevation—by the suffrages of their congregations—to the conspicuous uprightness of their lives. Such a one was Spyridion, of Cyprus, a shepherd in mind, speech, and dress, but with a turn for rustic humor. Around his name many legends have gathered, and none is more de-lightful than that which tells how he and his deacon set out for Nicaea mounted on two mules, a white and a chestnut. On the journey they came to an inn where they found a number of other bishops bound on the same errand. These prelates feared that so rustic a figure as Spyridion would bring discredit on their religion and appear in grotesque contrast with the splendor of the Imperial Court. So during the night they caused the two mules to be decapitated, thinking that they would thus prevent Spyridion from resuming his journey. The good Bishop was aroused before daybreak by his deacon, who told him of the disaster. Spyridion simply bade him attach the heads to the dead bodies, and, on this being done, the mules rose to their feet as though nothing unusual had happened. When day broke, it was found that the deacon had attached the heads to the wrong shoulders; the white mule now sported a chestnut head and the chestnut a white. Still, it was not thought necessary to repeat the miracle and change the heads, for the mules apparently suffered no inconvenience.

The preliminary meetings of the Council were held in the principal church of Nicaea and continued until the arrival of the Emperor, which was not until after July 3rd, the anniversary of his victory over Licinius. Then the state opening took place in the great hall of the palace. Eusebius gives us a graphic account of the memorable scene. Special invitations had been sent to all whose presence was desired, and these had entered and taken their places in grave and orderly fashion on either side of the hall. Then expectant silence fell upon the company. As the moment for the Emperor's entry approached, some of the members of his immediate entourage began to arrive, but Eusebius is careful to mention that there were no guards or officers in armour, "only friends who avowed the faith of Christ." At the signal that Constantine was at hand, the whole assembly swept to its feet, and the Emperor passed through their midst like "some heavenly angel of God, clad in glittering raiment that seemed to gleam and flash with bright effulgent rays of light, encrusted as it was with gold and precious stones". Yet, though Constantine was thus dazzling in externals, it was evident—at least to the penetrating eye of the courtier bishop—that his mind was "beautified by pity and godly fear". For was not this revealed by his downcast eyes, his heightened colour, and his modest bearing? Advancing to the upper end of the hall, Constantine stood facing the assembly, while a low golden stool was brought for him, and then, when the bishops motioned to him to be seated, he took his seat, and the whole audience followed his example. Beyond doubt, most of the bishops then gazed for the first time upon the Emperor to whom they could not be sufficiently grateful for all he had done for the Church, and Constantine himself might well be flattered and pleased at the homage, evidently sincere, that was being offered to him, as well as a little nervous at the thought that these were the principal ministers and representatives of the God to whom he had tendered allegiance. There would have been no downcast eye, no blush, no marked modesty of carriage, we may suspect, if it had been a council of augurs and flamens that Constantine had summoned. In that case the Emperor would have been perfectly at his ease as he advanced up the hall, conscious that he was the supreme head of all the priesthoods represented in his presence, and that he was not only worshipper but worshipped.

Then, says Eusebius, after a few introductory words of welcome had been spoken, the Emperor rose and delivered a brief address in Latin which was presently translated into Greek. He expressed his delight at finding himself in the presence of such a Council, "united in a common harmony of sentiment," and prayed that no malignant enemy might avail to disturb it, for "internal dissensions in the Church of God were far more to be feared than any battle or war". In well chosen language he explained the overwhelming importance of unity and implored his hearers as "dear friends, as ministers of God, and as faithful servants of their common Lord and Savior", to begin from that moment to discard the causes of dissension which had existed among them and loosen the knots of controversy by the laws of peace. The excellent impression created by this speech was intensified by the next act of the Emperor. On his arrival at Nicaea he had found awaiting him a great number of petitions addressed to him by the bishops accusing one another of heresy, or political intrigue, or too strenuous activity on behalf of the fallen Licinius. Socrates, indeed, says that "the majority of the Bishops" were leveling charges against one another. But they received no encouragement from Constantine. Seated there among them he produced the incriminatory documents from the folds of his toga, called for a brazier, and threw the rolls upon the fire, protesting with an oath that not one of them had been opened or read. "Christ", he said, "bids him who hopes for forgiveness forgive an erring brother". It was a dignified and noble rebuke. The story reads best in this, its simplest form. Theodoretus amplifies the Emperor's rebuke and puts into his mouth the dangerous doctrine that, if bishops sin, their offences ought to be hushed up, lest their flock be scandalized or be encouraged to follow their example. He would even, lie said, throw his own purple over an offending bishop to avoid the evils and contagion of publicity.

Such was the opening of the Council. The Emperor had scored a great personal triumph and had set the bishops a notable example of magnanimity. But it was not imitated. No sooner had the actual business of the Council begun than the flood-gates of controversy were opened. According to Eusebius, the Emperor remained to listen to their mutual recriminations, giving ear patiently to all sides, and doing what he could to assuage animosities by making the most of everything that seemed to tend towards compromise. Unfortunately, the reports of the Council are strangely incomplete. It is not even explicitly stated who presided. The presidency of the Emperor was one only of honor; the actual presidents were probably the legates of Pope Sylvester, viz., Hosius of Cordova and the two presbyters, Vito and Vincentius. But into the controversy which rages round this point we need not enter.

The general feeling of the Council was not long in declaring itself. Arius, who was regarded as a defendant on his trial, made his position absolutely clear. He did not envelop himself, as he might have done, in a cloud of metaphysics from which it would have been difficult to gather his precise meaning. On the contrary, he seems to have come prepared with a résumé of his doctrines, and to have been ready to defend his outposts as resolutely as his citadel. Immediately, therefore, the Council became split up into contending parties. There were the out-and-out Arians, few but formidable, and the out-and-out Trinitarians, led with great ability by the young Athanasius, whose reputation steadily rose as the days passed by. There was also a middle party, led by Eusebius of Nicomedia and supported by Eusebius of Caesarea, whose intellectual and personal sympathies lay with Arius rather than with Athanasius, though they saw that the great majority of the Council were against them, and that Arius and his opinions were sure of excommunication. Theirs was what we may call the "cross-bench mind". They doubtless felt, what many who approach this controversy at the present day feel, that if once appeal is made to Reason, there must be no further appeal beyond that to Faith, as to a higher Court. Those who invoke Reason must not turn round, when they find themselves driven into an ugly corner, and condemn "the Pride of Reason". In our view, Eusebius of Nicomedia was not the malignant, self-seeking, and entirely worldly prelate he is so often represented as having been, but a Bishop who honestly regretted that this question had been raised at all, inasmuch as he foresaw that it must rend the Church in twain. He would have preferred, that is to say, that the exact nature of the Sonship of Christ should not be made a matter of close definition, should not be made a point of doctrine whereon salvation depended, should not be inserted in a creed but left rather to the individual conscience or to the individual intellect. Once the question was raised, his intellectual honesty led him to side with Arius, but he considered that to tear the indivisible garment of Christ was a crime to be avoided at any cost. Eusebius was bent upon a compromise. Arius was his old friend, and his patron, the Emperor, passionately desired unity. The personal wish of the monarch would be sure to have some, though we cannot say precisely how much, weight with him in determining his policy.

Some of the sessions of the Council were marked by uproar and violence. Athanasius declares that when the bishops heard extracts read from the Thalia of Arius, they raised the cry of "impious", and closed their eyes and shut their ears tight against the admission of such appalling blasphemy. There is a legend, indeed, that St. Nicholas, Bishop of Myra, was so carried away by his indignation that he smote Arius a terrific blow upon the jaw for daring to give utterance to words so vile. Theodoretus declares that the Arians drew up the draft of a creed which they were willing to subscribe and had it read before the Council. But it was at once denounced as a "bastard and vile-begotten document" and torn to pieces. Then a praiseworthy attempt was made to begin at the beginning. The proposition was put forward that the Son was from God. "Agreed", said the Trinitarians; "Agreed", said the Arians, on the authority of such texts as "There is but one God, the Father, of whom are all things", and "All things are become new and all things are of God".

"But will you agree", asked the Trinitarians, "that the Son is the true Power and Image of the Father, like to Him in all things, His eternal Image, undivided from Him and unalterable?"

"Yes", said the Arians after some discussion among themselves, and they quoted the texts: "Man is the glory and image of God. For we which live are always delivered unto death for Jesus' sake, and In him we live and move and have our being"

"But will you admit", continued the Trinitarians, "that the Son is Very God?"

"Yes", replied the Arians, "for he is Very God if he has been made so".

Athanasius tells us that while these strange questions and answers were being tossed from one side of the Council to the other, he saw the Arians "whispering and making signals one to the other with their eyes". It is to be regretted that we have no independent account. The savage abuse with which Athanasius attacks the Arians in his Letter to the African Bishops makes his version of what took place at the Council exceedingly suspect. He speaks of their "wiliness," and delivers himself of the sarcasm that as they were cradled in ordure their arguments also partook of a similar character. Most of the vilification in the opening stages of the Arian controversy—at any rate most of that which has survived—seems to have been on the Trinitarian side.

The word Homoousion had at length been uttered and, strangely enough, by Eusebius of Nicomedia, though it was soon to become the rallying cry of his opponents. He had employed it, apparently, to clinch the argument against the Trinitarians, for, he said, if they declared the Son to be Very God, that was tantamount to declaring that the Son was of one substance with the Father. Greatly, no doubt, to his surprise, it was seized upon by his opponents as the word which, of all others, precisely crystallized their position and their objections to Arianism. But before the fight began to rage round this word, the moderates came forward with another suggestion of compromise. Eusebius of Caesarea read before the Council the confession of faith which was in use in his diocese, after having been handed down from bishop to bishop. The Emperor had read it and approved; perhaps, he urged, it might similarly commend itself to the acceptance of all parties in the Council. The creed began as follows:

"I believe in one God, the Father Almighty, maker of all things both visible and invisible, and in one Lord Jesus Christ, the Word of God, God of God, Light of Light, Life of Life, the only-begotten Son, the First-born of every creature, begotten of the Father before all worlds, by whom also all things were made. Who for our salvation was made flesh and lived amongst men, and suffered, and rose again on the third day, and as-cended to the Father, and shall come in glory to judge the quick and the dead. And I believe in the Holy Ghost".

Eusebius, in writing later to the people of his diocese, said that when this creed was read out, "no room for contradiction appeared; but our most pious Emperor, before anyone else, testified that it comprised most orthodox statements. He confessed, moreover, that such were his sentiments, and he advised all present to agree to it, and subscribe to its articles with the insertion of the single word one in substance".

Indeed, little objection could be taken to the creed of Eusebius, which might have been subscribed to with equal sincerity by Arius and Alexander. But the great problem, which had brought the Council together, would have remained entirely unsettled. The creed was not sufficient precise. It left openings for all kinds of heresies. The Trinitarians, therefore, insisted upon inserting a few words which should more precisely define the relationship between the Father and the Son and their real nature and substance, and should retain undiminished the majesty and Godhead of the Son. They put forward the simple antithesis "begotten not made" in reference to the Son, whereby the Arian doctrine that the Son was a creature was effectually negatived. And they also adopted as their own the word which has made the Council famous alike with believers and with skeptics—the word Homoousion.

Dean Stanley, in his History of the Eastern Church, has well said that this is "one of those remarkable words which creep into the language of philosophy and theology and then suddenly acquire a permanent hold on the minds of men". It was a word with a notable, if not a very remote past. It had been orthodox and heretical by turns, a fact which is not surprising when we consider the vagueness of the term ousia and the looseness with which it had been employed by philosophical writers.

"It first distinctly appeared", says Dean Stanley, "in the statement, given by Irenaeus, of the doctrines of Valentins; then for a moment it acquired a more orthodox reputation in the writings of Dionysius and Theognostus of Alexandria; then it was colored with a dark shade by association with the teaching of Manes; next proposed as a test of orthodoxy at the Council of Antioch against Paul of Samosata, and then by that same Council was condemned as Sabellian".

Obviously, therefore, it was not a word to command instantaneous acceptance; its old associations lent a certain specious weight to the repeated accusation of the Arians that the Trinitarians were importing into the Church fantastic subtleties borrowed from Greek philosophy, and were encrusting the simple faith and the simple language of Christ and the apostles with alien thoughts and formula. Athanasius meets that argument with a tu quoque, asking where in Scripture one can find the phrases which Arius had made his own. Modern theologians have replied with much greater force that this importation of philosophy into the Christian religion was inevitable.

"The Church", says Canon Bright, "had come out into the open, had been obliged to construct a theological position against the tremendous attacks of Gnosticism and to provide for educated enquirers in the great centres of Greek learning. She had become conscious of her debt to the wise".

Elsewhere, in the same chapter, he says: "It would, indeed, have been childish to attempt to banish metaphysics from theology. Any religion with a doctrine about God or man must, as such, be metaphysical." And for the Arians to complain of the borrowing of technical terms from philosophy by their opponents was palpably absurd. The whole raison d'être of the Arian movement was its professed rationalism, its appeal to reason and logic, its consciousness, in other words, "of its debt to the wise", and its desire to be able to debate boldly with the enemy in the gate. Really, therefore, the adoption of such a term was of great practical convenience, especially when once its meaning was rigidly defined. The Homoousion, whereby the Word or the Son was declared to be of one essence or substance with the Father, asserted the undiminished Divinity of the Son of God, through whom salvation came into the world.

It is for theologians to expand upon such a text, but it needs no theologian to point out the obvious truth that any diminution of the majesty of the Son of God must have impaired the vitality and converting power of Christianity. The word, therefore, was eagerly adopted by those who had been commissioned to draw up a creed to meet the views of the orthodox majority of the Council. That creed was at length decided upon; Hosius of Cordova announced its completion; and it was read aloud for the first time to the Council, apparently by Hermogenes, subsequently Bishop of Caesarea in Cappadocia. It ran as follows:

"We believe in one God, the Father Almighty, Maker of all things both visible and invisible. And in one Lord Jesus Christ, the Son of God, begotten of the Father, only begotten, that is from the substance of the Father, God of God, Light of Light, very God of very God, begotten not made, being of one substance with the Father, by whom all things were made, both in heaven and earth. Who for us men and for our salvation came down and was made flesh, and was made man, suffered and rose on the third day, ascended into the heavens and will come again to judge the quick and the dead. And we believe in the Holy Spirit".

Such was the text of the famous document which ever since has borne the title of the Nicene Creed. It has been added to during the centuries. It has even lost one or two of its qualifying and explanatory sentences. But these modifications have not touched its central theses, and, above all, the Homoousion remains.

In order to make the position absolutely clear and preclude even the most subtle from placing an heretical interpretation upon the words employed, there was added a special anathema of the Arian doctrines.

"But those who say, Once He was not, and Before He was begotten, He was not, and He came into existence out of what was not, or those who profess that the Son of God is of a different person or substance, or that He was made, or is changeable or mutable—all these are anathematized by the Catholic Church".

This was the formal condemnation of Arianism in all the Protean shapes it was capable of assuming, and the vast majority of the bishops cordially approved.

But what of Arius and his friends, and what of the Eusebian party? Interest centered in the action of the latter. Would they accept the text and sign? Or would they hold fast to the condemned doctrines? They loudly protested, of course, against the anathema, and the Homoousion in the creed itself was repugnant to their intellect. Eusebius of Caesarea asked for a day in which to consider the matter. Then he signed, and wrote a letter to his flock at Caesarea excusing and justifying his conduct, and explaining in what sense he could conscientiously subscribe to the Homoousion. He bowed to the clear verdict of the majority and to the passionate wish of the Emperor. Constantine insisted that the creed should be accepted as the final expression of Catholic belief, though he would have been just as ready to accept the creed of Eusebius himself. The presence or absence of the Homoousion was of little consequence to him. What he wanted was unity, and he was determined to have it, for he was already threatening recalcitrants with banishment. Eusebius of Caesarea signed. He submitted, in other words, when the Church, meeting in Council, had spoken. The Palestinian and Syrian bishops who had supported him in the debates followed his example, complying, we are told, with eagerness and alacrity.

Eusebius of Nicomedia, Theognis of Nicaea, and Maris of Chalcedon made a rather more resolute stand. According to one account, they consulted Constantia, the Emperor's sister, and she persuaded them to sign on the ground that they ought to merge their individual scruples in the will of the majority, lest the Emperor should throw over Christianity in disgust at the dissension among the Christians. According to another story, Constantia recommended them to insert an "iota" into the text of the creed, and thus change the Homoousion into the Homoiousion, to which they could subscribe without violence to their consciences. They could admit, that is to say, that the Son was of "like" substance to the Father when they could not admit that He was of "same" substance. The story is obviously a fiction and part of the campaign of calumny against Eusebius of Nicomedia. He and his two friends signed the creed—not fraudulently or with mental reservations as the story suggests—but for precisely the same reason that Eusebius of Caesarea had signed it. It was the Emperor's wish and they were willing to accept the decision of the Council, but they still stood out against signing the anathema. Two of them, Eusebius and Theognis, were deprived of their sees and sent into exile. Whether their degradation and exile were due wholly to this refusal is doubtful, though as an interesting parallel it may be pointed out that Eusebius, Bishop of Vercelli, and Dionysius, Bishop of Milan, were exiled by the Emperor Valens in 355 because they refused to subscribe the condemnation of Athanasius at the Third Council of Milan. Arius and his two most faithful supporters were excommunicated and banished and their writings, notably the Thalia, were burnt with ignominy.

The labors of the Council were not yet concluded. The Bishops decided that Easter should be observed simultaneously throughout the Church, and that the Judaic time should give way to the Christian. They then drew up what are known as the Canons of Nicaea. We may indicate some of the more important, as, for example, the Fifth, which provided that all questions of excommunication should be discussed in provincial councils to be held twice a year; the fourth, that there should be no less than three bishops present at the consecration of every bishop, and the fifteenth, which prohibited absolutely the translation of any bishop, presbyter, or deacon from one city to another. Some of the canons, such as the twentieth, which prohibited kneeling during church worship on Sundays and between Easter and Pentecost; and the eighteenth, which rebuked the presumption of deacons, have merely an antiquarian interest. The seventeenth forbade all usury on the part of the clergy; the third enacted that no minister of the Church, whatever his rank, should have with him in his house a woman of any kind, unless it were a mother, a sister, or an aunt, or someone quite beyond suspicion. While this canon was under discussion, one of the most exciting debates of the Council took place. The proposal was made that all the married clergy should be required to separate from their wives, and this received a considerable measure of support. But the opposition was led by the confessor Paphnutius, whose words carried the more weight from the fact that he himself had been a lifelong celibate. He debated the subject with great warmth, maintaining at the top of his shrill voice that marriage was honorable and the bed undefiled, and so brought a majority of the assembly round to his way of thinking.

Then at last this historic Council was ready to break up. But before the bishops separated, the Emperor celebrated the completion of his twentieth year of reign by inviting them all to a great banquet.

"Not one of them", says Eusebius, "was missing and the scene was of great splendor. Detachments of the bodyguard and other troops surrounded the entrance of the palace with drawn swords and through their midst the men of God proceeded without fear into the innermost apartments, in which were some of the Emperor's own companions at table, while others reclined on couches laid on either side".

He gave gifts to each according to his rank, singling out a few for special favor. Among these was Paphnutius. Socrates says that the Emperor had often sent for him to the palace and kissed the vacant eye socket of the maimed and crippled confessor. Acesius the Novatian was another, though he steadily refused to abate one jot or tittle of his old convictions. Constantine listened without offence, as the old man declared his passionate belief that those who after baptism had committed a sin were unworthy to participate in the divine mysteries, and merely remarked, with sportive irony, "Plant a ladder, then, Acesius, and climb up to Heaven alone!"

At the closing session the Emperor delivered a short farewell speech, in which his theme was again the urgent need of unity and uniformity within the Christian Church. He implored the bishops to forget and forgive past offences and live in peace, not envying one another's excellencies, but regarding the special merit of each as contributing to the total merit of all. They should leave judgment to God; when they quarreled among themselves they simply gave their enemies an opportunity to blaspheme. How were they to convert the world, he asked, if not by the force of their example? And then he went on to speak plain common sense. Men do not become converts, he said, from their zeal for the truth. Some join for what they can get, some for preferment, some to secure charitable help, some for friendship's sake. "But the true lovers of true argument are very few: scarce, indeed, is the friend of truth". Therefore, he concluded, Christians should be like physicians, and prescribe for each according to his ailments. They must not be fanatics: they must be accommodating. Constantine could not possibly have given sounder advice to a body of men whose besetting sin was likely to be fanaticism and not laxity of doctrine. The passage, therefore, is not without significance. The Church had already begun to act upon the State; here was the State palpably beginning to react upon the Church— in the direction of reasonableness, compromise, and an accommodating temper. Then, after begging the bishops to remember him in their prayers, he dismissed them to their homes, and they left Nicaea, says Eusebius, glad at heart and rejoicing in the conviction that, in the presence of their Emperor, the Church, after long division, had been united once more.

Constantine evidently shared the same conviction. He had no doubt whatever that the Arian heresy was finally silenced. So we find him writing to the church at Alexandria, declaring that all points whirls seemed to be open to different interpretations have been thoroughly discussed and settled. All must abide by the chose jugée. Arius had been proved to be a servant of the Devil. Three hundred bishops had said it, and "that which has commended itself to the judgment of three hundred bishops cannot be other than the doctrine of God, seeing that the Holy Spirit, dwelling in the minds of so many honorable men, must have thoroughly enlightened them as to the will of God". He took for granted, therefore, that those who had been led away by Arius would return at once to the Catholic fold. The Emperor also wrote another letter, which he addressed "To the Churches", in which he declared that each question at issue had been discussed until a decision was arrived at "acceptable to Him who is the inspector of all things", and added that nothing was henceforth left for dissension or controversy in matters of faith. Most of the letter, indeed, consists of argument showing the desirability of a uniform celebration of Easter, but one can see that the leading thought in the writer's mind is that the last word had at length been uttered on the cardinal doctrines of the Christian Faith. The Council had been a brilliant success. The three hundred bishops announced to the Catholic Church the decisions of their "great and holy Synod", with the explicit declaration that "all heresy has been cut out of the Church." Arius was banished and Eusebius of Nicomedia with him. The triumph of orthodoxy seemed finally assured.

THE MURDERS OF CRISPUS AND FAUSTA

WE saw in the last chapter how Constantine presided over the deliberations of the bishops at Nicaea, mild, benignant, gracious, and condescending. It is a very different being whom we see at Rome in 326, suspicious, morose, and striking down in blind fury his own gallant son. The contrast is startling, the cause obscure and mysterious, but if the secret is to be discovered at all, it is probably to be found in the jealousies which raged in the Imperial House.

We must look a little closer at the family of Constantine. The Emperor himself was in the very prime of middle age, just turning his fiftieth year. His eldest son, by his first marriage with Minervina, was the hope of the Empire. Crispus, as we have seen, had won distinction on the Rhine, and had just given signal proof of his capacity by his victories over the navy of Licinius in the Hellespont, which had facilitated the capture of Byzantium. He was immensely popular, and the Empire looked to him, as it had looked to Tiberius and Drusus three centuries before, as to a strong pillar of the Imperial throne.

But Crispus—if the usually accepted theory be right —had a bitter and implacable enemy in the Empress Fausta, who regarded him as standing in the path of her own children, and menacing their interests by his proved merit and abilities. The eldest of her sons, who bore his father's name, was not yet in his teens; the second, Constantius, had been born in 319; the third, Constans, was a year younger. Her three daughters were infants or not yet born. These three young princes, like Caius and Lucius,—to pursue the Augustan parallel,—threatened rivalry to Crispus as they grew up, the more so, perhaps, because Constantine had always possessed the domestic virtues which were rare in a Roman Emperor. In his young days one of the court Panegyrists had eulogized him as a latter-day miracle—a prince who had never sowed any wild oats, who had actually had a taste for matrimony while still young, and, following the example of his father, Constantius, had displayed true piety by consenting to become a father. Another Panegyrist praised him for "yielding himself to the laws of matrimony as soon as he ceased to be a boy", and Eusebius, more than once, emphasizes his virtues as a husband and parent. Constantine, we suspect, was a man easily swayed by a strong-minded woman, ambitious to oust a step-son from his father's favor.

There was yet another great lady of the reigning house whose influence upon the Emperor has to be taken into account. This was his mother, Helena, now nearly eighty years of age, but still vigorous and active enough in mind and body to undergo the fatigues of a journey to Jerusalem. Eusebius dwells upon the estimation in which Constantine held his mother, to whom full Imperial honours were paid. Golden coins were struck in her honor, bearing her effigy and the inscription, "Flavia Helena Augusta". She amassed great riches, and although it is impossible directly to trace her influence upon State affairs, there is reason to believe that Helena, who owed her conversion, according to Eusebius, to the persuasion of her son, was a woman of pronounced and decided character and a great power at court.

There was also Constantine's half-sister, Constantia, the widow of Licinius, whose intercession with her brother had secured for her defeated husband an ill-kept promise of pardon and protection. Constantia was to exhibit even more striking proof of her influence a little later on by her skillful advocacy of the cause of Arius and Eusebius of Nicomedia, and her share in procuring the banishment of Athanasius. These great ladies move in shadowy outline across the stage; we can scarcely distinguish their features or their form; but we think we can see their handiwork most unmistakably in the appalling tragedies which we now have to narrate.

In 326 Constantine went to Rome to celebrate the completion of his twentieth year of reign. Diocletian had done the same—the only occasion upon which that great Emperor had ever set foot in the ancient capital, and even then he made all possible haste to quit it. But whereas Diocletian had travelled thither with the intention of abdicating immediately afterwards, Constantine had no such act of self-abnegation in his mind. Yet he was in no festival mood. Not long after his arrival, there took place the ancient ceremony known as the Procession of the Knights, who rode to the Capitol to pay their vows to Jupiter—the religious ceremony which attended the annual revision of the equestrian lists. Constantine contemptuously stayed within his palace on the day and disdained to watch the Knights ride by. His absence was made the pretext for some street rioting, which, we can hardly doubt, had been carefully engineered beforehand. Rome, still overwhelmingly pagan in its sympathies, had doubtless heard with bitter anger how the Emperor, the head of the old national religion, had been taking part in a General Council of the Christian Church, had admitted bishops and confessors to the intimacy of his table, and had boldly declared himself the champion of Christianity. Constantine's pointed refusal to countenance a time-honored ceremony which, while itself of no extraordinary importance, might yet be taken as typical of the ancient order of things, would easily serve as pretext for a hostile demonstration. Demonstrations in Rome no longer menaced the throne now that the barracks of the Praetorians were empty, but the incident would serve to confirm the suspicions already clouding the mind of the Emperor.

We can read those suspicions most plainly in an edict which he had issued at Nicomedia a few months before. It was addressed to his subjects in every province, and in it the Emperor invited all and sundry to come forward boldly and keep him well informed of any secret plotting of which they happened to be cognizant. No matter how lofty the station of the conspirator might be, whether governor of a province, officer of the army, or even friend and associate of the Emperor, if any one discovered anything he was to tell what he knew, and the Emperor would not be lacking either in gratitude or substantial reward. "Let him come without fear", ran the edict, "and let him address himself to me! I will listen to all: I will myself conduct the investigation: and if the accuser does but prove his charge, I will vindicate my wrongs. Only let him speak boldly and be sure of his case!"

The hand which wrote this was the hand which had flung unread into the brazier at Nicaea, the incriminating petitions of the bishops. What had taken place in the interval that he should issue an edict worthy of a Domitian? The authorities give not the slightest hint. Was there some great conspiracy afoot, in the meshes of which Constantine feared to become entangled, but so cunningly contrived that the Emperor could only be sensible of its existence, without being able to lay hands on the intriguers? Was paganism restless in the East as we have seen it restless in Rome, at the triumph of its once-despised and always detested rival? We do not know. Quite possibly it was, though with the downfall of Licinius its prospects seemed hopeless. Unless, indeed, there was some member of the Imperial Family upon whom paganism rested its hopes and to whom it looked as its future deliverer! Was Crispus such a prince? Again we do not know. There is not a scrap of evidence to bear out a theory which has only been framed as a possible explanation of the dark mystery of his fate.

Eutropius, whose character sketches, for all their brevity, usually tally well with known facts, calls Crispus a prince of the highest merit. Why then did Constantine turn against him? We may, perhaps, see the first sign of the changed relationship in the fact that in 323 the Caesarship of Gaul was taken from Crispus and given to the young Constantius, then a child of seven. So far as is known, no compensating title or command was offered in exchange, which looks as though Constantine was disinclined to trust his eldest son any longer and preferred to keep him in surveillance by his side. The father may have been jealous of the prowess and popularity of the son; the son may have been ambitious, as Constantine himself had been in his young days, and have deemed that his services merited elevation to the rank of an Augustus. According to the system of Diocletian, twenty years of sovereignty were held to be long enough for the welfare alike of sovereign and of the Empire. Constantine's term was running out. The system was not yet formally abandoned; is it unreasonable to suppose that Crispus considered he had claims to rule, or that Constantine, resolved to keep what he had won, became estranged from one whom he knew he was not treating with generosity or with justice?

As we have said, there is no evidence of any disloyalty on the part of Crispus, but he may have let incautious expressions fall from his lips which would be carried to the ears of his father, and he may have chafed to see himself supplanted by the young princes, his half-brothers. The boy Caesar, Constantius, was named consul with his father for the festival year 326, a distinction which Crispus may justly have thought to belong by right to himself, and he may have seen in this another proof of the of the Empress Fausta, and of her influence over the Emperor. Possibly Crispus was goaded by anger into some indiscreet action, which confirmed Constantine's suspicions; possibly even he committed some act of disobedience which gave Constantine the excuse he sought for. At any rate, in the July or August of 326, Crispus was arrested in Rome and summarily banished to Pola in Istria. Tidings of his death soon followed. Whatever the manner of his death, whether he was beheaded or was poisoned or committed suicide, all the authorities agree that he came to a violent end and that the responsibility rests upon his father, Constantine. Nor was Crispus the only victim. With him fell Licinianus, the son of Licinius and Constantia. He was a promising lad who could not have been more than twelve years of age and could not, therefore, have been guilty of any crime or intrigue against his uncle.

One cannot pass by altogether without mention the story of Zosimus that the reason of Fausta's implacable hatred of Crispus was not ambition for her own children, but a still more ungovernable and much less pardonable passion. Zosimus declares that Fausta was enamored of her step-son, who rejected her overtures, and so fell a victim, like another Hippolytus, to the vengeance of this Roman Phaedra. Most modern historians have rejected the story, as emanating from the lively imagination of a Greek at a loss for a plausible explanation of a mysterious crime, and we may, with tolerable certainty, acquit Fausta of so disgraceful a passion. If, as we suppose, she was the untiring enemy of Crispus, it is at once more charitable and more probable to suppose that the motive of her hate was her fierce ambition for her own sons. For the moment the Empress conquered. But her triumph did not last long. Eutropius tells us that soon afterwards—mox—a vague word equally applicable to a period of days, weeks, or even months—Fausta herself was put to death by Constantine. What was her offence? Philostorgius declares that she was discovered in an intrigue with a groom of the stables—an amour worthy of Messalina herself. But the story stands suspect, especially when taken in conjunction with the legend of her passion for Crispus. The one seems invented to bolster up the other and add to its verisimilitude. The truth is that nothing is known for certain; and the whole episode was probably kept as a profound palace secret. One circumstance, however, mentioned by Aurelius Victor and by Zosimus, merits attention. Both declare that the Empress-mother, Helena, was furious at the murder of Crispus. Zosimus says that she was greatly distressed at her grand-son's suffering, and could hardly contain herself at the news of his death. Aurelius Victor adds that the aged Empress bitterly reproached her son for his cruelty. Evidently, Helena favored Crispus, the son of Minervina—who, like herself, had been forced by the exigencies of State to quit her hus-band's house, and make room for an Emperor's daughter,—in preference to the children of Constantine and Fausta; evidently therefore, Helena and Fausta were rival influences at court, each striving for ascendency. If Crispus's death betokened that Fausta had gained the upper hand, the death of Fausta showed that Helena had succeeded in turning the tables. When Helena violently reproached her son for slaying Crispus, we may be sure that she was aiming her shafts through Constantine at Fausta, and that when she succeeded in rousing the Emperor to remorse she succeeded also in kindling his resentment against his wife. It is said that Fausta was suffocated in a hot bath, but every detail is open to challenge. Eusebius passes over the entire episode without a word. He is not only silent as to the death of Fausta but also as to the death of Crispus. The courtly Bishop refuses to turn even a single look towards the crime-stained Palatine, on whose gates some lampoon writer had set a paper with the bitter epigram:

"Who will care to seek the golden age of Saturn? Ours is the age of jewels, but jewels of Nero's setting"

If Constantine, like Saturn, had devoured his children and had lapsed for the moment into a savage tyrant of Nero's pattern, it was not for Eusebius to judge him. He was writing for edification. Constantine had averred his willingness to cast his cloak over a sinning bishop lest scandal should arise; ought not an ecclesiastical historian to cast the cloak of charitable silence over the crimes of a most Christian Emperor? When, therefore, Eusebius describes how, after the death of Licinius, men cast aside all their former fears, and dared to raise their long-downcast eyes and look up with a smile on their faces and brightness in their glance; how they honored the Emperor in all the beauty of victory and "his most orderly sons and Heaven-beloved Caesars"; and how they straightway forgot their old troubles and all unrighteousness, and gave themselves up to an enjoyment of their present good things and their hope of others to come; it is a healthy corrective to recall the murderous outbreak of ungovernable wrath which made Rome shudder as it listened to the whispered tale of what was taking place in the recesses of the Palatine. The entire subject is one on which it is as fascinating as it is easy to speculate. On the whole, it seems most likely that Constantine's fears had been worked upon to such an extent that he believed himself surrounded by traitors in his own family, that the Empress Fausta had been the leading spirit in the plot to ruin Crispus, and that when the Emperor discovered his mistake he turned in fury upon his wife. It may be, as Eutropius suggests, that his mental balance had been upset by his extraordinary success, that his prosperity and the adulation of the world had been too much for him. That is a charitable theory which, in default of a better, we, too, may as well adopt.

We need not doubt the sincerity of his repentance. Zosimus depicts the Emperor remorsefully begging the priests of the old religion to purify him from his crime, and says that when they sternly refused, Constantine turned to accept the soothing offices of a wandering Egyptian from Spain. Another account, current among pagans, was that he applied for comfort to the philosopher, Sopater, who would have nothing to say to so heinous a sinner, and that he then fell in with certain Christian bishops, who promised him full forgiveness at the price of repentance and baptism. The motive of these legends is as obvious as their falsity. The pagans, in defiance of chronology, sought to explain the Emperor's conversion to Christianity as a result of the murders that lay heavy upon his soul, murders so revolting as only to admit of pardon in the eyes of Christians. Among the late legends of the Byzantine writer Codinus, we find the story that Constantine raised to the memory of Crispus a golden statue, which bore the inscription, "To the son whom I unjustly condemned", and that he fasted and refused the comforts of life for forty days. Of even greater interest is the legend that Constantine was baptized by Sylvester, the Bishop of Rome, and, in gratitude for the promise of pardon, bestowed upon the see of Rome the damnosa hereditas of the Temporal Power.

There is no necessity to discuss at length the once famous, but now simply notorious, Donation of Constantine. The legend is so grotesque that one wonders it ever imposed on the credulity even of the most ignorant. For it represented Constantine as being smitten with leprosy for having persecuted the Church and for having driven the good Pope Sylvester into exile. The Emperor consulted soothsayers, priests, and physicians in turn, and was at last informed that his only chance of cure lay in bathing in the blood of little children. Forthwith, a number of children were collected for this dreadful purpose, but their cries awoke the pity of Constantine and he gave them respite. Then, as he slept, Peter and Paul appeared to him in a dream and bade him let the children go free, recall Sylvester from exile, and submit at his hands to the rite of baptism. This was done; the baptism was administered; Constantine was cured of the leprosy, and in return he made over to Sylvester and his successors full temporal dominion over the city of Rome, the greater part of Italy, and certain other provinces. Such is the story, which was long accepted without demur and confidently appealed to as the origin of the Temporal Power. It is now universally admitted that the whole legend is a fraud and the letter of Constantine to Sylvester announcing the Donation a forgery of the eighth century. Constantine never persecuted the Church; he never had leprosy; he never contemplated bathing in infants' blood; he did not receive the rite of baptism until he was on his death-bed, and he did not hand over to the Pope the fee simple and title deeds of Rome and Italy. The Donation of Constantine belongs to the museum of historical forgeries.

But if the repentance of Constantine did not take the form of stupendous endowments for the Bishop of Rome, we may be tolerably sure that it did manifest itself in the increased zeal of the Emperor for the building of churches, and especially in his munificence to the Christians of Rome. It is tempting, also, to connect with Constantine's remorse and his mother's sorrow for the murder of her grandson the pilgrimage of Helena to Palestine and Jerusalem, which followed almost immediately. Around that visit there clustered many legends which, as time went on, multiplied amazingly. Of these the most famous is that which is known as the Invention of the Cross. This, in its fullest form many centuries after the event, ran something as follows: When Helena reached Jerusalem she asked to be shown the Holy Sepulchre. But no one could tell her where the exact spot was. Buildings had been erected upon Mount Calvary and the adjoining land; a temple of Venus was still standing near the place where the body of Christ must have been laid. Helena instituted a careful search, and the authority of the Emperor's mother would be warrant sufficient for the disturbance of the occupiers. At first their toil met with no success. Then a very clever Jew came forward with a story that he had heard of an old tradition that the site of the Sepulchre lay in such and such a spot; the direction of the excavation was entrusted to him; and the searchers were soon rewarded by finding not only the cave where Christ had lain, but also three crosses. These, it was at once determined, must have been the crosses on which Christ and the two malefactors had suffered. But which had borne the Savior? There was nothing to show, but so sacred an object was sure to be invested with wonder-working powers, and the test was, therefore, easy. So they brought to the spot a dying woman—according to one version, she was already dead—and touched her with the wood of the three crosses. At contact with the first two no change was visible; but the touch of the third recalled her to sensibility and perfect health, and the true Cross stood at once revealed to the adoring worship of all believers. In the wood were two nails. Helena had them carefully sent to Constantine, and he, we are told, had one of them inserted—as something far more precious than rubies—in the Imperial crown, while from the other he fashioned a bit for his horse.

Such is the legend in its most complete form. It directly associates the finding of the Cross with Helena's visit to Jerusalem, and attributes also to her the magnificent church which was raised in the latter part of the reign of Constantine on the site of the Holy Sepulchre. But it must also be added that the first historical mention of the "Invention" is seventy years after the discovery was supposed to have taken place. Eusebius, in describing Helena's pilgrimage, knows nothing of the finding of the Cross, and, while he speaks of the discovery of the Sepulchre, he does not associate it with Helena, though he attributes to her piety the new church at Bethlehem. It was Constantine, according to Eusebius, who built the church on the site of the Holy Sepulchre, and beautified the cave of Bethlehem and the site of the Ascension, but of the finding of the Cross there is not a word—a significant silence, which can only mean that the legend was not yet current when Eusebius composed his "Life" of Constantine. What cannot well be doubted is that the site of the Sepulchre was discovered and cleared in Constantine's reign. The Emperor built upon it one of his finest churches, but popular tradition, with a sure eye for the romantic and the extraordinary, preferred to attribute the origin of the noblest shrine in Palestine to the pious enthusiasm of the aged Helena. Her pilgrimage over, Helena died not long afterwards, and was buried by Constantine with full military honours "in the royal tombs of the reigning city". The phrase points clearly to Constantinople as the place of burial, though Rome also claims this honor.

History is silent as to the events of the next few years. But as the Empire had been free both from civil and foreign war since the downfall of Licinius, we may accept the general statement of Eusebius "that all men enjoyed quiet and untroubled days". Peace was always the greatest interest of the Roman Empire, but it was rarely of long continuance, and in 330 and the two following years we find the Emperor campaigning in person against the Goths and the Sarmatae. The account of these wars in the authorities of the period is so confused and contradictory that it is impossible to obtain a connected narrative.

It was the old familiar story over again. The barbarians had come raiding over the borders. There seems to have been fighting along the entire north-eastern frontier, from the great bend of the Danube to the Tauric Chersonese. Constantine and the legions drove the enemy back, won victories chequered by minor reverses, and finally the Emperor was glad enough in 332 to come to terms with the chiefs of the Gothic nation. Mention is made of a handsome subsidy paid by Constantine to the

Gothic kings, which certainly does not suggest the overwhelming triumph of the Roman arms of which Eusebius speaks when he says that the Emperor was the first to bring them under the yoke and taught them to acknowledge the Romans as their masters. As for the Sarmatae, Eusebius declares that they had been obliged to arm their slaves for their assistance against the attacks of the Scythians, that the slaves had revolted against their old masters, and that in despair the Sarmatae turned to Constantine and asked for shelter on Roman territory. Some of them, says Eusebius, were received into the legions; others were distributed as farmers and tillers of the soil throughout the frontier provinces; and all, he declares, confessed that their misfortunes had really been a blessing in disguise, inasmuch as it had enabled them to exchange their old state of barbarian savagery for the Roman freedom. Probably we shall not be far wrong if we place a different interpretation on the words of Eusebius, and see in the transference of these Sarmatians to the Roman provinces a confession of weakness on the part of Constantine. They were not captives of war. They were rather invited over the borders to keep their kinsmen out, and the Roman Emperor paid for his new subjects in the shape of a handsome subsidy. There can be no other meaning of the curious words of Eutropius that Constantine left behind him a tremendous reputation for generosity with the barbaric nations. Money was not so plentiful in Constantine's exchequer that he gave subsidies for nothing. The suggestion is not that he suffered defeat and bought off hostility; it is rather that he thought it worthwhile, after vindicating the honor of the Roman arms, to pay for the friendship of the vanquished.

On the Eastern frontier peace had remained unbroken throughout Constantine's long reign. Persia had been so shattered by Galerius that King Narses made no attempt to renounce the humiliating treaty which had been imposed upon him. His son, Hormisdas, had likewise acquiesced in the loss of Armenia and what were known as the five provinces beyond the Tigris, and when Hormisdas died, leaving a son still unborn, there was a long regency during which no aggressive movement was made from the Persian side. However, this son, Sapor, proved to be a high-spirited, patriotic, and capable monarch, who was determined to uphold and assert the rights of Persia. It is not known how the peaceful relationship, which had so long subsisted between his country and Rome, came to be broken. According to Eusebius, Sapor sent an embassy to the Emperor, which was received with the utmost cordiality, and Constantine, we are told, took the opportunity of sending back by these same envoys a letter commending to his favorable regard the Christians of Persia. The document contained a very tedious and involved confession of faith by the Emperor, who affirmed his devotion to God and declared his horror at the sight and smell of the blood of sacrifice. "The God I serve", said Constantine, "demands from His worshippers nothing but a pure mind and a spirit undefiled". Then he reminded Sapor how the persecutors of the Church had been destroyed root and branch, and how one of them, Valerian, had graced the triumph of a Persian king. He, therefore, confidently committed the Christians, who "honored by their presence some of the fairest regions of Persia," to the generosity and protection of their sovereign.

This remarkable letter suggests that Sapor had been alarmed at the growth of Christianity in his dominions, and by no means looked upon his Christian subjects as lending lustre and distinction to his realm. Whether he replied to what he may well have regarded as a veiled threat, we do not know, but in 335 we hear of what Eusebius calls "an insurrection of barbarians in the East", and Constantine prepared for war against Persia. In other words, Sapor had fomented an insurrection in the provinces beyond the Tigris and was claiming his lost heritage. Constantine laid his military plans before the bishops of his court. These declared their intention of accompanying him into the field, to the great delight, we are assured, of the Emperor, who ordered a tent to be made for his service in the shape of a church, while Sapor, in alarm, sent envoys to sue for a peace which the most peaceful-minded of kings was only too ready to grant. Such is the story of Eusebius, but it is evident that the Eastern legions had been carefully mobilized, and, whether such a peace was granted or not, the death of Constantine in 337 was the signal for a renewal of the old conflict between the two great empires of the world, and for a war which lasted without intermission through the reigns of Constantine's sons and that of his nephew Julian.

THE FOUNDATION OF CONSTANTINOPLE

WE come now to the greatest political achievement of Constantine's reign—the foundation of a new Rome. Let us ask at the outset what led him to take a step so decisive as the transference of the world's metropolis from the Italian peninsula to the borders of Europe and Asia. The assignation of merely personal motives will not suffice. We are told by Zosimus that Rome was distasteful to Constantine, because it reminded him of the son and the wife who had fallen victims to his savage resentment. He was uneasy in the palace on the Palatine, whose very stones suggested murder and sudden death, and whose walls were cognizant of unnumbered treasons. What Zosimus says may very well be true. Constantine's conscience was likely to give him less peace in Rome than elsewhere. But the personal wishes of even the greatest men cannot bind the generations which come after them. There have been cities founded by the caprice of royal tyrants which have flourished for a season and then vanished. Seleucia is perhaps the most striking example, and scarcely a mound remains to mark its site. But most of the historic cities of the world owe their greatness and their permanence not to the whims of royal founders, but to geographical and strategic position. Rome was not uncrowned by Constantine because he could not forget within its walls the crimes which had stained his hands with blood.

It is also to be remembered that others had already set the example of despoiling of her dignities the ancient Queen of the Nations. We have seen how in the western half of the Empire great Imperial cities had been rising within easy reach of the frontiers. In far-off Britain London might be the most opulent city, but York was the chief residence of the Cesar of the West when he visited the island. In Gaul Treves had outstripped Lyons in dignity and wealth, and was now the centre of military and administrative power. Even in Italy Milan had grown at the expense of Rome; it was nearer to the frontier and, therefore, nearer to the armies. Rome lay out of the way. Diocletian, again, had favored Nicomedia in Bithynia. In other words, Rome was ceasing to be the one centre of gravity of the ancient world, or, to express the same truth in another form, the Roman world was ceasing to be one. Diocletian had practically acknowledged this when he founded his system of Augusti and Caesars. With the subdivision of administrative and executive power there naturally ceases to be one supreme metropolis. It would be a mistake to suppose that Constantine, in founding a new Rome, deliberately hastened the rapid tendency towards separation. The very name of New Rome which he gave his city indicates his belief that he was merely moving Rome from the Tiber to the Bosphorus—merely changing to a more convenient site. But the fact that this name dropped out of use almost at once, and that the city was called after him, not in Latin but in Greek, shows how strongly the current was flowing towards political division.

But what attracted Constantine towards Byzantium? Precisely, of course, those advantages of situation which have attracted modern statesmen. Everyone knows the story of how, after the Peace of Tilsit, the Tsar Alexander constantly pressed Napoleon to allow him to take Constantinople. Napoleon at length told his secretary, M. de Méneval, to bring him the largest map of Europe which he could procure, and, after poring over it for some time, he looked up and exclaimed, "Constantinople! Never! It is the Empire of the world". Was Napoleon right? The publicists of today return different answers. The Mediterranean is not the all-important sea it once was, and the strategical importance of Constantinople has been greatly modified by the Suez Canal and the British occupation of Egypt. But if Napoleon's exclamation seems rather theatrical to us, it would not have seemed so to Constantine, whose world was so much smaller than ours and presented such different strategical problems calling for solution. Constantine had won the world when he defeated Licinius and captured Byzantium: he determined to keep it where he had won it.

It is said by some of the late historians that he was long in coming to a decision, and that he carefully weighed the rival claims of other cities.

There was his birthplace, Naissus, in Pannonia, though we cannot suppose that Constantine seriously thought of making this his metropolis. There was Sardica on the Danube, the modern Belgrade and capital of Servia, a city well adapted by its position for playing an important role in history, and conveniently near the most dangerous frontier of the Empire. "My Rome is at Sardica", Constantine was fond of declaring at one period of his career, according to a tradition which was perpetuated by the Byzantine historians. Another possible choice was Nicomedia, which had commended itself to Diocletian, and, finally, there was Salonica, which even now has only to fall into capable hands to become one of the most prosperous cities of eastern Europe.

According to Zosimus, even when Constantine had determined to found his new city at the point where Europe and Asia are divided by the narrow straits, he selected first the Asiatic side. The historian says that he actually began to build and that the foundations of the abandoned city were still to be seen in his day between Troy and Pergamum. But the story is more than doubtful. Legend has naturally been busy with the circumstances attending the Emperor's final choice of Byzantium. Was it inspired, as some say, by the flight of an eagle from Chrysopolis towards Byzantium? Or, while Constantine slept in Byzantium, did the aged tutelar genius of the place appear to him in a dream and then become transformed into a beautiful maiden, to whom he offered the insignia of royalty? Interesting as these legends are, we need seek no further explanation of Constantine's choice than his own good judgment and experience. He was fully aware of the extraordinary natural strength of Byzantium, for his armies had found great difficulty in taking it by assault; the supreme beauty of the site and its many other qualifications for becoming a great capital were manifest to his eyes every time he approached it. Byzantium had long been one of the most renowned cities of antiquity. Even in the remotest times the imagination of the Greeks had been powerfully affected by the stormy Euxine that lay in what was to them the far north-east, guarding the Golden Fleece and the Apples of the Hesperides, a wild region of big rivers, savage lands, and boisterous seas. Daring seamen of Megara, in the seventh century BC, had effected a landing at the mouth of the Bosphorus, where Io had fled across from Europe to Asia, turning their galleys up the smooth estuary that still bears its ancient name of the Golden Horn. Apollo had told them to fix their habitation "over against the city of the blind," and this they had rightly judged could be no other than Chalcedon, for men must needs have been blind to choose the Asiatic in preference to the European shore.

The little colony founded by Byzas, the Megarian, had prospered marvelously, though it had experienced to the full all the vicissitudes of fortune. It had fallen before the Persian King Darius; it had been wrested from him after a long siege by Pausanias, the hero of Plataea, when the Greeks rolled back the tide of invasion. In turn the subject and successful rival of Athens, Byzantium gained new glory by withstanding for two years the assaults of Philip of Macedon. Thanks to the eloquence of Demosthenes, Athens sent help in the shape of ships and men, and, in commemoration of a night attack of the Macedonians successfully foiled by the opportune rising of the moon, Byzantium placed upon her coins the crescent and the star, which for four centuries and a half have been the familiar symbols of Turkish sovereignty. Byzantium grew rich on commerce. It was the port of call at which every ship entering or leaving the Bosphorus was bound to touch; no craft sailed the Euxine without paying dues to the city at its mouth. Polybius, in a very interesting passage, points out how Byzantium occupied "the most secure and advantageous position of any city in our quarter of the world, as far as the sea is concerned". Then he continues:

"The Pontus, therefore, being rich in what the rest of the world requires to support life, the Byzantines are absolute masters in this respect. For the first necessaries of existence, cattle and slaves, are admittedly supplied by the region of the Pontus in better quality and greater profusion than elsewhere. In the matter of luxuries, they supply us with honey, wax, and salt fish, while they take our superfluous olive oil and wines".

It was Byzantium, therefore, which kept open the straits, and Polybius speaks of the city as a common benefactor of the Greeks. When the Romans began to appear on the scene as a world-power, Byzantium made terms with the Senate. It well suited the Roman policy to have a powerful ally on the Bosphorus, strong in the ships in which Rome was usually deficient. As a libera et federata civitas, Byzantium enjoyed a more or less prosperous history until the days of Vespasian, who stripped it of its privileges. These were restored, but a shattering blow overtook the city at the close of the second century, when Septimus Severus took it by storm. Angry at its long resistance, Severus leveled its fortifications to the ground,—a work of endless toil, for the stones and blocks had been so clamped together that the walls were one solid mass. However, before he died, he repented him of the destruction which he had wrought and gave orders for the walls to be built anew. It was the Byzantium as rebuilt by Severus that Constantine determined to refound on a far more splendid scale.

No subsequent historian has improved upon the glowing passage in which Gibbon summarizes the incomparable advantages of its site, which appears, as he well says, to have been "founded by Nature for the centre and capital of a great monarchy." We may quote the passage in full from his seventeenth chapter:

"Situated in the forty-first degree of latitude—practically the same, it may be noted, as that of Rome, Madrid, and New York—the imperial city commanded from her seven hills the opposite shores of Europe and Asia; the climate was healthy and temperate; the soil fertile; the harbor secure and capacious; and the approach on the side of the continent was of small extent and easy of defence. The Bosphorus and Hellespont may be considered as the two gates of Constantinople; and the prince who procured those important passages could always shut them against a naval enemy and open them to the fleets of commerce. The preservation of the Eastern provinces may, in some degree, be ascribed to the policy of Constantine, as the barbarians of the Euxine, who, in the preceding age, had poured down their armaments into the heart of the Mediterranean, soon desisted from the exercise of piracy and despaired of facing this insurmountable barrier. When the gates of the Hellespont and Bosphorus were shut, the capital still enjoyed, within their spacious inclosure, every production which could supply the wants, or gratify the luxury, of its numerous inhabitants. The seacoasts of Thrace and Bithynia, which languish under the weight of Turkish oppression, still exhibit a rich prospect of vineyards, of gardens and plentiful harvests;

and the Propontis has ever been renowned for an inexhaustible store of the most exquisite fish, that are taken in their stated seasons without skill and almost without labor. But, when the passages of the Straits were thrown open for trade, they alternately admitted the natural and artificial riches of the North and South, of the Euxine and the Mediterranean. Whatever rude commodities were collected in the forests of Germany and Scythia, as far as the sources of the Tanais and the Borysthenes, whatever was manufactured by the skill of Europe and of Asia, the corn of Egypt and the gems and spices of the farthest India, were brought by the varying winds into the port of Constantinople, which, for many ages, attracted the commerce of the ancient world".

From a strategical point of view, it was of inestimable advantage that the capital and military centre of the Empire should be within striking distance of the route taken by the nomad populations of the East as they pressed towards the West, at the head of the Euxine. The Scythians, the Goths, and the Sarmatae had all crossed that great region; the Huns were to cross it in the coming centuries. Placed on shipboard at Constantinople, the legions of the Empire could be swiftly conveyed into the Euxine, and could penetrate up the Danube, Tanais, or Borysthenes to confront the invaders where the danger threatened most.

The story of how Constantine marked out the boundaries of his new capital is well known. Not content with the narrow limits of the ancient city—which included little more than the district now known as Seraglio Point—Constantine crossed the old boundary, spear in hand, and walked with his attendants along the shores of the Propontis, tracing the line as he went. His companions expressed astonishment that he continued so far afield, and respectfully drew the Emperor's attention to the enormous circuit which the walls would have to enclose. Constantine rebuked them. "I shall still advance," he said, "until He, the invisible guide who marches before me, thinks it right to stop." The legend is first found in Philostorgius, and it is not of much importance. But Constantine, as usual, took care to foster the belief that his will was God's will, even in the matter of founding Constantinople, and that he had but obeyed the clearly expressed command of Heaven. In one of his edicts he incidentally refers to Constantinople as the city which he founded in obedience to the mandate of God. It is a phrase which has meant much or little according to the character of the kings who have employed it. With Constantine it meant much, and, above all, he wished it to mean much to his subjects.

Archeologists have not found it an easy task to trace the line of the walls of Constantine, especially on the landward side. It followed the coast of the Propontis from Seraglio Point, the Emperor adding height and strength to the wall of Severus and extending it to the gate of St. Emilianus, which formed the south-west limit of his city. This section was thrown down by an earthquake and had to be rebuilt by Arcadius and Theodosius II. From St. Emilianus the landward wall, with seven gates and ninety-five towers, stretched across from the waters of the Propontis to those of the Golden Horn, which was reached, it is supposed, at a point near the modern Djubali Kapou. This was demolished when the city had outgrown it, and Theodosius erected the new great wall which still stands almost unimpaired. The course of the old one can hardly be traced, but it is generally assumed that it did not include all the seven hills of Constantinople, though New Rome, like Old Rome, delighted in the epithet of Septicollis, -the Seven-Hilled. Along the Golden Horn no wall was built until five centuries had elapsed. On this side Constantine considered that the city was adequately protected by the waters of the estuary, closed against the attack of an enemy by a huge iron chain, supported on floats, which stretched from the Acropolis of St. Demetrius across to the modern Galata. Confidence in the chain— some links of which are still preserved in the Turkish arsenal—seems to have been thoroughly justified. Only once in all the many sieges of Constantinople was it successfully pierced, when, in 1203, the Crusading Latins burst in upon the capital of the East.

Within the area we have described, great if compared with the original Byzantium, but small in comparison with the size to which it grew by the reign of Theodosius II, Constantine planned his city. Probably no great capital has ever been built so rapidly. It was finished, or so nearly finished that it was possible to hold a solemn service of dedication, by May, 330—that is to say, within four years. Throughout that period Constantine seems to have had no thought for anything else. He urged on the work with an enthusiasm equal to that which Dido had manifested in encouraging her Tyrians to raise the walls of Carthage.

The passion for bricks and mortar consumed him. Like Augustus, he thought that a great imperial city could not be too lavishly adorned as a visible proof of present magnificence and a guarantee of future permanence. Nor was it in Constantinople alone that he built. Throughout his reign new public buildings kept rising in Rome, Jerusalem, Antioch, and the cities of Gaul. His impatience manifested itself in his letters to his provincial governors. "Send me word", he wrote imperiously to one of them, "not that work has been started on your buildings, but that the buildings are finished". To build Constantinople he ransacked the entire world, first for architects and builders, and then for art treasures. With such impetuous haste there was sure to be scamped work. Some of the buildings crumbled at the first slight tremor of earthquake or did not even require that impulse from without to collapse into ruin. It is by no means impossible that the havoc which seems to have been wrought in Constantinople by earthquakes during the next two or three centuries was largely due, not to the violence of the seismic disturbances but to insecure foundations and bad materials. The cynical Julian compared the city of Constantine to the fabled gardens of Adonis, which were planted afresh each morning and withered anew each night. Doubtless there was a substantial basis of fact for that bitter jibe.

Yet, when all allowances are made, it was a marvelous city which Constantine watched as it rose from its foundation. Those who study the archeology of Constantinople in the rich remains which have survived in spite of Time and the Turk, are surprised to find how constantly the history of the particular spot which they are studying takes them straight back to Constantine. Despite the multitude of Emperors and Sultans who have succeeded him, each anxious to leave his mark behind him in stone, or brick, or marble, Constantinople is still the city of Constantine. In the centre, he laid out the Augusteum, the ancient equivalent, as it has well been pointed out, of the modern Place Imperiale. It was a large open space, paved throughout in marble, but of unknown shape, and historians have disagreed upon the probability of its having been circular, square, or of the shape of a narrow rectangle. It was full of noble statuary, and was surrounded by an imposing pile of stately buildings. To the north lay the great church of Sancta Sophia; on the east the Senate House of the Augustum, so called to distinguish it from the Senate House of the Forum; on the south lay the palace, entered by an enormous brazen gate, called Chalce, the palace end of the Hippodrome, and the Baths of Zeuxippus. The street connecting the Augustum with the Forum of Constantine was known as or Middle-street, and was entered on the western side. In the Augustum, which later Emperors filled with famous statues, there stood in Constantine's day a single marble column known as the Milion—from which were measured distances throughout the Empire,—a marble group representing Constantine and Helena standing on either side of a gigantic cross, and a second statue of Helena upon a pedestal of porphyry. It was in this Augustum, moreover, that was to stand for a thousand years the huge equestrian statue of Justinian, known through all the world and described by many a traveler before the capture of the city by the Turks, who broke it into a thousand pieces.

To the west of the Augustum lay the Forum of Constantine, elliptical in form and surrounded by noble colonnades, which terminated at either end in a spacious portico in the shape of a triumphal arch. In the centre, which, according to an old tradition, marked the very spot on which Constantine had pitched his camp when besieging Licinius, stood, and still stands, though in sadly mutilated and shattered guise, the Column of Constantine, which has long been known either as the Burnt Pillar, owing to the damage which it has suffered by fire, or as the Porphyry Pillar, because of the material of which it was composed. There were eight drums of porphyry in all, brought specially from Rome, each about ten feet in height, bound with wide bands of brass wrought into the shape of laurel wreaths. These rested upon a stylobate of white marble, some nineteen feet high, which in turn stood upon a stereobate of similar height composed of four spacious steps. Sacred relics were enclosed—or are said to have been enclosed—within this pediment, including things so precious as Mary Magdalene's alabaster box, the crosses of the two thieves who had suffered with Christ upon Mount Calvary, the adze with which Noah had fashioned the Ark out of rough, primeval timber, and— in strange company—the very Palladium of ancient Rome, transported from the Capitol to an alien and a rival soil. At the foot of the column there was placed the following inscription: "0 Christ, Ruler and Master of the world, to Thee have I now consecrated this obedient city and this sceptre and the power of Rome. Guard and deliver it from every harm".

At the summit of the column was a colossal statue of Apollo in bronze, filched from Athens, where it was believed to be a genuine example of Pheidias. But before the statue had been raised into position, it suffered unworthy mutilation. The head of Apollo was removed and replaced by a head of Constantine. This may be interpreted as a confession of the sculptors of the day that they were unable to produce a statue worthy of their great Emperor; but the fact that a statue of Apollo was chosen for this doubtful honor of mutilation is worth at least passing remark, when we remember that before his conversion Constantine had selected Apollo for special reverence. It is certainly strange that the first Christian Emperor should have been willing to be represented, on the site which was ever afterwards to be associated with his name, by a statue round which clustered so many pagan associations. He did not even disdain the pagan inscription, "To Constantine shining like the Sun"; nor did he reject the pagan attribute of a radiated crown around the head. In the right hand of Apollo the old Greek artist had placed a lance; in the left a globe. That globe was now surmounted by a cross and lo! Apollo had become Constantine; the most radiant of the gods of Olympus had become the champion of Christ upon earth. The fate of this statue—which was held in such superstitious reverence that for centuries all horsemen dismounted before passing it, while below it, on every first day of September, Emperor, Patriarch, and clergy assembled to chant hymns of prayer and praise—may be briefly told. In 477 the globe was thrown down by an earthquake. The lance suffered a like fate in 541, while the statue itself came crashing to earth in 1105, killing a number of persons in its fall. The column was then surmounted by a cross, and fire and time have reduced it to its present almost shapeless and unrecognizable mass.

Close to the Augustum there began to rise the stately magnificence of the Imperial Palace, the Great Palace, as it was called to distinguish it from all others. This was really a cluster of palaces spread over an enormous area, a self-contained city within itself, strongly protected with towers and walls. Here were the Imperial residences, gardens, churches, barracks, and baths, and for eight hundred years, until this quarter was forsaken for the palace of Blachernae in another region of the city, Emperors continued to build and rebuild on this favored site. In later years the Great Palace consisted of an interconnected group of buildings bearing such names as Chrysotriklinon, Trikonchon, Daphne,—so called from a diviner's column brought to Constantinople from the Grove of Daphne near Antioch,—Chalce, Boucoleon, and Manavra. One at least of these dated back to Constantine. This was the Porphyry Palace, with a high pyramidal roof, constructed of porphyry brought especially from Rome. It was dedicated to the service of the ladies of the Imperial Family, who retired thither to be away from the vexations, intrigues, and anxieties of everyday life during the time of their pregnancy. In the seclusion of this Porphyry Palace they were undisturbed and secure, and the children born within walls thus sacred to Imperial maternity were distinguished by the title of "Porphyrogeniti", which plays so prominent a part in Byzantine history.

Constantine built below ground as well as above. One of the principal drawbacks—perhaps the only one—to the perfect suitability of the site of Constantinople was that it contained very few natural springs. Water, therefore, had to be brought into the town by gigantic aqueducts and stored in cisterns, some small, some of enormous size, which must have cost fabulous sums. The two greatest of these are still in good preservation after nearly sixteen centuries of use. One is the Cistern of Philoxenos, called by the Turks Bin Bir Derek, or the Thousand and One Columns. The columns stand in sixteen rows of fourteen columns each, each column consisting of three shafts, and each shaft being eighteen feet in height, though all the lower and most of the middle tiers have long been hidden by masses of impacted earth. Philoxenos, whose name is thus immortalized in this stupendous work, came to Constantinople from Rome at the request of the Emperor, and lavished his fortune upon the construction of this cistern in proof of his public spirit and in order to please his master. Assistance was also invited from the public. And just as in our own day subscriptions are often coaxed out of reluctant purses by deft appeal to the harmless vanity which delights to see one's own name inscribed upon a foundation stone, so in this Cistern of Philoxenos there are still to be deciphered upon the columns the names of the donors, names, as Mr. Grosvenor points out in his most interesting account of these cisterns, which are wholly Greek. "It is a striking evidence", he says, "how little Roman was the Romanized capital, that every inscription is in Greek". The second great cistern is the Royal or Basilike Cistern, begun by Constantine and restored by Justinian, which is called by the Turks Yeri Batan Serai, or the Underground Palace. This is supported by three hundred and thirty-six columns, standing twelve feet apart in twenty-eight symmetrical rows. The cistern is three hundred and ninety feet long and a hundred and seventy-four feet wide, and still supplies water from the Aqueduct of Valens as fresh as when its first stone was laid.

The chief glories of Constantinople, however, were the Hippodrome and the churches. With the latter we may deal very briefly, the more so because the world-renowned St. Sophia is not the St. Sophia which Constantine built, but the work of Justinian. Constantine's church, on which he and many of his successors lavished their treasures, was burnt to the ground and utterly consumed in the tumult of the Nika which laid half the city in ashes. Nor had St. Sophia been intended to be the metropolitan church. That distinction belonged to the church which Constantine had dedicated not to the Wisdom but to the Peace of God, to St. Irene. It, too, shared the fate of the sister church in the tumult of the Nika, and was similarly rebuilt by Justinian. This was regarded as the Patriarchal church and called by that name, for here the Patriarch conducted the daily services, since the church had no clergy of its own. It was at the high altar of St. Irene that the Patriarch Alexander in 335 prayed day and night that God would choose between himself and Arius; while the answer—or what was taken for the answer—was delivered at the foot of Constantine's Column. It was in this church nearly half a century later that the great Arian controversy was ended in 381, and here that the Holy Spirit was declared equal to the Father and the Son. Since the Ottoman conquest this church—the sole survivor of all that in Byzantine times once stood in the region of what is now the Seraglio—has been used as an arsenal and military museum. On its walls hang suits of armor, helmets, maces, spears, and swords of a bygone age, while the ground floor is stacked with modern rifles. The temple of "the Peace that

Passeth Understanding" has been transformed into a temple of war. Mr. Grosvenor well sums up its history in the fine phrase, "Saint Irene is a prodigious hearthstone, on which all the ashes of religion and of triumph and surrender have grown cold".

There is yet another church in Constantinople which calls for notice. It is the one which Constantine dedicated to the Holy Trinity, though its name was soon afterwards changed to that of the Holy Apostles, in honor of the remains of Timothy, Andrew, and Luke, the body of St. Mathias, the head of James, the brother of Jesus, and the head of St. Euphemia, which were enshrined under the great High Altar. So rich a store of relics was held to justify the change of name. It was from the pulpit of this Church of the Holy Apostles that John Chrysostom denounced the Empress Eudoxia, but the chief title of the building to remembrance is that it was for centuries the Mausoleum of Constantinople's Emperors and Patriarchs. None but members of the reigning house, or the supreme Heads of the Eastern Church, were accorded burial within its walls. Constantine built a splendid Heroon at the entrance, just as Augustus had built a magnificent Mausoleum on the Field of Mars. When it could hold no more, Justinian built another. Each monarch, robed and crowned in death as in life, had a marble sarcophagus of his own; no one church in the world's history can ever have contained the dust of so much royalty, sanctity, and orthodoxy. Apart from the rest lay the tombs of Julian the Apostate and the four Arian Emperors, as though cut off from communion with their fellows, and removed as far outside the pale as the respect due to an anointed Emperor would permit. It was not the conquering Ottoman but the Latin Crusaders, the robbers of the West, who pillaged the sacred tombs, stole their golden ornaments, and flung aside the bones which had reposed there during the centuries.

We pass from the churches to the Hippodrome, a Campus Martius and Coliseum combined, which now bears the Turkish name of Atmeidan, a translation of its ancient Greek name. Its glories have passed away. It has shrunk to little more than a third of its original proportions, and is merely a rough exercise ground surrounded by houses. But it preserves within its attenuated frame three of the most famous monuments of antiquity, around which it is possible to recreate its ancient splendors. These three monuments are the Egyptian obelisk, the Serpent Pillar, and a crumbling column that looks as though it must snap and fall in the first storm that blows. They preserve for us the exact line of the old spina, round which the charioteers used to drive their steeds in furious rivalry. The obelisk stood exactly in the centre of the building, which was shaped like a narrow magnet with long arms. From the obelisk to the middle of the sphendone—that is to say, the curving top of a magnet, or the loop of a sling—was 695 feet, while the width was 395 feet. The Hippodrome, therefore, was nearly 1409 feet long by 400 wide, the proportions of three and a half to one being those of the Circus Maximus at Rome. It lay north-north-east, conforming in shape to the Augustum. The Hippodrome had been begun in 203 by Severus, to whom belongs the credit of having conceived its stupendous plan, but it had remained uncompleted for a century and a quarter.

At the northern end, reaching straight across from side to side, was a lofty structure, raised upon pillars and enclosed within gates. Here were the stables and storehouses, known to the Romans by the name of Carceres and to the Greeks as Mangana. Above was a broad tribunal, in the centre of which, and supported by marble pillars, stood the Kathisma, with the throne of the Emperor well in front. This, in modern parlance, was the Royal Box, and, when the Emperor was present, the tribunal below was thronged with the high dignitaries of State and the Imperial Bodyguard, while, in front of the throne, but at a rather lower level, was the pillared platform, called the Pi, where stood the royal standard-bearers. Behind this entire structure, fully three hundred feet wide and so spacious that it was dignified with the name of palace and contained long suites of royal apartments, was the Church of St. Stephen, through which, by means of a spiral stairway, access was obtained to the Kathisma. It was always used by the Emperor on his visits to the Hippodrome, and was considered to be profaned if trodden by meaner mortals. The palace, raised as it was over the stables of the Hippodrome and looking down the entire length of the arena, had no communication with the body of the building, and on either side the long arms of the Hippodrome terminated in blank walls. The first tier of seats, known as the Bouleutikon or Podium, was raised thirteen feet above the arena. This was the place of distinction. At the back rose tier upon tier, broken half-way by a wide passage, while at the very top of all was a broad promenade running right round the building from pole to pole of the magnet.

This was forty feet above the ground, and the benches and promenades were composed of gleam-ing marble raised upon arches of brick. There was room here for eighty thousand spectators to assemble in comfort, and one seems to hear ringing down the ages the frenzied shouts of the multitudes which for centuries continued to throng this mighty building, of which now scarce one stone stands upon another. Mr. Grosvenor very justly says that "no theatre, no palace, no public building has today a promenade so magnificent. Within was all the pomp and pageantry of all possible imperial and popular contest and display; without, piled high around, were the countless imposing structures of that city which for more than half a thousand years was the most elegant, the most civilized, almost the only civilized and polished city in the world. Beyond was the Golden Horn, crowded with shipping; the Bosphorus in its winding beauty; the Marmora, studded with islands and fringing the Asiatic coast, the long line of the Arganthonius Mountains and the peaks of the Bithynian Olympus, glittering with eternal snow—all combining in a panorama which even now no other city of mankind can rival".

In the middle of the arena stood the spina, a marble wall, four feet high and six hundred feet long, with the Goal of the Blues at the northern end facing the throne, and that of the Greens facing the sphendone. The spina was decorated with the choicest statuary, including the three surviving monuments. Of these the Egyptian obelisk, belonging to the reign of Thotmes III, had already stood for more centuries in Egypt than have elapsed since Constantine transported it to his new capital. When it arrived, the engineers could not raise it into position and it remained prone until, in 381, one Proclus, a prefect of the city, succeeded in erecting it upon copper cubes. The shattered column belongs to a much later epoch than that of Constantine. It was set up by Constantine VIII Porphyrogenitus, and once glittered in the sun, for it was covered with plates of burnished brass. The third, and by far the most interesting monument of the three, is the famous column of twisted serpents from Delphi. Its romantic history never grows dull by repetition. For this is that serpent column of Corinthian brass which was dedicated to Apollo by the thankful and exultant Greeks after the battle of Plataea, when the hosts of the Persian Xerxes were thrust back from the soil of Greece never to return. It bears upon its coils the names of the thirty-one Greek cities which fought for freedom, and there is still to be seen, inscribed in slightly larger characters than the rest, the name of the Tenians, who, as Herodotus tells us, succeeded in proving to the satisfaction of their sister states that they deserved inclusion in so honorable a memorial. The history of this column from the fifth century before the Christian era down to the present time is to be read in a long succession of Greek, Roman, medieval, and modern historians; and as late as the beginning of the eighteenth century the three heads of the serpents were still in their place. But even in its mutilated state there is perhaps no relic of antiquity which can vie in interest with this column, associated as it was in the day of its fashioning with Pausanias and Themistocles, with Xerxes and with Mardonius. We have then to think of it standing for seven centuries in the holiest place of all Hellas, the shrine of Apollo at Delphi. There it was surmounted by a golden tripod, on which sat the priestess who uttered the oracles which, in important crises, prompted the policy and guided the development of the cities of Greece. The column is hollow, and it is possible that the mephitic exhalations, which are supposed to have stupefied the priestess when she was possessed by the god, mounted up the interior of the spiral. The golden tripod was stolen during the wars with Philip of Macedon; Constantine replaced it by another when he brought the column from Delphi to Constantinople. And there, surviving all the vicissitudes through which the city has passed, still stands the column, still fixed to the pedestal upon which Constantine mounted it, many feet below the present level of the Atmeidan, still an object of superstition to Christian as well as to the Turk, and owing, no doubt, its marvelous preservation to the indefinable awe which clings, even in ruin, to the sacred relics of a discredited religion.

To the Hippodrome itself there were four principal entrances. The gate of the Blues was close by the Carceres or Mangana, on the western side, with the gate of the Greens facing it. At the other end, just where the long straight line was broken and the building began to curve into the sphendone, was a gate on the eastern side which bore the ill-omened name of the Gate of the Dead, opposite another, the name of which is not known. The gate of the Blues—the royal faction—was the grand entrance for all state processions. Such was the outward form of the famous Hippodrome, and Mr. Grosvenor justly dwells on the imposing vastness and beauty of its external appearance.

"The walls were of brick, laid in arches and faced by a row of Corinthian pillars. What confronted the spectator's eye was a wall in superposed and continuous arches, seen through an endless colonnade. Seventeen columns were still erect upon their bases in 1529. Gyllius, who saw them, says that their diameter was three and eleven-twelfths feet. Each was twenty-eight feet high, and pedestal and capital added seven feet more. They stood eleven feet apart. Hence, deducting for the gates, towers, and palace, at least two hundred and sixty columns would be required in the circuit. If one, with the curiosity of a traveler, wished to journey round the entire perimeter, he must continue on through a distance of three thousand and fifteen feet, before his pilgrimage ended at the spot where it had begun; and ever, as he toiled along, there loomed into the air that prodigious mass, forty feet above his head. No wonder that there remained, even in the time of the Sultan Souleiman, enough to construct that most superb of mosques, the Souleimanieh, from the fallen columns, the splintered marbles, the brick and stone of the Hippodrome".

But it was not merely the shell of the Hippodrome that was imposing by reason of its size and magnificence. It was filled with the choicest art treasures of the ancient world. Constantine stole masterpieces with the catholicity of taste, the excellence of artistic judgment, and the callous indifference to the rights of ownership which characterized Napoleon. He stripped the world naked of its treasures, as St. Jerome neatly remarked. Rome and its conquering proconsuls and propertors had done the same. Constantine now robbed Rome and took whatever Rome had left. Greece was still a fruitful quarry. We have already spoken of the Serpent Column, which was torn from Delphi. The historians have preserved for us the names of a number of other famous works of art which adorned the spina and the promenade of the Hippodrome. There was a Brazen Eagle, clutching a writhing snake in its talons and rising in the air with wings outspread; the Hercules of Lysippus, of a size so heroic that it measured six feet from the foot to the knee; the Brazen Ass and its driver, a mere copy of which Augustus had offered to his own city of Nicopolis founded on the shores of Actium; the Poisoned Bull; the Angry Elephant; the gigantic figure of a woman holding in her hand a horse and its rider of life size; the Calydonian Boar; eight Sphinxes, and last, but by no means least, the Horses of Lysippus. These horses have a history with which no other specimens of equine statuary can compare. They first adorned a temple at Corinth. Taken to Rome by Memmius when he laid Corinth in ashes, they were placed before the Senate House. Nero removed them that they might grace his triumphal arch; Trajan, with juster excuse, did the same. Constantine had them sent to Constantinople. Then, after nearly nine centuries had passed, they were again packed up and transported back to Italy. The aged Dandolo had claimed them as part of his share of the booty and sent them to Venice. There they remained for almost six centuries more until Napoleon cast covetous eyes upon them and had them taken to Paris to adorn his Arc de Triomphe. On his downfall Paris was compelled to restore them to Venice and the horses of Lysippus paw the air once more above the roof of St. Mark's Cathedral.

We have thus briefly enumerated the most magnificent public buildings with which Constantine adorned his new capital, and the choicest works of art with which these were further embellished. The Emperor pressed on the work with extraordinary activity. No one believes the story of Codinus that only nine months elapsed between the laying of the first stone and the formal dedication which took place in the Hippodrome on May 11th, 330, but it is only less wonderful that so much should have been done in four years. The same untrustworthy author also tells a strange story of how Constantine took advantage of the absence of some of his officers on public business to build exact models of their Roman mansions in Constantinople, and transport all their household belongings, families, and households to be ready for them on their return as a pleasant surprise. What is beyond doubt is that the Emperor did offer the very greatest inducements to the leading men of Rome to leave Rome for good and make Constantinople their home. He even published an edict that no one dwelling in Asia Minor should be allowed to enter the Imperial service unless he built himself a house in Constantinople. Peter the Great issued a like order when he founded St. Petersburg and opened a window looking on Europe. The Emperor changed the destination of the corn ships of Egypt from Rome to Constantinople, established a lavish system of distributions of wheat and oil and even of money and wine, and created at the cost of the treasury an idle and corrupt proletariate. He thus transported to his new capital all the luxuries and vices of the old.

ARIUS AND ATHANASIUS

WE have seen how, at the conclusion of the Council of Nicaea, it looked as if the Church had entered into her rest. The day of persecution was over; Christianity had found in the Emperor an ardent and impetuous champion; a creed had been framed which seemed to establish upon a sure foundation the deepest mysteries of the faith; heresy not only lay under anathema, but had been reduced to silence. Throughout the East— the West had remained practically untroubled—the feeling was one of confidence and joy. Constantine rejoiced as though he had won a personal victory; his subjects, we are told, thought the kingdom of Christ had already begun. When Gregory, the Illuminator of Armenia, met his son, Aristaces, returning from Nicaea and heard from his lips the text of the new creed, he at once exclaimed: "Yea, we glorify Him who was before the ages, by adoring the Holy Trinity and the one Godhead of the Father, and of the Son and of the Holy Ghost, now and forever, through ages and ages".

Moreover, the Emperor's violent edicts against the Arians, and the banishment of Eusebius and Theognis, all indicated a settled and rooted conviction which nothing could shake, while the death of the Patriarch Alexander of Alexandria and the election of Athanasius in his stead must have strengthened enormously the Catholic party in Egypt and, indeed, throughout the East. Alexander had died within a few months of his return from Nicaea, in the early part of 326. He is said, when on his death-bed, to have foretold the elevation of Athanasius and the trials which lay before him. He had called for Athanasius—who at the moment was away from Egypt—and another Athanasius, who was present in the room, answered for the absent one. The dying man, however, was not deceived and said: "Athanasius, you think you have escaped, but you will not; you cannot". We need not recount the stories which the malignity of his enemies invented in order to cast discredit upon Athanasius' election. There is no reason to doubt either its validity or its overwhelming popularity in Alexandria, where, while the Egyptian bishops were in session, the Catholics outside the building kept up the unceasing cry: "Give us Athanasius, the good, the holy, the ascetic". The election was not unanimous. Evidently some thought the situation required a conciliatory demeanor towards the beaten Arians. But that was not the view of the majority, who, by choosing Athanasius, set the best fighting man on their side upon the throne of St. Mark. They did wisely. Tolerance was not properly understood in the fourth century.

The outward peace lasted little more than two years. Unfortunately, we are almost entirely in the dark as to what took place during that time, beyond the certain fact of the recall of Arius, Eusebius, and Theognis. Arius had been banished to Galatia; then we read of the sentence being partially revoked, and the only embargo placed upon his freedom of movement was that he was forbidden to return to Alexandria. Did this take place before the recall of Eusebius and Theognis? Socrates gives the text of a strange letter written by these two prelates to the principal bishops of the Church, in which they definitely say that, inasmuch as Arius has been recalled from exile, they hope the bishops will use their influence with the Emperor on their behalf.

"After closely studying the question of the Homoousion", they say, "we are wholly intent on preserving peace and we have been seduced by no heresy. We subscribed to the Creed, after suggesting what we thought best for the Church, but we refused to sign the anathema, not because we had any fault to find with the Creed, but because we did not consider Arius to be what he was represented as being. The letters we had received from him and the discourses we had heard him deliver compelled us to form a totally different estimate of his character".

The authenticity of this letter has been sharply called in question, for there is no other scrap of evidence confirming the statement that Arius was recalled before Eusebius and Theognis—in itself a most improbable step. Constantine had issued an edict that any one concealing a copy of the writings of Arius and not instantly handing it over to the authorities to be burnt, should be put to death, and it is much more probable that Arius was recalled after, rather than before, Eusebius of Nicomedia. The "History" of Socrates contains many letters of doubtful authenticity and some which are, beyond dispute, forgeries. Among the latter we may certainly include the portentously long document in which Constantine is represented as making a grossly personal attack on the banished Arius. We will content ourselves with quoting the most vituperative passage:

"Look! Look all of you! See what wretched cries he utters, writhing in pain from the bite of the serpent's tooth! See how his veins and flesh are poison-tainted and what agonized convulsions they excite! See how his body is wasted away with disease and squalor, with dirt and lamentation, with pallor and horror! See how he is withered up with a thousand evils! See how horrible to look upon is his filthy tangled head of hair; how he is half dead from top to toe; how languid is the aspect of his haggard, bloodless face; how madness, fury, and vanity, swooping down upon him together, have reduced him to what he is—a savage and wild beast! He does not even recognize the horrible situation he is in. I am beside myself with joy, he says, I dance and leap with glee; I fly; I am a happy boy again".

Assuredly this raving production never came from the pen of Constantine, and it bears no resemblance to his ordinary style. The resounding platitude with which it opens, "An evil interpreter is really the image and counterpart of the Devil," leads us confidently to acquit the Emperor of its authorship and ascribe it to some anonymous and unknown ecclesiastic desirous at once of edifying and terrifying the faithful.

We can only surmise the circumstances which worked upon the Emperor's mind and caused his complete change of front with respect to Arianism and its exponents. Sozomen, indeed, attributes it wholly to the influence of his sister, Constantia. According to an Arian legend quoted by that historian, it was revealed to the Princess in "a vision from God" that it was the exiled bishops who held the true orthodox doctrine and, therefore, that they had been unjustly banished. She worked upon the impressionable mind of her brother, and the two bishops were recalled. When Constantine asked whether they still held the Nicene doctrines to which they had subscribed, they replied that they had assented, not from conviction, but from the fear lest the Emperor should be disgusted at the dissensions among the Christians, and revert to paganism. This curious story certainly tends to confirm the tradition that it was Constantia who was the court patroness of the Arians. She had been for years Empress in the palace of Nicomedia, and it is easy to suppose that the very able Bishop of that city had established a strong ascendency over her mind, long before the Arian controversy arose.

The upshot of the whole matter—however the change was brought about—was that in the year 329, the Arian and Eusebian party was paramount at the Imperial Court. They had persuaded the Emperor that theirs was the party of reason, and that those who persisted in troubling the peace of the Church by holding extreme views and seeking to impose rigorous tests were the followers of the new Patriarch of Alexandria. They had subscribed to the Nicene Creed or to a Creed which—so they persuaded the Emperor—was practically indistinguishable from it, and they now plotted, with great skill and adroitness, to undermine the position of Athanasius. How they conducted the intrigue we do not know, but it is significant that after the break up of the Council of Nicaea we hear no more, during Constantine's lifetime, of his long-trusted adviser Hosius, Bishop of Cordova. The dreadful tragedies in the Imperial Family had taken place at Rome in the summer of 326. It is possible that Hosius made no secret of his horror at these monstrous crimes and retired to his Spanish bishopric, and that Eusebius of Nicomedia, when brought into communication with Constantine, was not so exacting in his demand for a show of penitence and proved more skillful in allaying the Emperor's remorse. Be that as it may, as soon as Eusebius felt assured of his position, he lost no time in prosecuting a vigorous campaign against those who had triumphed over him at Nicaea. The first blow was directed against Eustathius, the Bishop of Antioch, who was charged with heresy, profligacy, and tyranny by the two Eusebii and a number of other bishops, then on their way to Jerusalem. Whether the charges were well founded or not, the tribunal was a prejudiced one and the sentence of deprivation and banishment passed upon Eustathius was bitterly resented in Antioch.

After certain other bishops had met with a like fate, the Eusebii flew at higher game and attacked Athanasius. They had already entered into an under' standing with the Meletian faction in Egypt, who carefully kept alive the charges against Athanasius, and now they again took up the cudgels on behalf of Arius. Eusebius wrote to the Patriarch asking him to restore Arius to communion on the ground that he had been grievously misrepresented. Athanasius bluntly refused. Arius, he said, had started a deadly heresy; he had been anathematized by an Ecumenical Council: how, then, could he be restored to communion? Eusebius and Arius appealed to the Emperor. Constantine, who had previously ordered Arius to attend at court and promised him signal proof of his regard and permission to return to Alexandria, sent a peremptory message to Athanasius bidding him admit Arius. When Athanasius, on the score of conscience, returned a steady refusal, the Emperor angrily threatened that, if he did not throw open his church doors to all who desired to enter, he would send an officer to turn him out of his church and expel him from Alexandria. "Now that you have full knowledge of my will", he added, "see that you provide uninterrupted entry to all who wish to enter the church. If I hear that you have prevented any one from joining the services, or have shut the doors in their faces, I will at once dispatch some one to deport you from Alexandria". The threat did not terrify Athanasius, who declared that there could be no fellowship between heretics and true believers. Nor was the Imperial officer sent.

Then began an extraordinary campaign of calumny against the Patriarch, who was accused of taxing Egypt in order to buy a supply of linen garments, called sticharia, for his church; of instigating one Macarius to upset a communion table and break a sacred chalice; of murdering a Meletian bishop named Arsenius, who was presently found alive and well; and of other crimes equally preposterous and unfounded. It was the Meletian irreconcilables in Egypt who brought these calumnies forward, but Athanasius had no doubt that the moving spirit was none other than Eusebius himself. And his enemies, whoever they were, were untiring and implacable. As soon as one calumny was refuted, they were ready with another, and all this time there was Eusebius at the Emperor's side, continually suggesting that with so much smoke there needs must be some fire, and that Athanasius ought to be called upon to clear himself, lest the scandal should do injury to the Church. Constantine summoned a council to try Athanasius in 333, and fixed the place of meeting in Caesarea,—a tolerably certain proof that the two Eusebii were acting in concert. For some reason not stated the bishops did not assemble until the following year, and then Athanasius refused to attend. Not until 335 did Athanasius stand before his episcopal judges at Tyre.

Accompanied by some fifty of his suffragans, Athanasius had made the journey, only to find himself confronted by a packed council. All his bitterest enemies were there; all the old unsubstantiated charges were resuscitated. His election was said to be uncanonical; he was charged with personal unchastity and with cruelty towards certain Meletian bishops and priests; and, most curious of all, the ancient calumnies of "The Broken Chalice" and "The Dead Man's Hand" were revived and pressed, as though they had never been confuted. With respect to the latter charge, Athanasius enjoyed one moment of signal triumph. After his accusers had caused a thrill of horror to pass through the Council by producing a blackened and withered hand, which they declared to belong to the missing Bishop Arsenius, who was supposed to have suffered foul play, Athanasius asked whether any of those present had known Arsenius personally. A number of bishops claimed acquaintance, and then Athanasius gave the signal for a man, who was standing by closely muffled in a cloak, to come forward. "Lift up your head!" said Athanasius. The unknown did so, and lo! it was none other than Arsenius himself. Athanasius drew aside the cloak, first from one hand and then from the other. "Has God given to any man", he asked quietly, "more hands than two?" His enemies were silenced, but only for the moment. One of them, cleverer than the rest, immediately exclaimed that this was mere sorcery and devil's work; the man was not Arsenius; in fact, he was not even a man at all, but a mere counterfeit, an illusion of the senses produced by Athanasius' horrible proficiency in the black art. And we are told that this ingenious explanation proved so convincing to the assembly, and created such a fury of resentment against Athanasius, that Dionysius, the Imperial officer who had been deputed by Constantine to represent him at the Council, had to hurry Athanasius on shipboard to save him from personal violence.

There was clearly so little corroborative evidence against Athanasius that the Council dared not convict him. But, as they were equally determined not to acquit him, they appointed a commission of enquiry to collect testimony on the spot in the Mareotis district of Egypt with respect to the story of the Broken Chalice. The six commissioners were chosen in secret session by the anti-Athanasian faction. Athanasius protested without avail against the selection: they were all, he said, his private enemies. The commission sailed for Egypt, and Athanasius determined, with characteristic boldness, to go to Constantinople, confront the Emperor, and appeal for justice and a fair trial at the fountain-head. Athanasius met the Emperor as he was riding into the city, and stood before him in his path. What followed is best told by Constantine himself in a letter which he wrote to the Bishop of Tyre. Here are his own words:

"As I was returning on horseback to the city which bears my name, Athanasius, the Bishop, presented himself so unexpectedly in the middle of the highway, with certain individuals who accompanied him, that I felt exceedingly surprised on beholding him. God, who sees all, is my witness that at first I did not know who he was, but some of my attendants, having ascertained this and the subject of his complaint, gave me the necessary information. I did not accord him an interview, but he persevered in requesting an audience, and, although I refused him and was on the point of ordering that he should be removed from my presence, he told me, with greater boldness than he had previously manifested, that he sought no other favor of me than that I should summon you hither, in order that he might, in your presence, complain of the injustice that had been done to him".

Such boldness had the success it deserved. Constantine evidently made enquiries from Count Dionysius, and, discovering that the Council at Tyre was a mere travesty of justice, ordered the bishops to come forthwith to Constantinople. But before these instructions reached them they had received the report of the Egyptian commissioners, and, on the strength of it, had condemned Athanasius by a majority of votes, recognized the Meletians as orthodox, and, adjourning to Jerusalem for the dedication of the new church, had there pronounced Arius to be a true Catholic and in full communion with the Church. The Emperor's letter, which began with a reference to the "tumults and disorders" which had marked their sessions, was a plain intimation that he disapproved of their proceedings, and only six bishops, the two Eusebii and four others, travelled up to Constantinople. Arrived there, they changed their tactics, and recognizing that the old charges against Athanasius had fallen helplessly to the ground, they invented another which was much more likely to have weight with the Emperor. They accused him of seeking to prevent the Alexandrian corn ships from sailing to Constantinople. Egypt was the granary of the new Rome as well as of the old, and upon the regular arrival of the Egyptian wheat cargoes the tranquility of Constantinople largely depended. Athanasius protested that he had entertained no such designs. He was, he said, simply a bishop of the Church, a poor man with no political ambition or taste for intrigue. His enemies retorted that he was not poor, but wealthy, and that he had gained a dangerous ascendency over the turbulent people of Alexandria. Constantine abruptly ended the dispute by banishing Athanasius to Treves, and the Patriarch had no choice but to obey. He arrived at his city of exile in 336, and was received with all honor by the Emperor's son Constantine, then installed in the Gallic capital as the Cesar of the West. This is tolerably certain proof that the Emperor did not regard him as a very dangerous political opponent, but banished him rather for the sake of religious peace. Constantine was weary of such interminable disputations and such intractable disputants.

The exile of Athanasius was of course a signal victory for the Eusebians and for Arius. With the Patriarch of Alexandria thus safely out of the way, they might look forward with confidence to gaining the entire court over to their side and still further consolidating their position in the East. Arius returned in triumph to Alexandria, where he had not set foot for many years. But his presence was the signal for renewed popular disturbance. The Catholics remained faithful to their Bishop in exile—St. Antony repeatedly wrote to Constantine, praying for Athanasius' recall—and Alexandria was in tumult. Constantine refused to reconsider the sentence of banishment on Athanasius, but he checked the violence of the Meletian schismatics by banishing John Arcaph from Alexandria, and he hurriedly recalled Arius to Constantinople. The heresiarch was summoned into the presence of the Emperor, who by this time was once more uneasy in his mind. Constantine asked him point blank whether he held the Faith of the Catholic Church. "Can I trust you?" he said; "are you really of the true Faith?" Arius solemnly affirmed that he was and recited his profession of belief. "Have you abjured the errors you used to hold in Alexandria?"" continued the Emperor; "will you swear it before God?". Arius took the required oath, and the Emperor was satisfied. "Go", said he, "and if your Faith be not sound, may God punish you for your perjury".

This strange scene is described by Athanasius himself, who had been told the details by an eye-witness, a priest called Macarius. According to Socrates, Arius subscribed the declaration of the Faith in Constantine's presence, and the historian goes on to recount the foolish legend that Arius wrote down his real opinions on paper, which he carried under his arm, and so could truly swear that he "held " the sentiments he had written. Arius then demanded to be admitted to communion with the Church at Constantinople, as public testimony to his orthodoxy, and the Patriarch Alexander was ordered to receive him. Alexander was a feeble old man of ninety-eight but he did not lack moral courage. He told the Emperor that his conscience would not allow him to offer the sacraments to one whom, in spite of the recent declarations of the bishops at Jerusalem, he still regarded as an archheretic. He was not troubled, says Socrates, at the thought of his own deposition; what he feared was the subversion of the principles of the Faith, of which he regarded himself as the constituted guardian. Locking himself up within his church—the Church of St. Eirene—he lay prostrate before the high altar and remained there in earnest supplication for many days and nights. And the burden of his prayer was that if Arius's opinions were right he (Alexander) might not live to see him enter the church to receive the sacrament, but that, if he himself held the true Faith, Arius the impious might be punished for his impiety.

The aged Bishop was still calling upon Heaven to judge between Arius and himself and declare the truth by some manifest sign, when the time appointed for Arius to be received into communion was at hand. Arius was on his way to St. Eirene.

He had quitted the palace—says Socrates—attended by a crowd of

Eusebian partisans, and was passing through the centre of the city, the observed of all observers. He was in high spirits—as well he might be, for it was the hour of his supreme triumph. Then the blow fell. As he drew near the Porphyry Pillar in the Forum of Constantine he was suddenly taken ill. There was a public lavatory close by and he withdrew to it. When he did not return his friends became alarmed. Entering the place, they found him dead of a violent hemorrhage, with bowels protruding and burst asunder, like the traitor Judas in the Field of Blood. One can imagine the extraordinary sensation which the news must have caused in Constantinople as it flew from mouth to mouth. Not only the Patriarch Alexander, but all the orthodox, attributed Arius' sudden and awful end to the direct interposition of Providence in answer to their prayers. In an instant, we are told, the churches were crowded with excited worshippers and were ablaze with lights as for some happy festival.

On the superstitious mind of the Emperor so tragic a death naturally made a deep impression. He was, says Athanasius, amazed. Doubtless he believed that Arius had deceived him and that God had answered his prayer to punish the perjurer. The Eusebians were "greatly confounded". Some hinted at poison, others at magic; others were content to look no further than natural causes.   The general verdict of antiquity, however, was almost unanimous in ascribing the death of Arius to the anger of an offended Deity. It is a view which still finds adherents. Cardinal Newman, for example, declares:

"Under the circumstances a thoughtful mind cannot but account this as one of those remarkable interpositions of power by which Divine Providence urges on the consciences of men in the natural course of things, what their reason from the first acknowledges, that He is not indifferent to human conduct. To say that these do not fall within the ordinary course of His governance is merely to say that they are judgments, which in the common meaning of the word stand for events extraordinary and unexpected".

But that is a matter which need not be discussed here. What is more important to our purpose is to point out that the death of Arius does not seem to have affected the state of religious parties at Constantinople. It did not shake the position of Eusebius of Nicomedia, who continued to enjoy the confidence of the Emperor and to act as the keeper of his conscience.

CONSTANTINE'S DEATH AND CHARACTER

IT seems incontestable that Constantine degenerated as he grew older. Certainly his popularity tended to decrease. This, however, is the usual penalty of length of reign, and in itself would not count for much. But one cannot overlook the cumulative evidence which is to be found in the authorities of the period. Eusebius himself admits that unscrupulous men often took advantage of the piety and generosity of the Emperor, and many of the stories which he tells in Constantine's praise prepare us for the charges which were brought against him by the pagan historians. For example, Eusebius declares that whenever the Emperor heard a civil appeal, he used to make up out of his private purse the amount in which the losing party was mulcted, on the extraordinary principle that both the winner and the loser ought to leave their sovereign's presence equally satisfied. Such a theory would speedily beggar the richest treasury. Aurelius Victor preserves a popular saying which shows the general estimation in which Constantine's memory was held. Men used to say that for the first ten years of his reign he was a model sovereign, for the next twelve he was a brigand, and for the last ten a spendthrift heir, so called because of his preposterous extravagance. He was nick-named Trachala, the obvious reference of which would be to his short, thick neck; but Aurelius Victor appears to associate it in some way with the meaning of "scoffer" (irrisor).

In greater detail Zosimus accuses Constantine of wasting the public money on useless buildings. As a pagan, he would naturally regard expenditure upon the construction of sumptuous Christian churches as money thrown away, but it is perfectly certain that the state of the Imperial resources did not justify the Emperor in lavishing vast sums upon churches in all parts of the Empire. If we consider what must have been the capital cost of his churches in Rome, Constantinople, Jerusalem, Bethlehem, Mamre, and Antioch,—to mention only a few places, —and remember that he was constantly urging the bishops to keep building and constantly sending instructions to his vicars to make handsome subsidies out of the State funds, we cannot but conclude that the grumbling of the pagan tax payer was thoroughly well justified. Constantine, indeed, seems to have been as entêté in the matter of building churches as was in our day the mad King Ludwig of Bavaria in the building of royal castles. Nor was this the only form in which the passion for bricks and mortar—il mal di pietra—seized him. He built a new basilica even in Rome—though he rarely set foot in the city. In Constantinople he must have sunk millions of unproductive capital, which were far more urgently required for the development of agriculture and commerce. In one epigrammatic sentence Zosimus sums up his indictment by saying that Constantine thought to gain distinction by lavish outlay. He also wasted the public revenue on unworthy and useless favorites, whom he taught, in the phrase of Ammianus Marcellinus, to open their greedy jaws. Zosimus says bluntly that in his opinion it was Constantine who sowed the seeds of the ruinous waste and destruction that prevailed when he wrote his history, and he roundly declares that the Emperor devoted his life to his own selfish pleasures.

There is another character sketch of Constantine which has survived for us, drawn by an even more bitter enemy than the historian Zosimus. It is to be found in that amusing and extraordinary jeu d'esprit which bears the name of The Cosars, from the pen of the Emperor Julian. Julian detested the very memory of Constantine the Great, whom he regarded as the arch-apostate from the ancient religion, and, thus, when he introduced him into the presence of the deities of Olympus, it was really to pour ridicule and contempt upon his pretensions.

Julian describes him, at the first mention of his name, as a man who has seen considerable fighting, but has become soft through self-indulgence and luxury. The deities of heaven are represented as sitting in conclave, while the deified Emperors approach to join in their councils. Julian runs over the list of the great Emperors, introducing them one by one and making each sit by the side of the god whom he most resembles in character. But when Constantine's turn comes, it is found that he has no such archetype. No god will own him as his protégé or pupil, and so, after some hesitation, Constantine runs up to the Goddess of Luxury, who embraces him as her own darling, dresses him up in fine clothes, and, when she has made him smart, hands him over to her sister, the Goddess of Extravagance. The irony was bitter, and the shaft sped home.

The ascetic Julian does not spare his august relative, whose title to the epithet of "Great" he would have laughed to scorn. He declares that Constantine's victories over the barbarians were victories pour rire; he represents him as a crazy being in love with the moon, like that half-witted Emperor of the Claudian house, who used to stand at night in the colonnades of his palace and beg the gracious Queen of the Sky to come down to him as she had come down to Endymion. Julian puts into his mouth a grotesque speech in which he makes Constantine claim to have been a greater general than Alexander because he fought with Romans, Germans, and Scythians and not with mere Asiatics; greater than Julius Cesar or than Augustus because he fought not with bad men but with good; and greater even than Trajan, because it is a finer thing to win back what you have lost than merely to acquire something new. The speech was received with ridicule by the gods, and then Hermes pointedly asked Constantine in the Socratic manner, "How would you define your ideal?"; "To have great riches", was Constantine's reply, "and to be able to give away lavishly, and satisfy all one's own desires and those of one's friends". The answer is significant. Julian, like Constantine's other critics, keeps harping on the same string. It is the luxury, extravagance, and self-indulgence of the Emperor that he singles out as the most glaring defect of his character and his squandering of the Imperial resources upon effeminate and un-Roman pomps, useless buildings, and greedy and unworthy favorites. Silenus, the bibulous buffoon of Olympus, a moral rebuke from whose lips would be received with shouts of laughter, tells Constantine with mock gravity that he has led a life fit only for a cook or a lady's-maid, and so the episode ends. We cannot doubt that there was quite sufficient of truth in these accusations to make the sharp-witted Greeks of the Empire, for whom Julian principally wrote, thoroughly enjoy his biting sarcasms.

But we must be careful not to push too far any argument based upon this lampoon of Julian or upon the obvious bias of Zosimus. They disclose to us, undoubtedly, the least worthy side of Constantine's character, viz., a tendency to effeminacy and luxury, and it is morally certain that no one who had given way to his worst passions, as Constantine had done in Rome in the year 326, could ever be quite the same man again. He had on his conscience the assassination of his son and wife. These were but two out of a terribly long list of victims, which included his father-in-law, Maximian; his brother-in-law, Licinius, and Licinius's young son, Licinianus; another brother-in-law, the Caesar Bassus; and many more besides. Some fell for reasons of State—"it is only the winner", as Marcus Antonius had said three centuries before, "who sees length of days"—but there was also the memory, even in the case of some of these, of broken promises and ill-kept faith. Constantine's Christianity was not of the kind which permeates a man's every action and influences his entire life; or, if that he claimed for him, it must at least be admitted that there were periods in his career when he suffered most desperate lapses from grace.

On the whole perhaps the general statement of Eutropius, which we have already quoted, that Constantine degenerated somewhat as he grew older, fairly meets the case. It is worthwhile, indeed, to quote the reasoned estimate which this excellent epitomist gives of the Emperor's character. He says:

"At the opening of his reign Constantine was a man who challenged comparison with the best of Princes; at its close he merited comparison with those of average merit and demerit. Both mentally and physically his good points were beyond computation and conspicuous to all. He was passionately set on winning military glory; and in his campaigns good fortune attended him, though not more than his zealous industry deserved ... He was devoted to the arts of peace and to the humanities, and he sought to win from all men their sincere affection by his generosity and his tractability, never losing an opportunity of enriching his friends and adding to their dignity".

This estimate agrees in its main particulars with that of Aurelius Victor, who, after speaking of his wonderful good luck in war and his avidity for praise, eulogizes his exceptional versatility, his zeal for literature and the arts, and the patient ear which he was always ready to lend to any provincial deputation or complaint.

We have spoken of a marked degeneracy observable in Constantine as his life drew to a close. Perhaps the clearest proof of this is to be found in a momentous step taken by him in 335, when he divided the sovereignty of the world among his heirs. Such a partition meant the stultification of his political career, for he thus destroyed at a blow the political unity which he had so laboriously restored out of the wreck of the system of Diocletian.

Eusebius gives us the truth in a single sentence when he says that Constantine treated the Empire for the purposes of this division as though he were apportioning his private patrimony among members of his own family. He was much more concerned to make handsome provision for his sons and nephews than to secure the peace and well-being of his subjects. Crispus had now been dead nine years, and the three sons of Constantine and Fausta were still young, the eldest being only just twenty-one. Eusebius tells us how carefully they had been trained. They had been instructed in all martial exercises, and special professors had been engaged to make them proficient in political affairs and a knowledge of the laws. Their religious education had been personally supervised by their father, who zealously sowed "the seeds of godly reverence" and impressed upon them that "a know-ledge of God, who is the king of all things, and true piety were more deserving of honor than riches or even than sovereignty itself". Admirable precepts and Eusebius declares again and again that this "Trinity of Princes"—so he calls them in one place—were models of deportment, modesty, and piety. Unfortunately, we know how emphatically their future careers belied their early promise and the eulogies of the Bishop of Caesarea. We do not doubt his statement that Constantine spared no effort to educate them aright, but it was most unfortunate that the remarkable success of their father's political career bore testimony rather to the efficacy of ambition without scruple than of "godly reverence and true piety".

In this new partition of the Empire the Caesarship of the West, including

Gaul, Britain, and Spain, fell to Constantine, the eldest of the three princes. To the second, Constantius, were assigned the rich provinces of the East, including the seaboard provinces of Asia Minor, together with Syria and Egypt. Constans, the youngest, received as his share Italy, Elyria, and Africa. But there was still a goodly heritage left over, sufficient to make a handsome dowry for a favorite daughter. This was Constantina, eldest of the three daughters of Constantine and Fausta, and she had been married to her half-cousin, Annibalianus, whose father had been the second son of Constantius Chlorus and Theodora. To support worthily the dignity of his new position as son-in-law of Constantine, the new title of Nobilissimus was created in his honor, and a kingdom was made for him out of the provinces of Pontus, Cappadocia, and Lesser Armenia. Gibbon expresses surprise that Annibalianus, "of the whole series of Roman Princes in any age of the Empire", should have been the only one to bear the name of Rex, and says that he can scarcely admit its accuracy even on the joint authority of Imperial medals and contemporary writers. The explanation is surely to be found in the fact that Pontus, Cappadocia, and Lesser Armenia had for centuries been accustomed to be ruled by a king and that, in creating a new kingdom, Constantine simply retained the title which would be most familiar to the subjects over whom Annibalianus was to rule. Annibalianus was himself a second son: his elder brother, Dalmatius, was raised to the full title of Caesar and given command over the important provinces of Thrace and Macedonia, with Greece thrown in as a make-weight. The position was a very important one, for it fell to the Caesar of Thrace to guard the frontier chiefly threatened by the Goths, and we may suppose, therefore, with some probability that Dalmatius—who had been consul in 333— had given proof of military talent.

But to what extent, we may ask, was this a real partition? In what sense were the Caesars independent of Constantine himself? Eusebius expressly tells us that each was provided with a complete establishment, with a court, that is to say, which was in every respect a miniature copy of the court at Constantinople. Each had his own legions, bodyguards, and auxiliaries, with their due complement of officers chosen, we are told, by the Emperor for their knowledge of war and for their loyalty to their chiefs. It is hardly to be supposed that Constantine contemplated retirement: had he done so, he would have retired at the Tricennalia which he celebrated in the following year. In all probability, he did not intend that his supreme power should be one whit abated, though he was content to delegate his administrative authority to others acting under his strict supervision. His Caesars, in short, were really viceroys, though it is difficult to understand how such an arrangement can have worked harmoniously without some modification of the powers of the four Praetorian prefects. But the division, as we have said, was not made in the interests of the Empire but in the interests of the Princes of the Blood, and it was one which could not possibly endure. As soon as Constantine died chaos and civil war were bound to ensue, and, as a matter of fact, did ensue. For there is no evidence that the Emperor made any arrangement as to who should succeed him on the throne. Constantinople itself lay in the territory assigned to Dalmatius; yet it was entirely unreasonable to suppose that the three sons of Constantine would acquiesce in leaving the capital to the quiet possession of their cousin. The division of the Empire, therefore, in 335 carried with it the early ripening seeds of civil war, bloodshed, and anarchy. If the system of Diocletian had proved unworkable, because it took no account of the natural desire of a son to succeed his father, the system of Constantine was even worse. It was absolutely certain that of the five heirs the three sons would combine against the two cousins, whom they would regard as interlopers, and that then the three brothers would quarrel among themselves, until only one was left.

Constantine's reign was now hastening to its end. In 336 he celebrated his Tricennalia, and his courtiers would not fail to remind him that he alone, of all the successors of the great Augustus, had borne such length of days in his left hand and such glory in his right. The principal event of the festival seems to have been the dedication at Jerusalem of the sumptuous Church of the Anastasis on the site of the Holy Sepulchre. As we have seen in another chapter, the year was one of acute religious contention, rendered specially memorable by the awe-inspiring death of Arius, and the Emperor's last months of life must have been embittered by the thought that, despite all his efforts, religious unity within the Church seemed as far as ever from realization.

Eusebius tells us that Constantine sought to find a remedy in the hot baths of Constantinople for the disorder from which he was suffering, and then, obtaining no relief, crossed the straits to Drepanum, or Helenopolis, as it was now called in honor of the Emperor's mother. There his malady grew worse and special prayers were offered for his recovery in the Church of Lucian the Martyr.

But Constantine had a presentiment that the end was near, and he determined, therefore, that the time had come for him formally to become a member of the Christian Church and so obtain purification for the sins which he had committed in life. Falling upon his knees on the church floor, he confessed his sins, received the laying-on of hands, and so became a catechumen. Then, travelling down to the palace which stood on the outskirts of Nicomedia, the now dying Emperor summoned to his side a number of bishops and made confession of his faith. He told them that the moment for which he had thirsted and prayed had come at last, the moment when he might receive "the seal which confers immortality". He had hoped, he said, to be baptized in Jordan: God had willed otherwise and he bowed to His will. But he assured them that his resolve was not due to any passing whim. He had fully made up his mind, that even if recovery were vouchsafed him, he would set before himself such rules and conduct of life as would be becoming to God.

Eusebius of Nicomedia then performed the rite of baptism. Constantine, clad in garments of shining white, lay upon a white bed, and, down to the hour of his death, refused to touch the purple robes he had worn in life. "Now", he exclaimed, with all the fervor of a neophyte, "now I know in very truth that I am blessed; now I have confidence that I am a partaker of divine light". When his captains came to take leave of him and wept at the thought of losing their chief, he told them that he had the assurance of having been found worthy of eternal life, and that his only anxiety was to hasten his journey to God. He wished to die, and the wish was soon granted. Constantine drew his last breath on May 22d, 337.

They bore the body, enclosed in a golden coffin covered by a purple pall, from Nicomedia to Constantinople and placed it with great pomp in the throne room of the palace. There the dead Emperor lay in state, guarded night and day by the chief officers of the army and the highest officials of the court. Even in death, says Eusebius, he still was king, and all the elaborate bowings and genuflexions with which men had entered his presence in his lifetime were still observed. Constantine's illness had declared itself very suddenly, and had run its course so quickly that not one of his sons was at hand to take up the reins of administration. It looks too as though the Emperor had made no preparations with a view to his demise, but had left his three sons and his two nephews to determine among themselves who should be supreme. His second son, Constantius, was the first to arrive at Constantinople, and it was he who arranged the obsequies of his father. We are told that the Roman Senate earnestly desired the body of the Emperor to be laid to rest in the old capital and sent deputations begging that this last honor should not be denied them. But it had been Constantine's express wish to be buried in the Church of the Apostles, at Constantinople, where he had prepared a splendid sarcophagus, and there can have been no hesitation as to the choice of a resting-place. The body was borne with an imposing military pageant to the Church. Constantius was the chief mourner, but he and his soldiers quitted the sanctuary before a word of the burial-service was spoken or a note of music sounded. He was not a baptized Christian and, therefore, could not be present as the last rites were performed. The great Emperor was buried by the bishops, priests, and Christian populace, whose zealous champion he had been and to whose undying gratitude he had established an overwhelming title. Coins were struck bearing on one side the figure of the Emperor with his head closely veiled, and, on the other, representing Constantine seated in a four-horse chariot, and being drawn up to heaven by a celestial hand stretched out to him from the clouds. It was a device which could offend neither Christian nor pagan. To the former it would recall the triumphant ascent of Elijah; the latter would regard it as the token of a natural apotheosis. The hand might equally well be the hand of God or of Jupiter.

Such is the story of the Emperor's baptism, death, and burial as recounted by Eusebius. There is, however, one important detail to be added and one important question to be asked. Constantine was baptized by an Arian bishop. To the Athanasian party and to the ecclesiastical historians of succeeding ages this was a lamentable circumstance which greatly exercised and troubled their minds. It sorely grieved them to think that their patron Constantine should have been admitted into the communion of the faithful by the dangerous heretic who had been the bitterest enemy of their idol, Athanasius. But with a forbearance to which they were usually strangers, they agreed to pass over the episode in comparative silence and remember not the shortcomings but the virtues of the first Christian Emperor.

It still remains to be asked why Constantine did not formally enter the Church until he was on his death-bed. There had been no lukewarmness about his Christianity. He was not one to be afflicted with doubts. There had never been any danger of his reverting to paganism. In the last few years, indeed, he had been distracted by the clamour of Arians and Athanasians, and his was a mind upon which a clever and acute ecclesiastic, who enjoyed his confidence, could play at will. When Hosius of Cordova stood by his side he was the champion of the Catholic party; when Hosius fell from favor and Eusebius of Nicomedia took his place Constantine strongly inclined to the Arian side. But in neither case was there any doubt of his Christianity. Why then did he not become a member of the Church? Was it because the rite of baptism conferred immediate forgiveness of sin and therefore a death-bed baptism infallibly opened the gate of Heaven? By putting off entrance into the Church until the hour had come after which it was hardly possible to commit sin, did Constantine count upon making sure of eternal happiness? Such is the motive assigned by some historians. It certainly is not a lofty one. Yet the idea may very well have presented itself to Constantine's mind and the impression left by Eusebius's narrative is that Constantine only determined to receive the rite because he felt his end to be near and dared not put it off any longer. On the other hand, Constantine's statement that his ambition had been to be baptized in Jordan is rather against this theory. Possibly, too, he was to some degree influenced by the wish not to alienate entirely the support of his pagan subjects, especially the more fanatical of them, who would bitterly resent their Chief Pontiff becoming a baptized member of the Christian Church. No one can say, but we shall be the better able to form an opinion if we look a little more closely at the religious life and policy of Constantine.

Eusebius represents the daily life of the Emperor on its religious side to have been almost that of a monk or of a saint. Every day, we are told, he used to retire for private meditation and prayer. He delighted in delivering sermons and addresses to his courtiers, Bible in hand. He would begin by exposing the errors of polytheism and by proving the superstition of the Gentiles to be a mere fraud and cloak for impiety, and would then expound his theory of the sole sovereignty of God, the workings of Providence, and the sureness of the Judgment, in-variably concluding with his favorite moral that God had given to him the sovereignty of the whole world. Such a discourse could not possibly be short, but Constantine liked his religious exercises long. He once insisted on standing throughout the reading of an elaborate disquisition by Eusebius himself, who evidently tired of the exertion and begged that the Emperor would not fatigue himself further. But Constantine was resolved to hear it out, and the courtier Bishop, while profoundly flattered at the compliment, ruefully admitted that the thesis was very long. Probably the courtiers found it interminable. But it was their duty to listen, applaud, and appear duly impressed when, for example, Constantine traced on the ground the dimensions of a coffin, and solemnly warned them against covetousness by the reminder that six feet of earth was the utmost they could hope to enjoy after death, and they might not even get so much as that if burial were refused them or they were burnt or lost at sea. No one ever accused Constantine of covetousness; his failing was reckless extravagance, and we fear he is to be num-bered among those who

"Compound for sins they are inclined to

By damning those they have no mind to".

Constantine ordered all the bishops throughout the Empire to offer up daily prayers for him; he had coins struck at the Imperial mints which depicted him with eyes uplifted to heaven, and he had pictures of himself—probably in mosaic—set over the gates of his palaces, in which he was seen standing erect with hands in the attitude of prayer. For our part we like better the chapters in which Eusebius describes the Emperor's open-handed generosity to the poor and needy and to the orphan and the widow, extols the kind-heartedness which was carried to such a length as to raise the question whether such clemency was not excessive, and claims that his most distinctive and characteristic virtue was the love of his fellow-men, a virtue which the typical Roman rarely developed to his full capacity.

Constantine's whole career testified to the zeal with which he had embraced Christianity. We have seen the enthusiasm with which he set to work to build churches throughout the Empire. In Rome there are ascribed to him the Church of Saint Agnes, the Church of St. John Lateran, and another which stood on part of the site of the present St. Peter's. In Constantinople he built the Churches of the Apostles, St. Eirene, and St. Sophia. In Jerusalem he built the Church of the Anastasis as the crowning memorial of his thirty years of reign, and in Antioch, Nicomedia, and a score of other cities his purse was constantly at the service of the Faith. The building of churches was a passion with him, and he also took care that they were provided with the Scriptures. Eusebius gives the text of a letter written to him by the Emperor ordering fifty copies of the Scriptures to be executed without delay. Constantine published an edict commanding that the Lord's day should be scrupulously observed and honored, and that every facility should be given to Christian soldiers to enable them to attend the services. Even his pagan soldiers were to keep that day holy by offering up a prayer to the "King of Heaven", in which they addressed him as the "Giver of Victory, their Preserver, Guardian, and Helper".

"Thee alone we know to be God; Thee alone we recognize as King; Thee we invoke as Helper; from Thee we have gained our victories; through Thee we are superior to our enemies. To Thee we give thanks for the benefits we now enjoy; from Thee we look for our benefits to come. All of us are Thy suppliants: and we pray that Thou wilt guard our King Constantine and his pious sons long, long to reign over us in safety and victory".

No pagan soldier could be offended at being required to offer this prayer to the King of Heaven. If he were sincere in his faith he would hope that it might reach the throne of Jupiter; Constantine evidently expected that, as it was addressed to the King of Heaven, it would be intercepted in mid-course and wafted to the throne of God. He was at any rate determined that no soldier of his, whether pagan or Christian, should wear on his shield any other sign than that of the Cross—"the salutary trophy".

But what was Constantine's policy towards the old religion? Let us look first at the explicit statements of Eusebius. He says in one place that "the doors of idolatry were shut throughout the whole Roman Empire for both laity and military alike, and every form of sacrifice was forbidden". In another passage he says that edicts were issued "forbidding sacrifice to idols, the mischievous practice of divination, the putting up of wooden images, the observance of secret rites, and the pollution of cities by the sanguinary combats of gladiators". In a third passage he speaks of Constantine's having "utterly destroyed polytheism in all its variety of foolishness". Eusebius also tells us that Constantine was careful to choose, whenever possible, Christian governors for the provinces, while he forbade those with Hellenistic, i.e., pagan, sympathies to offer sacrifice. He also ordered that the synodal decrees of bishops should not be interfered with by the provincial authorities, for, adds Eusebius, he considered a priest of God to be more entitled to honor than a judge. The same authority expressly states that Constantinople was kept perfectly free from idolatry in every shape and form, and was never polluted with the blood or smoke of sacrifice, and the general impression which he leaves upon the reader's mind is that paganism was proscribed and the practice of the old religion declared to be a crime.

It is evident, however, that this was not the case. Eusebius, as usual, supplies the corrective to his own exaggerations. He quotes, for example, in full the text of an edict which Constantine addressed to the governors of the East, wherein it is unequivocally laid down that complete religious freedom is to be the standing rule throughout the Empire. He beseeches all his subjects to become Christians, but he will not compel them. "Let no one interfere with his neighbor. Let each man do what his soul desires". This edict was issued after the overthrow of Licinius and is remarkable chiefly for the fervent profession of Christianity which the Emperor makes in it. "I am most firmly convinced", he says, "that I owe to the most High God my whole soul, my every breath, my most secret and inmost thoughts". And then he continues: "Therefore, I have dedicated my soul to Thee, in pure blend of love and leant For I truly adore Thy name, while I reverence Thy power which Thou hast manifested by many proofs and made my faith the surer".

But did Constantine maintain this attitude of strict neutrality, only tempered by ardent prayer that his pagan subjects might be brought to a knowledge of the truth? In its entirety he certainly did not, and it was impossible that so zealous a convert should. When the smiles of Imperial favor were withdrawn from the old religion it was inevitable that the Imperial arm which protected it should grow slack in its defence. Yet, throughout his reign Constantine never forgot that the majority of his subjects were still pagan, despite the hosts of conversions which followed his own, and he took care not to press too hardly upon them and not to goad the more fanatical upholders of the old regime to the recklessness of despair. We have seen how the Emperor refused to witness the procession of the Knights in Rome at the time of his Vicennalia. He also forbade his statue or image to be placed in a pagan temple. But he, nevertheless, retained through life the office of Pontifex Maximus, and as such continued to be supreme head of the pagan religion. Nor was it until the time of Gratian fifty years afterwards that this title—no doubt in deference to the repeated representations of the bishops—was dropped by the Christian Emperors. Some historians have expressed surprise that so enthusiastic a convert to Christianity should have been willing to remain Chief Pontiff; a few have even been genuinely concerned to explain and excuse his conduct. But Constantine was statesman as well as convert. If he had resigned the Chief Pontificate that office might conceivably have passed into dangerous hands. By holding it as an absolute sinecure, by never performing its ceremonial duties or wearing its distinctive robes, Constantine did far more to destroy its influence than if he had resigned it. Imperial titles, moreover, sometimes signify very little. Everyone knows the gibe of Voltaire at the Holy Roman Empire which was neither holy, nor Roman, nor an Empire. For centuries after the loss of Calais the lilies of France were quartered on the Royal arms of Great Britain, and the coins of our Protestant monarch still bear the F. D. bestowed by the Pope upon the eighth Henry. The King of Portugal is still Lord of All the Indies. It is not titles that count but actions. Whether or not Constantine's ecclesiastical friends were troubled by his retaining the title, we may be sure the question never troubled the Emperor himself, as the title of "Supreme Head of the

English Church" is said to have troubled the scrupulous conscience of James II after he became a convert to Rome. But in the latter case the practical advantages of retention outweighed the shock to consistency in the eyes of those whom James consulted.

Constantine helped forward the conversion of the Empire with true statesmanlike caution, desirous above all things to avoid political disturbance. He abolished outright, we are told, certain of the more offensive and degraded pagan rites, to which it was possible to take grave exception on the score of decency and morality. For example, some Phoenician temples at Heliopolis and Aphaca, where the worship of Venus was attended with shameless prostitution, were ordered to be pulled down. The same fate befell a temple of Aesculapius at Egaea, and a college of effeminate priests in Egypt, associated with the worship of the Nile, was disbanded and its members, according to Eusebius, were all put to death. But these are the only specific examples of repression instanced by Eusebius, and they assuredly do not suggest any general proscription of paganism. Eusebius is notoriously untrustworthy. He distinctly says that Constantine determined to purify his new capital of all idolatry, so that there should not be found within its walls either statue or altar of any false god. Yet we know that the philosopher Sopater was present at the ceremony of dedication and that he enjoyed for a time the high favor of the Emperor, though he was subsequently put to death on the accusation of the prefect Ablavius, who charged him with delaying the arrival of the Egyptian corn ships by his magical arts. We know too that there were temples of Cybele and Fortuna in the city, and Zosimus expressly declares that the Emperor constructed a temple and precincts for the Dioscuri, Castor and Pollux. At Rome the temple of Concord was rebuilt towards the close of his reign, and inscriptions show that the consuls of the year still dedicated without hindrance altars to their favorite deities. The famous altar of Victory, around which a furious controversy was to rage in the reign of Valentinian, at the close of the fourth century, still stood in the Roman Curia, and in the two great centers of Eastern Christianity, Antioch and Alexandria, the worship of Apollo and Serapis continued without intermission in their world-renowned temples.

No doubt in districts where the Christians were in a marked majority and paganism found only lukewarm adherents, there was occasional violence shown to the old temples and statues, especially if the governor happened to be a Christian. Ornaments might be stolen, treasures ransacked, and probably few questions were asked. Christianity had been persecuted so long and so savagely that when the day of revenge came, the temptation was too strong for human frailty to resist, and as long as there was no serious civil disturbance the authorities probably made light of the occurrence. Paganism was a dying creed; where it had to struggle hard to keep its head above water, the end was not long delayed. The case would be different where the temples were possessed of great wealth and where there were powerful priestly corporations to defend their vested interests. There can be no greater mistake than to suppose that Constantine declared war on the old religion. He did nothing of the kind. When he showered favors on the Christian clergy, what he did in effect was merely to raise them to the same status as that already enjoyed by the pagan priesthood. He did not take away the privileges of the colleges: and inscriptions have been found which tend to show that he allowed new colleges to be founded which bore his name. In short, to the old State-established and State-endowed religion he added another, that of Christianity, reserving his special favor for the new but not actively repressing the ancient. He had hoped to convert the world by his own example; but, though he failed in this, he never contemplated a resort to violence. His religious policy, throughout his reign, may fairly be described as one of toleration. That is what Symmachus meant when he said, half a century later, that Constantine had belonged to both religions.

There was one exception to this rule. Constantine came down with a heavy hand on secret divination and the practice of magic and the black arts. But other Emperors before him had done the same, Emperors whose loyalty to the Roman religion had never been questioned—for these mysterious rites formed no part of the established worship. They might be employed to the harm of the State; they might portend danger to the Emperor's life and throne. It was not for private individuals to experiment with and let loose the powers of darkness, for, as a rule, beneficent deities had no part or lot in these dark mysteries. As a Christian, Constantine would have a double satisfaction in issuing edicts against the wonder-working charlatans who abounded in the great cities; but the point is that in attacking them he was not technically attacking the old State religion. The public and official haruspices were not interfered with; if any devout pagan still desired to consult an oracle, no obstacle was placed in his way; and, as a tribute to the universal superstition of the age from which he himself was not free, even private divination was permitted when the object was a good one, such as the restoration of a sick person to health or the protection of crops against hail. But it is evident that Constantine and his bishops were far more apprehensive of evil from the unchaining of the Devil than expectant of good from the favor of the ministers of grace. They were terrified of the one: they indulged but a pious hope of the other. Nor was the Emperor successful in stamping out the private thaumaturgist. Human nature was too strong for him. Sileat perpetuo divinandi curiositas, ordered one of his successors in 358. But the curiosity to divine the future continued to defy both civil and ecclesiastical law.

A much bolder act, however, than the closing of a few temples on the score of public decency or the forbidding of private divination was the edict of 325, in which Constantine ordered the abolition of the gladiatorial shows. "Such blood-stained spectacles", he said, "in the midst of civil peace and domestic quiet are repugnant to our taste". He ordained, therefore, that in future all criminals who were usually condemned to be gladiators should be sent to work in the mines, that they might expiate their offences without shedding of blood. But it was one thing to issue an edict and another to enforce it. Whether Constantine insisted on the observance of this particular edict, we cannot say, but his successors certainly did not, for the gladiatorial spectacles at Rome were in full swing in the days of Symmachus, who ransacked the world for good swordsmen and strange animals. The cruenta spectacula, as Constantine called them, were not finally abolished until the reign of Honorius.

To sum up. The only reasonable view to take of the religious character of Constantine is that he was a sincere and convinced Christian. This is borne out alike by his passionate professions of faith and by the clear testimony of his actions. There are, it is true, many historians who hold that he was really indifferent to religion, and others who credit him with an easy capacity for finding truth in all religions alike. Professor Bury, for example, says that "the evidence seems to show that his religion was a syncretistic monotheism; that he was content to see the deity in the Sun, in Mithras, or in the God of the Hebrews". Such a description would suit the character of Constantius Chlorus perfectly, and it may very well have suited Constantine himself before the overthrow of Maxentius. There is a passage in the Ninth Panegyric which seems to have been uttered by one holding these views, and it is worth quotation, for it is an invocation to the supreme deity to bless the Emperor Constantine. It runs as follows:

Wherefore we pray and beseech thee to keep our Prince safe for all eternity, thee, the supreme creator of all things, whose names are as manifold as it has been thy will that nations should have tongues. We cannot tell by what title it is thy pleasure that we should address thee, whether thou art a divine force and mind permeating the whole world and mingled with all the elements, and moving of thine own motive power without impulse from without, or whether thou art some Power above all Heaven who lookest down upon this thy handiwork from some loftier arch of Nature.

Such a deity may have satisfied the philosophers, but it certainly was not the deity whom Constantine worshipped throughout his reign. Had he been indifferent to religion, or indifferent to Christianity, had he even been anxious only to hold the balance between the rival creeds, he would never have surrounded himself by episcopal advisers; never have set his hand to such edicts as those we have quoted; never have abolished the use of the cross for the execution of criminals or have forbidden Jews to own Christian slaves; never have called the whole world time and again to witness his zeal for Christ; never have lavished the resources of the Empire upon the building of sumptuous churches; never have listened with such extraordinary forbearance to the wranglings of the Donatists and the subtleties of Arians and Athanasians; never have summoned or presided at the Council of Nicaea; and certainly never have made the welfare of non-Roman Christians the subject of entreaty with the King of Persia. Constantine was prone to superstitions. He was grossly material in his religious views, and his own worldly success remained still in his eyes the crowning proof of the Christian verities. But the sincerity of his convictions is none the less apparent, and even the atrocious crimes with which he sullied his fair fame cannot rob him of the name of Christian. It was a name, says St. Augustine, in which he manifestly delighted to boast, mindful of the hope which he reposed in Christ.

THE EMPIRE AND CHRISTIANITY

THE reorganization of the Empire, begun by Diocletian, had been continued along the same lines by Constantine the Great. There were still further developments under their successors, but these two were the real founders of the Imperial system which was to subsist in the eastern half of the Empire for more than eleven hundred years. In other words, Diocletian and Constantine gave the Empire, if not a new lease of life, at least a new impetus and a new start, and we may here present a brief sketch of the reforms which they introduced into practically every sphere of governmental activity.

We have already seen how profoundly changed was the position of the Emperor himself. He was no longer essentially a Roman Imperator, a supreme War-Lord, a soldier Chief of State. He had become a King in a palace, secluded from the gaze of the vulgar, surrounded with all the attributes and ornaments of an eastern monarch, and robed in gorgeous vestments stiff with gold and jewels. Men were taught to speak and think of him as superhuman and sacrosanct, to approach him with genuflexion and adoration, to regard every office, however menial, attached to his person, as sacred. In speaking of the Emperor language was strained to the pitch of the ridiculous; flattery became so grotesque that it must have ceased to flatter. When Nazarius, for example, speaks of the Emperor's heart as "the stupendous shrine of mighty virtues", and such language as this became the recognised mode of addressing the reigning Sovereign, we see how far we have travelled not only from Republican simplicity, but even from the times of Domitian. The Emperor, in brief, was absolute monarch, autocrat of the entire Roman world, and his will and nod were law.

He stood at the head of a hierarchy of court and administrative officials, most minutely organized from the highest to the lowest. For purposes of Imperial administration, those next to the throne were the four Praetorian prefects, each one supreme, under the Emperor, in his quarter of the world. The Empire had been divided by Diocletian into twelve dioceses and these again into ninety-six provinces; Constantine accepted this division but apportioned the twelve dioceses into four prefectures, those of the Orient, Illyria, Italy, and Gaul. The four Pretorian prefects stood in relation to the Emperor—so Eusebius tells us—as God the Son stood in relation to God the Father. They wore—though not perhaps in the days of Constantine—robes of purple reaching to the knee; they rode in lofty chariots, and among the insignia of their office were a colossal silver inkstand and gold pen-cases of a hundred pounds in weight. Their functions were practically unlimited, save for the all-important exception that they exercised no military command. They had an exchequer of their own, through which passed all the Imperial taxes from their provinces; they had absolute control over the vicars of the dioceses beneath them, whom, if they did not actually appoint they at least recommended for appointment to the Emperor. In their own prefectures they formed the final court of appeal, and Constantine expressly enacted that there should be no appeal from them to the throne. They even had a limited power of issuing edicts. Thus in all administrative, financial, and judicial matters the four Praetorian prefects were supreme, occupying a position very similar to that of the Viceroys of the great provinces of China, save that they had no control over the troops within their territories.

Below these four prefects came the vicars of the twelve dioceses of the Oriens, Pontica, Asiana, Thracia, Moesia, Pannonia, Britannia, Galliae, Viennenses, Italia, Hispania, and Africa. Egypt continued to hold an unique position; its governor was almost independent of the prefect of the Orient, and was always a direct nominee of the Emperor. Then, below the twelve vicars came the governors of the provinces, the number of which constantly tended to increase, but by further subdivision rather than by conquest of new territory. Various names were given to these governors; they were rectores and correctores in some provinces, proesides in many more, consulares in a few of the more important ones, such as Africa and Italia. Each had his own entourage of minor officials,

223

and the hierarchical principle was observed as rigidly on the lowest rungs of the ladder as on the topmost. Autocrats arc obliged to rule through a bureaucracy, a broad-based pyramid of officialdom which usually weighs heavily upon the unfortunate taxpayer who has to support the entire structure.

A similar hierarchy of officials prevailed in the palace and the court, from the grand chamberlain down through a host of Imperial secretaries to the head scullion. The tendency of each was to magnify his office into a department, and to be the master of a set of underlings. And it was the policy of Constantine, as it had been the policy of Augustus, to invent new offices in order to increase the number of officials who looked to the Emperor as their benefactor.

In the conduct of State affairs the Emperor was assisted by an Imperial council, known as the consistarium principis. It included the four Pretorian prefects of whom we have spoken; the questor of the palace, a kind of general secretary of state; the master of the offices (magister officiorum), one of whose principal duties was to act as minister of police; the grand chamberlain (praepositus sacri cubiculi); two ministers of finance, and two ministers for war. One of the finance ministers was dignified with the title of count of the sacred largesses (comes sacrarum largitionum); the other was count of the private purse (comes rerum privatarum). The distinction was similar to the old one between the aerariumn and the fiscus, between, that is to say, the State treasury and the Emperor's privy purse. One of the two ministers for war had supreme charge of the infantry of the Empire; the other was responsible for the cavalry. Both also exercised judicial functions and sat as a court of appeal in all military cases wherein the State was interested, either as plaintiff or defendant.

There were still consuls in Rome, who continued to give their names to the year. All their political power had vanished, but their dignity remained unimpaired, though it was now derived not from the intrinsic importance of their office so much as from its extrinsic ornaments. To be consul had become the ambition not of the boldest but of the vainest. The protectorship had similarly fallen, but it still entailed upon the holder the expensive and sometimes ruinous privilege of providing shows for the amusement of the Roman populace. The number of praetors had fallen to two in Constantine's day: he raised it to eight, in accordance with his general regardlessness of expense, so long as there was outward magnificence. It is doubtful whether, during the reign of Constantine, there were consuls and preators in Constantinople. Certainly there was no urban prefect appointed in that city until twenty years after his death, and it seems probable that the Emperor did not set up in his new capital quite such a pedantically perfect imitation of the official machinery of Rome as has sometimes been supposed. His successors, however, were not long in completing what he had begun.

We pass to the senate and the senatorial order, with their various degrees of dignity, which Constantine and those who came after him delighted to elaborate. Every member of the senate was naturally a member of the senatorial order, but it by no means followed that every member of the order had a seat in the senate. The new senate of Constantinople, like its prototype at Rome, had little or no political power. It merely registered the decrees of the Emperor, and its function seems to have been one principally of dignity and ceremony. Membership of the senatorial order was a social distinction that might be held by a man living in any part of the Empire and was gained by virtue of having held office. The order was an aristocracy of officials and ex-officials, distinguished by resplendent titles, involving additional burdens in the way of taxation— the price of added dignity. A few of these titles are worth brief consideration. To the Emperor there were reserved the grandiloquent names of Your Majesty, Your Eternity, Your Divinity. Members of the reigning house were Most Noble (Nobilissimi). To the members of the senate, including the officials of the very highest rank, viz., the consuls, proconsuls, and prefects, there was reserved the title of Most Distinguished (Clarissimi), while officers of lower rank, members of the senatorial order but not of the senate, were Most Perfect (Perfectissimi) and Egregious (Egregii), the former being of a higher class than the latter. Such was the order of precedence in Constantine's reign, but there was a constant tendency for these honorable orders to expand, due, no doubt, entirely to the exigencies of the treasury. Thus the high rank of Clarissimi was bestowed on those who previously had been only Perfectissimi and Egregii, and two still higher orders of Illustres and

Spectabiles were created for the old Clarissimi and Perfectissimi. The two topmost classes were thus given an upward step.

Such was the new official aristocracy, while a rigid line of division, quite unknown to Republican and early Imperial Rome, was drawn between the civil and the military officers of the Empire. The military forces themselves were organized into two great divisions, (I) the troops kept permanently upon the frontiers, and (2) the soldiers of the line. The first were known as Limitanei (Borderers) or Riparienses (Guardians of the Shore), the second name being specially applied to the soldiers of the Rhine and the Danube. All these troops were stationed in permanent camps and forts, which often developed into townships, and it was a rare thing for a legion to be moved to another quarter of the Empire. Boys grew up and followed their fathers in the profession of arms in the same camp, and were themselves succeeded by their own sons. The term of service was twenty-four years, and these Limitanei were not only soldiers but tillers of the soil, playing a part precisely similar to the soldier colonists of Russia in her Far Eastern provinces. The soldiers of the line (Numeri), on the other hand, served for the shorter period of twenty years. They included the Palatini,—practically the successors of the old Praetorian Guard,—the crack corps of the army, who were divided into regiments bearing such titles as Scholares, Protectores, and Domestici, and enjoyed the privilege of guarding the Emperor's person. Most of the legions of the line were known as the Comitatenses. These were employed in the interior garrisons of the Empire, and Zosimus— whether justly or not, it is impossible to say—accuses Constantine of having dangerously weakened the frontier garrisons and withdrawn too many troops into the interior. The control of the army, under the Emperor and his two ministers for war, was vested by the end of the fourth century in thirty-five commanders bearing the titles of dukes and counts,—the latter being the higher of the two. Three of these were stationed in Britain, six in Gaul, one each in Spain and Italy, four in Africa, three in Egypt, eight in Asia and Syria, and nine along the upper and lower reaches of the Danube.

Such was the structure which rested upon the purse of the taxpayer and upon a system of finance inherently vicious and wasteful. The main support of the treasury was still, as it had always been, the land tax, known as the capitatio terrena, the old tributum soli. It was the landed proprietor (possessor) who found the wherewithal to keep the Empire on its feet. Diocletian had reorganized the census, and, in the interests of the treasury, had caused a new survey and inventory to be made of practically every acre of land in every province. By an ingenious device he had established a system of taxable units (jugum or caput), each of which paid the round sum of 100,0o0 sesterces or 1000 aurei. The unit might be made up of all sorts of land—arable, pasture, or forest —the value of each being estimated on a regular scale. Thus five acres of vineyard constituted a unit and were held to be equivalent to twenty acres of the best arable land, forty acres of second-class land, and sixty of third-class. Nothing escaped: even the roughest woodland or moorland was assessed at the rate of four hundred and fifty acres to the unit. The Emperor and his finance ministers estimated every year how much was required for the current expenses of the Empire. When the amount was fixed, they sent word throughout the provinces, and the various municipal curies, or town senates, knew what their share would be, for each town and district was assessed at so many thousand units, and each curia or senate was responsible for the money being raised. The curia was composed of a number of the richest landowners, who had to collect the tax from themselves and their neighbors as best they could. If, therefore, any possessor became bankrupt, the others had to make up the shortage between them. Those who were solvent had to pay for the insolvent. All loopholes of evasion were carefully closed. Land-owners were not permitted to quit their district without special leave from the governor; they could not join the army or enter the civil service. When it was found that large numbers were becoming ordained in the Christian Church to escape their obligations, an edict was issued forbidding it. Once a decurion always a decurion.

The provincial country landowner and the small farmer were almost taxed out of existence by this monstrous system. Every ten or fifteen years, it is true, a revision of the assessments took place, and there were certain officials, with the significant name of defensores, whose duty it was to prevent the provincials from being fleeced too flagrantly. But a man might easily be reduced to beggary by a succession of bad harvests before the year of revision came round, and the defensor's office was a sinecure except in the rare occasions when he knew that he would be backed at the headquarters of the diocese. During Constantine's reign, or at least during its closing years, there is overpowering evidence that the provincial governors were allowed to plunder at discretion. They imitated the reckless prodigality of their sovereign, who, in 331, was compelled to issue an edict to restrain the peculation of his officers. There is a very striking phrase in Ammianus Marcellinus who says that while Constantine started the practice of opening the greedy jaws of his favorites, his son, Constantius, fattened them up on the very marrow of the provinces. Evidently, the incidence of this land tax inflicted great hardships and had the mischievous result of draining the province of capital, and of dragging down to ruin the independent cultivator of the land. Hence districts were constantly in arrears of payment, and the remission of outstanding debt to the treasury was usually the first step taken by an Emperor to court popularity with his subjects.

In short, the fiscal system of the Empire, so far as its most important item, the land tax, was concerned, seemed expressly designed to exhaust the wealth of the provinces. It helped to introduce a system of caste, which became more rigid and cramping as the years passed by and the necessities of the treasury became more urgent. It also powerfully contributed to crush out of existence the yeoman farmer, whose insolvency was followed, if not by slavery, at any rate by a serfdom which just as effectually robbed him of freedom of movement. The colonus having lost the title-deeds of his own land became the hireling of another, paying in kind a fixed proportion of his stock and crops, and obliged to give personal service for so many days on that part of the estate where his master resided. The position of the poor colonus, in fact, became precisely similar to that of a slave who had not obtained full freedom but had reached the intermediate state of serfdom, in which he was permanently attached to a certain estate as, so to speak, part of the fixtures. He was said to be "ascribed to the land", and he had no opportunity of bettering his social position or enabling his sons to better theirs, unless they were recruited for the legions.

The land tax, of course, was not the only one, for the theory of Imperial finance was that everybody and everything should pay. Constantine did not spare his new aristocracy. Every member of the senatorial order paid a property tax known as "the senatorial purse", and another imposition bearing the name of aurum oblaticium, which was none the more palatable because it was supposed to be a voluntary offering. Any senator, moreover, might be summoned to the capital to serve as praetor and provide a costly entertainment—a convenient weapon in the hands of autocracy to clip the wings of an obnoxious ex-official. Another ostensibly voluntary contribution to the Emperor was the aurum coronarium, or its equivalent of a thousand or two thousand pieces of gold, which each city of importance was obliged to offer to the sovereign on festival occasions, such as the celebration of five or ten complete years of rule. Every five years, also, there was a lustralis collatio to be paid by all shopkeepers and usurers, according to their means. This was usually spoken of as "the gold-silver" (chrysargyrum), and, like "the senatorial purse," is said by some authorities to have been the invention of Constantine himself. Zosimus, in a very bitter attack on the fiscal measures of the Emperor, declares that even the courtesans and the beggars were not exempt from the extortion of the treasury officials, and that whenever the tribute had to be paid, nothing was heard but groaning and lamentation. The scourge was brought into play for the persuasion of reluctant tax-payers; women were driven to sell their sons, and fathers their daughters. Then there were the capitatio humana, a sort of poll-tax on all labourers; the old five per cent. succession duty; an elaborate system of octroi (portoria), and many other indirect taxes. We need not, perhaps, believe the very worst pictures of human misery drawn by the historians, for, in fairness to the Emperors, we must take some note of the roseate accounts of the official rhetoricians. Nazarius, for example, explicitly declares that Constantine had given the Empire "peace abroad, prosperity at home, abundant harvests, and cheap food." Eusebius again and again conjures up a vision of prosperous and contented peoples, living not in fear of the tax-collector, but in the enjoyment of their sovereign's bounty. But we fear that the sombre view is nearer the truth than the radiant one, and that the subsequent financial ruin, which overtook the western even more than the eastern provinces, was largely due to the oppressive and wasteful fiscal system introduced and developed by Diocletian and Constantine, and to the old standing defect of Roman administration, that the civil governor was also the judge, and thus administrative and judicial functions were combined in the same hands.

Here, indeed, lay one of the strongest elements of disintegration in the reorganized Empire, but there were other powerful solvents at work, at which we may briefly glance. One was slavery, the evil results of which had been steadily accumulating for centuries, and if these were mitigated to some extent by the increasing scarcity of slaves, the degradation of the poor freeman to the position of a colonus more than counterbalanced the resultant good. Population, so far from increasing, was going back, and, in order to fill the gaps, the authorities had recourse to the dangerous expedient of inviting ill the barbarian. The land was starving for want of capital and labor, and the barbarian colours was introduced, as we have seen in all earlier chapter, not, if the authorities are to be trusted, by tens, but by hundreds of thousands, "to lighten the tribute by the fruits of his toil and to relieve the Roman citizens of military service." This was the principal and certainly the original reason why recourse was had to the barbarian; the idea that the German or the Goth was less dangerous inside than outside the frontier, and would help to bear the brunt of the pressure from his kinsmen, came later. The result, however, of importing a strong Germanic and Gothic element into the Empire was one of active disintegration. Though they occupied but a humble position industrially, as tillers of the soil, they formed the best troops in the Imperial armies. The boast which Tacitus put into the mouth of a Gallic soldier in the first century, that the alien trooper was the backbone of the Roman army, was now an undoubted truth, and the spirit which these strangers brought with them was that of freedom, quite antagonistic to the absolutism of the Empire.

There was yet another great solvent at work,—in its cumulative effects the greatest of them all,—the solvent of Christianity, dissociating, as it did, spiritual from temporal authority, and introducing the absolutely novel idea of a divine law that in every particular took precedence of mundane law. The growth of the power of the Church, as a body entirely distinct from the State and claiming a superior moral sanction, was a new force introduced into the Roman Empire, which, beyond question, weakened its powers of resistance to outside enemies, inasmuch as it caused internal dissensions and divisions. The furious hatreds between Christianity and paganism which lasted in the West down to the fall of Rome, and the equally furious hatreds within the Church which continued both in East and West for long centuries, can only be considered a source of serious weakness. No one disputes that the desperate and murderous struggle between Catholic and Huguenot retarded the development of France and weakened her in the face of the enemy, and it stands to reason that a nation which is torn by intestinal quarrel cannot present an effective front to foreign aggression. It wastes against members of its own household part of the energy which should be infused into the blows which it delivers at its foe.

Christianity has always tended to break down dis-tinctions and prejudices of race. It has never done so wholly and never will, but the tendency is forever at work, and, as such, in the days of the Empire, it was opposed both to the Roman and to the Greek spirit. For though there had already sprung up a feeling of cosmopolitanism within the Empire, it cannot be said to have extended to those without the Empire, who were still barbarians in the eyes not only of Greek or Roman, but of the Romanized Celt and Iberian, whose civilization was no longer a thin veneer. When we say that Christianity was a disintegrating element in this respect, the term is by no means wholly one of reproach. For it also implies that Christianity assisted the partial fusion which took place when at length the frontier barriers gave way and the West was rushed by the Germanic races. These races were themselves Christianized to a certain extent. They, too, worshipped the Cross and the Christ, and this circumstance alone must, to a very considerable degree, have mitigated for the Roman provinces the terrors and disasters of invasion. It is true that the invaders were for the most part Arians,—though it is a manifest absurdity to suppose that the free Germans from beyond the Rhine understood even the elements of a controversy so metaphysical and so purely Greek,—and, when Arian and Catholic fought, they tipped their barbs with poison. "I never yet," said Ammianus Marcellinus, "found wild beasts so savagely hostile to men, as most of the Christians are to one another." But the fact remains that the German and Gothic conquerors, who settled where they had conquered, accepted the civilization of the vanquished even though they modified it to their own needs; they did not wipe it out and substitute their own, as did the Turk and the Moor when they appeared, later on, at the head of their devastating hordes. If therefore, Christianity tended to weaken, it also tended to assimilate, and we are not sure that the latter process was not fully as important as the former. The Roman Empire, as a universal power, had long been doomed; Christianity, in this respect, simply accelerated its pace down the slippery slope.

But other and more specific charges have been brought against Christianity. One is that it contributed largely to the depopulation of the Empire, which, from the point of view of the State, was an evil of the very greatest magnitude. The indictment cannot be refuted wholly. In the name of Christianity extravagant and pernicious doctrines were preached of which it would be difficult to speak with patience, did we not remember that violent disorders need violent remedies. No one can doubt the unutterable depravity and viciousness which were rampant and unashamed in the Roman Empire, especially in the East. If there was a public conscience at all, it was silent. Decent, clean-living people held fastidiously aloof and tolerated the existence of evils which they did nothing to combat. A strong protest was needed; it was supplied by Christianity. But many of those who took upon themselves to denounce the sins of the age felt compelled to school themselves to a rigid asceticism which made few allowances not only for the weaknesses but even for the natural instincts of human nature. The more fanatical among them grudgingly admitted that marriage was honorable, but rose to enthusiastic frenzy in the contemplation of virginity, which, if they dared not command, they could and did commend with all the eloquence of which they were capable. One cannot think without pity of all the self-torture and agonizing which this new asceticism—new, at least, in this aggravated form brought upon hundreds and thousands of men and women, whose services the State needed and would have done well to possess, but who cut themselves off from mundane affairs, and withdrew into solitudes, not to learn there how to help their fellow-men but consumed only with a selfish anxiety to escape from the wrath to come. They thought of nothing but the salvation of their own souls. It is impossible to see how these wild hermits, who peopled the Libyan deserts, were acceptable in the sight either of themselves, their fellows, or their God. Simon Stylites, starving sleepless on his pillar in the posture of prayer for weeks, remains for all time as a monument of grotesque futility. If charity regards him with pity, it can only regard with contempt those who imputed his insane endurance unto him for righteousness. No one can estimate the amount of unnecessary misery and sufferings caused by these extreme fanatics, who broke up homes without remorse, played on the fears and harrowed the minds of impressionable men and women, and debased the human soul in their frantic endeavor to fit it for the presence of its Maker. They stand in the same category as the gaunt skeletons who drag themselves on their knees from end to end of India in the hope of placating a mild but irresponsive god. Man's first duty may be towards God; but not to the exclusion of his duty towards the State.

It is not to be supposed, of course, that the majority of Christians were led to renounce the world and family life. The weaker brethren are always in a majority, and we do not doubt that most of the Christian priests were of like mind with their flock in taking a less heroic but far more common-sense view. It is also to be noted that the practical Roman temper speedily modified the extravagances of the eastern fanatics, and the asceticism of monks and nuns living in religious communities in the midst of their fellow-citizens, and working to heal their bodies as well as to save their souls, stands on a very different plane from the entirely self-centred eremitism associated with Egypt. By doing the work of good Samaritans the members of these communities acted the part of good citizens. Succeeding Emperors, whose Christianity was unimpeachable, looked with cold suspicion on the recluses of the deserts. Valens, for example, regarding their retirement as an evasion of their civic duties, published an edict ordering that they should be brought back; Theodosius with cynical wisdom said that as they had deliberately chosen to dwell in the desert, he would take care that they stopped there. But it is easy to exaggerate the influence wielded by extreme men, whose doctrines and professions only emerge from obscurity because of their extravagances. We must not, therefore, lay too much stress on the constant exhortations to celibacy and virginity which we find even in the writings of such men as Jerome and Ambrose. However zealously they plied the pitch-fork, human nature just as persistently came back, and the extraordinary outspokenness of Jerome, for example, in his letters to girls who had pledged themselves to virginity—an outspokenness based on the confident assumption that human, and more especially womanly, nature is weak and liable to err--shows that he was profoundly diffident of the success of his preaching. Nevertheless, when the counsel of perfection offered by the Church was the avoidance of marriage, it is a just charge against Christianity that it was in this respect anti-civic and anti-social.

On the other hand, it is to be remembered that this avoidance of marriage and its responsibilities was no new thing in the Roman Empire. For centuries the State had been alarmed at the growth of an unwillingness, manifested especially in the higher orders of society, to undertake the duties of parentage. Special bounties and immunities from taxation were offered to the fathers even of three children; checks were placed upon divorce; taxes were levied upon the obstinate bachelor and widower who clung to what he called the blessings of detached irresponsibility. These laws were all based on the theory that it is a man's civic duty to marry and give sons and daughters to the service of his country, and we find one of the Panegyrists declaring them to be the very foundation of the State, because they supply a nursery of youth and a constant flow of manly vigour to the Roman armies. Yet so powerful were the attractions of a childless life that the whole series of Julian laws on this subject had proved of little value, and Tacitus had declared that the remedy was worse than the disease. The motives of the luxurious voluptuary or the fastidious cynic were widely different from those of the Christian enthusiast for bodily purity, but by a curious irony they were directed towards the same object—the avoidance of matrimony.

There was also brought against Christianity the charge that it discouraged military service and looked askance upon the profession of arms. The accusation is true within certain limits. Christianity was and is a gospel of peace. Ideally, therefore, it is always antagonistic to war as a general principle, and there is always a considerable section of Christian opinion which is opposed, irrespective of the justice of the quarrel, to an appeal to arms. That section of Christian opinion was naturally at its strongest when the Roman Empire was pagan, and when it was practically impossible for a Christian to be a soldier without finding himself compelled to worship, at the altars of Rome, the Roman Emperor and the Roman gods. Omnismilitia est religio, Seneca had said most truly. There was a permanent altar fixed before the proetorium of every camp. That being the case, one can understand that the army was regarded with abhorrence by every Christian at a time when Christianity was a proscribed, or barely tolerated, religion, and hence the violent denunciations of the army and military service to be found in some of the early Fathers. Hence too the number of Christian soldier martyrs, who had been converted while serving in the ranks. But the whole case was changed when the Roman Emperor was a Christian, and the army took its oath to a champion and no longer to an enemy of the Church. The bishops at once changed front—they could not help themselves—and at the Council of Arles we have seen the Gallican bishops passing a canon anathematizing any Christian who flung down his arms in time of peace. There were still extremists, as there are today, who denounced war with indiscriminate censure; there must have been a much larger number who acquiesced in standing armies as a necessary evil, but themselves carefully kept aloof from service; the majority, as today, would recognize that the security of a State rests ultimately upon force, and would pray that their cause might be just whenever that force had to be put into operation. It is not Tertullian with his dangerous doctrine that politics have no interest for the Christian, that the Christian has no country but the world, and that Christ had bidden the nations disarm when he bade Peter put up his sword—it is not Tertullian who is the typical representative of the Church in its relations with the State and mundane affairs, but the broad-minded Augustine who, when nervous Christians appealed to him to say whether a Christian could serve God as a soldier, said that a man might do his duty to his God and his Emperor as well in a camp as elsewhere.

God-fearing men could spend their days in the legions without peril to their souls, but the atmosphere of a Roman camp, full as it was of barbarians and semi-barbarians, naturally cannot have been congenial to the Christian religion. In spite of the Labarum, service in the army was discountenanced by the more zealous Christian bishops. Yet nothing could be more unfair than to charge Christianity with having introduced into the Roman world the reluctance to carry arms. That reluctance dated back to the latter days of the Republic. Christianity merely intensified it.

Christianity, again, may be acquitted of having caused the decadence of literature and the arts. That decadence was of long standing. There had been a steady decline from the brilliant circle of Augustan poets and prose writers to the days of the Antonines. The third century had been utterly barren of great names. Literature had become imitation; originality was lost. Society was literary in tone; grammarians and rhetoricians flourished; learning was not dead but active; yet the results, so far as creative work was concerned, were miserably small. But if Christianity cannot be held responsible for the poverty of imagination in the ranks of pagan society, it must be held responsible for its own shortcomings. It often assumed an attitude of open hostility to the ancient literature, which was to be explained—and, so long as paganism was a living force, might be justified—by the fact that the poetry of Rome was steeped in pagan associations. Men to whom Jupiter was a false deity or demon; to whom the radiance of Apollo was hateful because it was a snare to the unwary; to whom the purity of Diana, the cold stateliness of Minerva, the beauty of Venus, and the bountifulness of Ceres, were all treacherous delusions and masks of sin, and all equally pernicious to the soul, found in the very charm of style and the seductiveness of language of the old poetry another reason for keeping it out of the hands of their children and for themselves eschewing its dangerous delights. It is difficult to blame them. Protestants and Catholics even of the present day are studiously ignorant of the special literatures of the other, and if the Christian eschewed the classical poets, the educated pagan was grotesquely ignorant of the Christian's "Holy Books."

But this point must not he pursued too far. Education itself was based on the ancient literature of Greece and Rome—there was, indeed, no-thing else on which to base it—and in the ablest and most cultured of the Christian writers the influence of the classical authors is evident on every page. Jerome dreamt that an angel came to rebuke him for his love of the rounded periods of Cicero. Augustine bewails the tears he had wasted on the moving story of the Fall of Troy, while his heart was insensible to the sufferings of the Son of God. Lines and half lines from Virgil, or the choice of a Virgilian epithet, betray the ineradicable influence of the Mantuan over Ambrose. Even the author of the De Mortibus Persecutorum, despite his ferocious hatred of paganism, takes evident pleasure in the Ciceronian flavor of his maledictions. Do what he would, the cultured and educated Christian could not escape from the spell of the poets of antiquity. There were, of course, narrow-minded fanatics in plenty who would cheerfully have burned the contents of every pagan library and have imagined that they were offering an acceptable sacrifice, and there were doubtless many more who, without vindictiveness towards the classics, were quite content with want of culture, deeming that ignorance was more becoming to Christian simplicity. The tendencies of Christianity, as compared with paganism, were not towards what we call the humanities and a liberal education, for the dominant feeling was that there was only one book in the world which really mattered, and that was the Bible. There was, it is true, a slight literary renaissance starting at the close of the fourth century, with which we associate the names of Ausonius, Paulinus of Nola, Prudentius, and Claudian. This was mainly Christian. Ausonius strictly followed classical models; the graceful yet vigorous hymns of Prudentius were an original and valuable contribution to literature; Claudian stands neutral. "The last of the classics," as Mr. Mackail has well said, "he is, at the same time, the earliest and one of the most distinguished of the classicists. It might seem a mere chance whether his poetry belonged to the fourth or to the sixteenth century." This literary renaissance, however, was a last flicker, and while we have to thank the Church for preserving the Latin tongue, we owe it little thanks—compared with the paganism it had overthrown—for its services to culture and the humanities. In the fifteenth and sixteenth centuries the classics had to be rediscovered and relearnt: the dead spirit of humanism had to be quickened to a new birth.

Hard things have been said of Christianity and its influence upon the Roman Empire, harder perhaps than the facts warrant, though the bitterness of many of the critics has been directly provoked by the boundless assumptions of the Christian apologists. Looking back dispassionately upon the period with which we have been dealing, it is not difficult to see why the Church triumphed and why the nations acquiesced as readily as they did in the downfall of paganism. The reason is that the world had grown stale. It had outlived all its old ideals. It was sick of doubt, weary of bloodshed and strife, and nervously apprehensive, we can hardly question, of the cataclysm that was to burst upon the West and submerge it before another century was over. The philosophies were worn out. The gods themselves had grown grey. There was a general atmosphere of numbness and decrepitude.

Men wanted consolation and hope. Christianity alone could supply it, and though Christianity itself had lost its early joyousness, freshness, and simplicity, it retained unimpaired its marvelous powers to console. To a world tired of questioning and search it returned an answer for which it claimed the sanction of absolute Truth. The old spirit was not wholly dead. One may see it revive from time to time in the various heresies which split the Church. But it was ruthlessly suppressed, and humanity had to purchase back its liberty of thought at a great price, ten or more centuries later, when the world realized that her ancient deliverer had herself become a tyrant. Nevertheless, few can seriously doubt that the triumph of the Christian Church was an unspeakable boon to mankind. The Roman Empire was doomed. Its downfall was certain and, on the whole, was even to be desired, so long as its civilization was not wholly wiped out and the genius of past generations was not wholly destroyed.

Made in the USA
Columbia, SC
16 September 2022

67399480R00130